STILL
BROKEN

STILL
BROKEN

A RECRUIT'S INSIDE ACCOUNT
OF INTELLIGENCE FAILURES,
FROM BAGHDAD TO THE PENTAGON

A. J. ROSSMILLER

PRESIDIO PRESS

BALLANTINE BOOKS • NEW YORK

Published in the United States by Presidio Press,
an imprint of The Random House Publishing Group,
a division of Random House, Inc., New York.

PRESIDIO PRESS and colophon are trademarks
of Random House, Inc.

Library of Congress Cataloging-in-Publication Data
Rossmiller, A. J.
Still broken : a recruit's inside account of intelligence failures,
from Baghdad to the Pentagon / A. J. Rossmiller.
p. cm.
ISBN-13: 978-0-89141-914-3
1. United States. Defense Intelligence Agency.   2. Rossmiller, A. J.
3. Intelligence officers—United States—Biography.   I. Title.
JK468.I6R677   2008
327.1273—dc22   2007032286

Printed in the United States of America on acid-free paper

www.presidiopress.com

9 8 7 6 5 4 3 2 1

First Edition

Book design by Victoria Wong

To those who fight

Although readers will find this obvious, I am legally obligated to say that the views expressed in this account are those of the author and do not reflect the official policy or position of the Department of Defense or the U.S. government.

Nearly all of the names used in this book are pseudonyms, and some identifying characteristics have been changed, in order to protect the privacy of my former coworkers. My friends and family are identified by their first names only, and the only government employees whose names I have not changed are those who receive extensive press coverage. For instances in which names are central to the narrative, I have changed them in a way that accurately reflects events as they occurred.

This is a nonfiction account. Events are rendered without exaggeration or modification to the best of my recollection and records. Whenever possible, I have recounted and confirmed conversations with the other participants to ensure precision. When it was not possible, I relied on my memory, contemporaneous emails, and the recollections of others. I have also resisted the (frequent) urge to sanitize or enhance my own reactions or impressions from the time.

The following description reflects just one person's experience in a broken system, but I believe it is largely representative of the whole. I hope it will in some small way help illuminate the continued problems we have in our military and intelligence structures—problems with very real consequences for our national security and, more immediately, for the tens of thousands of men and women injured and killed as a result.

STILL
BROKEN

I'm the kind of person the United States intelligence community claimed to want: young, committed, and passionate about our security, with an educational background in the Middle East. Willing—eager, even—to pass up the investment banking and consulting jobs my peers flocked to in favor of civil service, and ready to make a career of protecting the nation.

"Alex?"

"That's me. You're Josh, I take it?"

"Yup. Let me show you where our office is."

On my first day at the Defense Intelligence Agency, essentially the spy arm of the U.S. Department of Defense, I didn't have a desk. Or a computer. Or an assignment, really. I was relieved when Josh, a young, socially functional coworker, met me at the security desk, but when he took me upstairs to the office, much of my new team seemed surprised to see me. I had talked to Josh on the phone a few times in the months leading up to my arrival, and he was tremendously helpful regarding matters both large (What Washington, DC, neighborhoods are good to live in? What's the office environment like?) and small (Is there a dress code? Should I bring or buy lunch?). That first day, he helped me get a temporary security badge and process mountains of initial paperwork, and eventually we went to meet the rest of my team. It was a motley crew, but one that seemed dedicated to the work and ready to integrate their new charge.

I was barely a month out of college, having just graduated from Middlebury College in bucolic Middlebury, Vermont, and my life-long interest in law enforcement and intelligence had led me, through a circuitous route, to DIA.

I initially worked at the Air Force base where DIA is headquartered. The atmosphere of the office was mildly depressing: The building itself was run-down and dreary, and most of the employees had the rounded shoulders and shuffling gait that I hoped to avoid as my career progressed. The general reputation of intelligence analysts is that they're quirky introverts, and I didn't find that to be untrue. My favorite joke from those initial weeks: How do you spot an extroverted intelligence analyst? He looks at *your* shoes when he talks to you. But much of that reputation was due to the presence of so many intellectuals, especially those who were brilliant in one very specific area of military or political minutiae.

The culture and mood were clear from the beginning. As in many bureaucracies, the individuals were capable and helpful, but the system somehow managed to impede progress and common sense. Although my team ostensibly knew my start date months in advance, when I arrived it took weeks to get the requisite passwords and computer access, there was no established training program, and, perhaps most frustrating, I didn't have a set position for months. What I assumed was an aberration, however, turned out to be fairly typical as I swapped notes with other young employees.

My generation of analysts reflected a new direction for the agency, and for the intelligence community (IC) as a whole. In the late 1990s, and especially after 9/11, the IC increasingly hired generalists rather than people with narrow expertise, and many of my contemporaries had outlooks and goals similar to mine. I went into the business of intelligence because I passionately believe that those with the ability to contribute to their country also have a responsibility to do so. Idealistic, perhaps, but a belief I was willing to act on. Events in Afghanistan and Iraq, and, above all, the attacks against America on September 11, hugely amplified that feeling, and I believed that with my background I could make a positive contribution to my country. The attacks, which occurred during my time at Middlebury, were a tremendous motivation for me to pursue my interest and studies in international politics, especially in the Middle East. That day also felt like a personal affront: I grew up just outside New York City, and my father worked downtown. His building was so damaged on 9/11 that it was eventually condemned, and on that day he walked uptown through the shrapnel and soot that rained down on Lower Manhattan. I was always a highly motivated student, but during the fall after 9/11, I took it to another level.

I spent an absurd amount of time on schoolwork, reading, and keeping up with the news. When I did go out, I partied harder than I had before, hoping for fast relief from the self-imposed intensity. It was the best academic semester of my entire college career, and I studied through the night with regularity. During one all-nighter, a good friend, who lived across the hall, wandered in.

"AJ," she said, "your sleeping and eating habits need to change. Now."

I looked up at her, eyebrows raised.

"Look at you!" she insisted. "You have in front of you two empty water bottles, a bagel and cream cheese, and pills"—my migraine medicine. "That's always good. Why don't you put some Tabasco sauce in the water for sustenance? That'd be fantastic." Before I could respond, she rolled her eyes and ambled out.

When I wasn't working, I sometimes wondered if I should leave school and join the military; it felt wrong not to contribute in such a time of national need. The attack infuriated me, both for the loss of life and for what it represented: a rejection of American security and authority. September 11 was an assault on the moral ideals of America and an accusation of weakness. Power that is rejected in such a way cannot be maintained, and without an appropriate response, contempt replaces respect. I understood the importance of responding appropriately, in a way that reinforced both our virtues and our power, thereby reasserting justice and decency in the face of defiance.

I eventually decided that I could do the most good by continuing my education and staying focused on the future, though I knew my decision was a rationalization. There is some combination of courage and conviction that causes a person to act on his or her beliefs, some threshold that must be met with a combined amount of those two elements before an individual will put him- or herself on the line. Better and braver individuals with my feelings would have left immediately to join the fight, and I did not. I don't think there is too much shame in my decision to remain in school, but I certainly did not feel great about it.

Despite this decision—or perhaps partly motivated by it—I wanted even more to be part of the process after college. When I was lucky enough to get a job offer from DIA, I jumped at the chance, and many of my peers at the agency had similar motivations for joining: a combination of general patriotism, an interest in international relations, and the knowledge that the business of intelligence was once again a top priority for the security of the country.

I found in my initial months at DIA that most analysts were relatively segregated; we had little contact with colleagues outside our immediate teams, and at my first post I regularly interacted with fewer than a dozen people, basically my cubicle neighbors and institutional chain of command. Eventually, though, I met and talked to other entry-level employees. There was a noticeable generation gap, which I was told resulted from a hiring freeze (or significant reduction) from the late 1980s into the '90s. As the Cold War limped to its conclusion, intelligence, especially military intelligence, was devalued. After 9/11, however, intel was important again, and the intelligence community went on massive hiring binges. The old paradigm for hiring was to acquire specialists: people with advanced degrees in the specific area they'd be working on, whether Russian submarines, Chinese ICBMs, Colombian narcotics command-and-control structures, or a wide variety of other topics. The new plan was to hire generalists: smart people who knew how to think and analyze, and who could develop expertise in any issue. Graduate degrees in public policy, economics, and law became desirable, and even a few undergraduate political science majors—like me—slipped in.

The result is something of a disjointed workforce. The older generation was educated with a state-based, Cold War–focused approach and mind-set. For many of them, the phrase *nonstate actors* was a virtual non sequitur, and the agency was structured to focus on countries rather than elements that operated transnationally. The younger set, conversely, grew up with the reality of globalization and international interdependence. Many of the important things in our lives were not unique to a particular country, and we didn't remember a time before the Internet and cell phones and multinationals. To us, the concept of terrorist groups was the same general idea as the Internet, or even—and I draw a general analogy of global reach only, of course—companies like Nike, Microsoft, and Starbucks. We couldn't possibly imagine how analysts had done their job before computers and the Net, whereas our bosses had never heard of Wikipedia or decentralized social network theory. While many supervisors are making a valiant effort to catch up, it hasn't been an easy transition.

This shift, exacerbated by the generation gap, is further compounded by the high turnover in the intelligence community, especially of younger analysts, resulting in a lack of experienced middle management. During the 1990s people stagnated in jobs with reduced mobility, and generally speaking the most talented minds were still Soviet experts. As the next generation, the 9/11 generation, began to permeate the intelligence community, there were older people and younger people, and not many in between. At least, that's how it felt and appeared. We arrived in the middle of what should have been a great shift in resources and focus, but the personnel and leadership were struggling to keep up.

Generation Cold War and generation 9/11 were united, however, in their recognition of a sputtering bureaucracy. As I built an expertise in my assigned topics, I began to write reports on a variety of issues and events. Originally I thought that the point of these products was for subject matter experts (analysts) to synthesize issues to digestible pieces for use in decision making by supervisors and policymakers. I eventually learned, though, that products rarely reached their intended audience. Even when reports did go up the chain, the end result could be drastically different from the initial effort, as the editing process was largely indiscriminate. Sometimes it would take months for the appropriate people to read and sign off on assessments; other times a piece could make its way up the chain in just a couple of weeks. But it was not, as a rule, a nimble process. I thought, naïvely as it turned out, that the process was cumbersome because of the specific office in which I started.

As I settled in, I became accustomed to the environment and the culture of DIA. Although the official amount of current military in the agency is around 30 percent (with the other 70 percent civilian), the large number of prior, retired, and reserve military, as well as a phalanx of contractors—the vast majority of whom are former service members—gives it a distinctly military atmosphere. As I learned the methods and tools of intelligence analysis, I also learned how to identify the different uniforms, ranks, and, slowly but surely, some of the lingo. DIA is a joint environment, meaning that members of multiple armed services are included, so there was a lot to learn.

I heard of only one classmate from my high school graduating class of 180 going into the military. I knew one student from my college graduating class of about 550 who went into the military, and he was going straight to law school and then into the judge advocate general's (JAG) office. I had virtually no contact with the military or its personnel growing up, so it was an entirely new world. I was raised in the suburbs just north of New York City, where the armed forces weren't something most people thought about. Certainly my mind was on other things. However, I felt a debt to my nation for providing a structure that ensures the rights and responsibilities we take for granted, and I recognized my luck in having the familial support and education that allowed me to pursue a wide range of opportunities. I wanted to contribute to that system through working in government, and I could think of no better focus than intelligence.

Despite my lack of knowledge about the armed forces when I started at DIA, I was delighted to gain insight into a system and a group of individuals that I greatly respected. I had entered a secretive, insular world, dedicated to defending America at home and advancing her interests abroad, and I couldn't have been more pleased. For years I had hoped to have such an opportunity, and I never thought I would be able to do it so soon. I committed myself to learning and serving, and I kept my eyes and ears open.

I did have some of the misconceptions and presuppositions that come from any lack of contact with a group, one of which was a belief that virtually all service members are politically conservative. This turned out to be true in some ways, but not exactly how I'd expected. For example, the atmosphere within the military intelligence community, and within the military ranks in general, is, from my experience, positively poisonous toward some Bush administration leaders, especially former Secretary of Defense Donald Rumsfeld.

At first I thought the animosity came from his efforts to "modernize" the armed forces, but eventually it became clear that while the Bush administration talked a good game about supporting the military, many of the troops themselves were greatly dissatisfied with how the administration was dealing with military policy in general and Iraq in particular. I met person after person who in 2004 voted for a Republican for House, Senate, and governor, but John Kerry for president. Much of the military is ideologically conservative, but many felt their conservative ideals were being betrayed by an unrestrained executive branch. Further, issues such as lack of body armor, unprotected vehicles, and appalling policies regarding veterans that flare up only occasionally in the public consciousness are searing affronts to the servicemen and -women who have to face these betrayals on a daily basis.

The single most important issue at DIA was, of course, Iraq. The war in Iraq had superseded the efforts on most of our previous priorities, including terrorism, securing vulnerable weapons of mass destruction in unstable areas, and narco-trafficking, among others. Iraq was not the greatest threat to American interests, but we were hemorrhaging money and losing a steady stream of troops there, so the focus naturally shifted.

While many people I worked with were supportive of the war in theory, in practice they felt that leadership had taken its eye off the ball. Real terrorists—as opposed to infuriated nationalists who had no desire to export death—were being overlooked for a war that had neither clear goals nor an apparent endgame. The Powell doctrine of set goals and overwhelming force to achieve those objectives, once lauded by conservatives as an escape from the purported touchy-feely humanitarian interventionism of liberals, was gone. We were well into the Rumsfeld doctrine of light forces and technology supposedly winning quickly and cheaply. At the risk of inviting a million DoD budget jokes, you get what you pay for, and in the invasion of Iraq, as everyone now knows, we paid for far too few troops and a plan that failed to establish law and order. Military and intelligence personnel were accordingly pissed at leadership for screwing things up so badly.

Despite unhappiness with leadership and the bureaucracy, however, I and the vast majority of others at DIA were passionate about helping improve the situation in Iraq. Whether we agreed with the decision to invade, or how the campaign was waged, the general perception was that we should "win" and then get out as soon as possible. The goal for all of us was to help create a situation in which the troops could be responsibly redeployed. Our benchmarks for sensible redeployment varied, but we all knew that the faster the security situation in Iraq improved, the faster we could bring home the troops and put the focus back on international terrorism.

I frequently thought about the people in the field, both military and civilian, whom DIA supported from various sites throughout the United States. As time went by, I felt increasingly powerless and, deep down, craven. I was working in DC when tens of thousands of men and women were out contributing directly to the fight, many trying to bring some semblance of order to Iraq and still more working tirelessly in other areas of the world.

That feeling was accentuated by a specific incident within my team, one that probably had the greatest impact on my eventual decision to volunteer for service in Iraq. I knew that the agency asked for volunteers for missions to Iraq, but its method of doing so was inconsistent. Sometimes the notice would be posted on the internal website, other times an email would go out, and occasionally we'd hear about it by word of mouth. When I felt I had enough training and experience to contribute to any mission, I began to think about volunteering for overseas deployment, to Iraq or elsewhere. I am not a big fan of major change, and heading to a war zone involves quite a bit of it. Still, I couldn't quite rationalize a decision not to do everything I possibly could to help our most critical mission. It was a purely theoretical issue, however, as the agency hadn't called for a group of volunteers in months. With these considerations tickling the back of my mind, something happened that was unique in my experience but common in the military world: One of my colleagues was involuntarily deployed.

Air Force Technical Sergeant James Aiello was, to the best of my estimation, in his late thirties or early forties, and was a Marine trapped in the body of an Airman. He was smart, a tenacious worker, and a kind and helpful teammate. I didn't work especially closely with him, but he was a guy whom everybody liked and respected. His little cubicle was filled with two things: pictures of his family and awards. He had two towheaded young kids and a lovely wife, all of whom he appeared to dote on. The kind of family, by all appearances at least, that everybody hopes for.

I heard from a coworker that he was being sent to Iraq. The details of exactly how it happened are hazy; I think that he was sent to a DIA position in Iraq, which would explain why people referred to it as an involuntary deployment. In theory, virtually all military deployments are involuntary in that they are ordered. A unit is told where it's going, and when it's going there, and that is that. But with individuals who are detailed to specific environments, such as DIA, most have a reasonable expectation that they will be with those elements for the duration that they have been assigned. So an Army Sergeant who is assigned to DIA, for example, may volunteer to work at a DIA position abroad, but the average military intelligence officer working for DIA would not necessarily expect to be sent out of the country. It is possible that I remember the specifics of Aiello's case incorrectly, but the bottom line was that I knew he was told he had to go, and he was devastated.

It meant that for several months, his young kids—at a time when they needed their dad the most—would lose him. It meant that his wife would be left with all of her usual responsibilities plus all of his. It meant that yet another person was being sent into harm's way instead of being with family. And there I was, a young, single, able intelligence officer, watching this husband and father be sent away. I also knew that I had more education about the region, its people, and its culture than the vast majority of people working there, and I felt my knowledge and reality-based approach to analysis could benefit the war effort. I began to think seriously about submitting my name when the agency next asked for volunteers. If 130,000 troops could serve on the front lines, and if my coworkers were being sent involuntarily to do a job that I could do more easily, I simply couldn't justify staying in DC. I began talking to people who had gone before to get their opinions and perspectives. I knew the agency had encountered problems getting enough recruits the last time it had asked for volunteers, and I saw no reason that that would change.

Of course, I didn't realize at the time that one of the reasons absurd DIA had such difficulty in enlisting volunteers for overseas deployment was its internal processes. In early December I received an email indicating that DIA was establishing an analytical counterinsurgency (or COIN, as we called it) team to head to Iraq. The email said the agency needed people for a six-month rotation, but it did not say how many people, where they would be going, what they'd be doing, or when the mission would deploy. Also, because the news had filtered through down the chain of command within DIA, it was not a standardized message, so different offices got different information. But basically it was a cattle call for bodies with no additional details.

The cutoff time for volunteering was 0900 hours the next day. Fewer than twenty-four hours to decide whether you wanted to put your life on hold for six months (minimum) to head to a war zone for an unknown mission in an unknown place at an unknown time for an unknown duration. *No wonder they have such a hard time getting people to sign up,* I thought.

But my mind kept going back to the people whose lives were so adversely affected when they had to abandon their families, especially their kids, because nobody else would go. I thought about what I would have to do, logistically, if I left DC. My apartment, my car, all that stuff. Everything seemed doable, even given a potentially short time frame.

No one else on my team had any interest, and I had not told my boss that I was considering it, mostly because I'd thought there would be time to do so when a call for volunteers went out. I spent that afternoon talking to my coworkers, supervisors, and a few people who had previously completed an Iraq deployment. My leadership was supportive, if a little unhappy at the prospect of losing a good analyst from an already short-staffed group. They told me that my education and abilities would greatly benefit the mission, and that the experience would help my career. The mission, they said, sounded interesting, and, according to my boss, I'd learn more about the intelligence community in a six-month deployment than I would in six years at the headquarters. My colleagues thought I was crazy to go, saying it would be dangerous and ineffectual, but they did not impede the process.

I was lucky to get support from my office leadership; I later found out that some managers refused to submit the names of individuals who wanted to volunteer. These supervisors lied, especially to younger employees, by saying that they had the authority to deny approval for volunteer deployment. Much is made of turf wars among agencies, but those kinds of fights are just as vicious within agencies: The China office, to use a hypothetical example, does not want its new missile expert heading off to work on the Iraq counterinsurgency, and so supervisors were willing to lie and threaten to keep their people in place.

That evening I made three phone calls. I first called my parents, imagining how scared they would be and hoping neither would have a heart attack when I broached the subject. If they were worried when I'd tried to pursue a semester abroad in Beirut a few years earlier—a plan that was nixed after 9/11, leading me to go to Turkey instead—I figured they were going to be monumentally displeased with this development. When we spoke, I presented it as a possibility rather than a certainty ("a plan, not a commitment," as my mom would say), and they took it better than I had expected. I was anticipating tears and appeals to seek psychiatric help, so the actual response—"Are you out of your fucking mind?"—wasn't so bad. We talked it through, and they gamely promised to support whatever I decided. Next, I spoke to my two best friends in the world, starting with Jena, an ally since the sixth grade, and Justin, a smart and candid Texan. I trusted both to tell me what they honestly thought, and after talking it over with these confidants, I decided to do it.

I had a unique chance to actively help a problematic situation, and the ability, both intellectually and logistically, to take that opportunity. With my friends' and family's semi-blessing, I went in the next morning, in early December 2004, and asked my boss to submit my name.

In typical DIA fashion, we heard nothing—literally nothing, no acknowledgment, no further information, no indication that our names had even been received—for an entire month. I slowly met a few other people who had volunteered, but we didn't know if we'd be going, or if we were, when it would be, so we all just waited for more information. After the New Year, we finally got an email saying that we'd be leaving our regular offices almost immediately to start the training and education part of the deployment process, and we should prepare to leave in as early as a month or as far away as late spring. I was officially on my way to Iraq.

CHAPTER 2

The pre-deployment schedule was packed with training. Our group, about two dozen intelligence officers, was greatly varied. We had civilians and active duty, young and old, gregarious and reticent, and a few crazies.

As part of the preparation, we took classes on various aspects of Middle East history, counterinsurgency, and Iraq-specific issues; we prepared to work directly on human intelligence (HUMINT) matters; and, eventually, we did what virtually every DoD employee must do before deploying to Iraq: head to Fort Benning, Georgia.

Fort Benning housed the CONUS (continental United States) Replacement Center, or CRC, a processing operation for deployment. It's about two hours from Atlanta, where DIA shipped us on an early-morning Sunday flight. We arrived around lunchtime, found our barracks, unpacked, and had a few briefings before heading down to the chow hall for dinner and crashing early in preparation for the long days ahead.

Fort Benning has two primary purposes: preparing people to go abroad and the U.S. Infantry School. It's big, it's in the middle of nowhere, and civilians are a minuscule minority among the army folks. Needless to say, the dozen or so civilians in our group experienced significant culture shock. Army soldiers tend to speak primarily in acronyms and profanity, with the occasional regular word thrown in (compared with, for example, Marines, who speak in profanity with an occasional acronym thrown in, and the Air Force, which has a vocabulary of engineering terms and the occasional haughty profanity), so we had to pay close attention to figure out what was going on at any given moment. At Fort Benning many of us immediately learned a new word, an utterance that has dozens of meanings in the army. Pronounced *hoo-uh,* but without a pause between the two syllables, like *hooa,* the utterance was ubiquitous. For example, I was identified by the number 5350, so in the morning, after breakfast, I would head to formation, and when the drill sergeant yelled, *Number fifty-three fifty!,* I quickly replied *Hoo-ah, First Sergeant!* so he knew I wasn't some piece-of-shit civilian who had slept through the alarm, late for 0600 formation.

I was assigned to group one, which meant I had to get up the earliest but was also finished before most of the others, at least when we were on a staggered schedule. Monday was medical, all day, which meant getting stuck with needles. I got jabbed five different times, including once for blood and four vaccinations. That made it hard to put my shirt on in the morning for the rest of the week, but it was good to know that I did not have to worry about tetanus, hepatitis A, the flu, or, my personal favorite, typhoid fever. The army also proclaimed me free of all major communicable diseases, complimented my excellent blood pressure and cholesterol levels, and declared me fit for service in deployment. Everything took forever—I made sure to have a paperback with me at all times—but the delays were cheerfully accounted for by the unofficial motto of "Hurry up and wait."

The next day was Records and CIF (Central Issue Facility), so I spent the morning at various records and paperwork stations, including power of attorney, ID card (which alerted a hypothetical capturing enemy force that we were protected under the Geneva Conventions, a safeguard somewhat less comforting after Attorney General Gonzales identified them as "quaint"), assorted checklists, the chaplain (a required visit), dog tags, and, most disquieting, a last will and testament. The will brought the process much closer to reality. We had plenty of classes and presentations on first aid, IEDs (improvised explosive devices), wounds, and methods of attack, all of which were strong reminders of the seriousness of the preparation and training. But there was something about preparing and signing a will that was especially personal.

We got all our gear at CIF, including multiple uniforms, jackets, sleeping bags, belts, a Kevlar vest, pistol holster, Kevlar helmet, gas mask, and, for me, three pairs of size 15 boots (two desert and a cold-weather black). CIF took all day, so we were introduced to the scientific marvel that is the MRE (Meal Ready to Eat or, alternatively, Meals Rejected by Ethiopians). We figured out the water-activated heating pad and debated exactly how long the MREs would be good for as well as who got the best meal—my Cheese Tortellini lost out to a friend's Beef Enchilada.

We had plenty of classroom training, which was mostly tedious but occasionally entertaining. The sections on the region were like Middle East for Morons; the one-page summary of the "Culture Guide to Iraq," for example, included the helpful hints that "Arabs usually believe that many, if not most, things in life are controlled by the will of God (fate) rather than by human beings. That is why it is difficult to get an Arab to do any form of planning for the future" and "Arabs are an emotional people who use the power of emotion in forceful and appealing rhetoric that tends toward exaggeration. In their exaggeration, wish becomes blended and confused with reality." Hard to imagine why we have a difficult time with dealing with the Arab world.

The lectures also included some unique insight on media relations, such as this nugget of wisdom, advising us not to give interviews, particularly on tape: "If you try to get that tape, they're not going to give it up freely. You're gonna be butt-stroking him in the head." I woke up from my stupor for that comment, racing to make the obligatory butt-stroking joke to the soldier sitting next to me. He was not amused, but at least I knew how to handle the evil, manipulative, Trotskyite press.

Through it all, I was worried about an upcoming activity. Firearms training was, understandably, a required element, and I needed to "qualify," which basically meant shoot decently, with an M16 assault rifle and a 9mm Beretta handgun, which they said we would carry at all times in theater. I knew even then that the odds of me ever having to use a firearm in Iraq were minuscule, and the day I needed to defend myself with a handgun would be the day that Iraq had completely and totally collapsed, but I still had to be capable of carrying and shooting, which was a little disturbing. I was, as a coworker half-jokingly jibed, a commie from pinko blue America; I'd never seen a real gun, much less had to train with one.

All week I was asking people how to qualify, how the weapons worked, and, mostly kidding, where the on–off switches were located. Everybody said it was no problem, you just had to point and shoot, but I was convinced that when it came time to qualify I would somehow manage to be the first person to defy the odds and shoot myself with an unloaded pistol.

Late in the week, we spent a three-hour session going over the basics: how to assemble and disassemble, clean, oil, and love our weapons like extensions of our respective arms. Then we spent ten minutes talking about aim, which basically amounted to "line the sights up with each other and then add the target in at the end." *Yeah, right,* I thought. The next morning at the crack of dawn we headed out to the range, which was freezing and foggy, and there were about a dozen of us civilians in the midst of 250 or so soldiers. We made sure to be at the back of the line so nobody else would witness our expected horrible failures.

For weapons qualification, you get ten practice shots at the targets, which are set up on a thirty-five-meter range at various points. The targets pop up for about three seconds, and you try to hit them before they go down. Generally you get one or two more bullets in a magazine than you need—seven bullets to hit six targets, for example—then break and reload, five bullets to hit four targets, reload, and so on. The exercise mixes various distances, magazines, and numbers of targets, and you have to hit sixteen out of thirty (after the ten practice shots) to qualify.

I was freezing, nervous, and stiff from standing around for three hours. I stepped up to the range, turned off all emotion and nerves, and completely focused. I gingerly picked up the weapon, still slightly concerned about the presence of live ammo, and got set. The targets started popping up, and I started shooting, surprising myself by hitting what I thought were seven or eight of the targets during my practice session. (Sometimes you couldn't tell whether you hit them because they didn't just topple over—it was all determined by computer sensors, making it tough to judge.) I started to think that maybe I would be okay, and then the real qualification began.

I stepped off the range ten minutes later having hit twenty-seven out of thirty. Against all odds. The next best civilian score was a twenty-two, and I had somehow managed to shoot better than even the military guys in the group. The army officially qualified me as an Expert 9mm shooter, and the group spent that evening celebrating our successful shooting with six-packs of Icehouse.

Almost immediately after being notified of our impending deployment, we were in full preparation and training mode. We had briefings, meetings, briefings, briefings, and meetings. The time spent training and preparing was mostly a blur. I was increasingly cut off from friends and family due to the constant travel, and I was attempting to do the irritating things required by a six-month departure from normal life. We still knew few details about exactly when we would depart, but there was a first group (an advance team that would head over about a month earlier than the rest of us to set things up) and a second group, which I was in, scheduled to go over sometime in March. When we were home in DC, we had tons of assigned reading to do, but we never went more than about a week between trips to various trainings and orientations.

In between all the travel, I was frenetically trying to get my affairs in order. A coworker graciously allowed me to park my car at his house, I sublet my apartment, and I was even still teaching LSAT classes at night—the government does not pay very well, and I needed extra money, so my facility with standardized tests was put to good use. I took care of all the logistics, made trips to the Northeast to say good-bye to friends and family there, and visited my parents in London, where my dad's job had taken them a couple of years earlier. Meanwhile, the travel and training continued unabated.

The group was beginning to coalesce, and although we weren't all on the same training schedule, we became friendly. There is nothing like knowing you're heading into a war zone with somebody, even as a desk jockey, to facilitate bonding. As with all groups, sometimes we connected due to common interests, other times through humor and situational circumstances, and now and then through shared irritation with the group's social outliers. I was lucky because I already knew one member of the group, a fantastic woman whom I'd worked with in my first DIA assignment. We stuck together through much of the training, but eventually the group, roughly two dozen strong, bonded around the mutual experience.

Perhaps the most influential event for our collective unity was our driving and shooting training, which was terrifically fun. We went down to a racetrack in North Carolina for a week, very much looking forward to the activities. The first two days were spent on the track, driving sedans, Suburbans, and "disposables," which we crashed with. We did just about every cool thing I'd ever seen in a car commercial, plus some movie stunt stuff. We executed cone drills, forward and backward; we did stopping drills with and without antilock brakes; we learned how to go around corners at the maximum possible speed (spinning out onto the grass when we were too aggressive); and we tested the cars to see how long it would take to stop after slamming on the brakes at a hundred miles an hour. We also tried great things with the disposables, principally learning how to get cars out of our way, whether they were moving or stationary. My personal favorite, though, was the "J-turn," which is what you do when you're going in reverse very, very fast, and you want to turn around to go the other way.

In that drill I was going backward at thirty, forty, fifty miles an hour, and my instructor, who taught these classes when he wasn't busy with his usual professional race and rally driver job, calmly but insistently told me to go faster. Suddenly he said "Turn *now*," and I slammed on the brakes, spun the wheel, popped the car into drive while the back of the car whipped around, and gunned the engine forward just as I pulled back parallel with the road. Thrilling stuff. The next day was off-road SUV driving, in obstacle courses, through the woods, and, most important, getting stuck and then getting ourselves (and one another) unstuck.

Then began the weapons instruction, which was comprehensive and extremely helpful. We practiced taking apart, putting together, unholstering, aiming, etc., and the teachers were excellent. Our main instructor told us the average person can cover ten meters in just two seconds, so for us to be effective, we had to draw and put two rounds on target in that amount of time. Over and over we drew and aimed, from when we averaged about four seconds until we were all under two.

Beyond the 9mm, there was the M16, and although I felt comfortable with the handgun due to our previous instruction, it was still somewhat intimidating to shoot an assault rifle. We got about forty practice rounds, after which it was time for qualification. Continuing my unlikely record of success in this area, out of sixty rounds from a maximum of a hundred meters, I dropped just three outside the kill zone, none of which missed the target. I clocked in at 295 out of 300, with the second-best civilian score at 271, earning some respect along the way. Despite my near certainty that I would never actually utilize this newly discovered skill, I was proud of myself. Another rating of Expert. My family, naturally, was horrified.

I joked with them that far scarier than the weapons training was another fact I learned at CRC. One of our meetings focused on all the factors to be wary of: dangerous insurgents, roadside bombs, and random gunfire from idiotic local celebrations, among other things. I was dutifully writing it all down, taking it in stride when I heard the instructor say, "And of course, you all should remember that there's no alcohol in-theater." I shook the fog from my head. It turned out that U.S. Department of Defense and military personnel are not allowed to imbibe while stationed in a war zone. Something about not being intoxicated if something bad happened—I don't really know since I completely lost focus when the announcement was made. I'm not a huge drinker, but my colleagues and I bemoaned the regulation because we're allowed virtually zero other vices in our business. No drugs whatsoever, no excessive gambling or debt; indeed, a whole assortment of entertaining immoral and/or criminal activity ranging from mild to insane is frowned upon. So a weekend drink (or five) was all we had left for socially questionable behavior that wouldn't get us fired after a polygraph. On the bright side, we made bets about how much weight we would lose.

In the midst of this trip I also named our group, bestowing a moniker that was concurrently affectionate and self-mocking. We were officially the 101st Fighting Keyboarders, and the nickname quickly became popular. I stole it from the derisive nickname for so-called warbloggers, but it fit us better, really capturing the essence of sending a bunch of policy wonks into the middle of a war zone, gearing up for some serious combat typing.

The deployment was fast approaching. The week after I got back from North Carolina, my students took the LSAT, much to the relief of my schedule, and I went to New York and then London to say good-byes. Upon my return it was time to start packing, attend final meetings, and relax for a few days in anticipation of an intense six months. I made sure all the logistics were in order for my departure, had a farewell gathering in Washington, and then the day arrived. I was too busy to contemplate much of anything other than the details of getting ready. I wasn't scared, I wasn't excited, I just was. And then I was on the plane.

CHAPTER 3

Arriving in Iraq was like stepping onto another planet. We flew to Germany, then Doha, Qatar, and finally Baghdad. We flew in under the cover of night, performing the diving, corkscrew tactical landing required for security reasons. Nobody expects to be the first plane blown out of the sky or ambushed on the ground by insurgents, but we all wore our Kevlar vests and helmets just in case. The DIA group traveled with hundreds of troops heading to their various missions, and the general mood was grave. The trip is long and grueling. I gritted my teeth for the spiraling descent, and after days in transit, we hit the ground in Baghdad. I was exhausted, and in dire need of some time away from other people, but safe and sound.

"Head to that building over there!" The technician had to shout over the noise of airport activity, and we scampered to Baghdad airport's main "terminal." As I walked away from the plane, I remember thinking, *This isn't so bad . . . once I get away from the heat of the engines, it won't be too hot.* The engines were already off. Whoops.

The first thing I noticed coming off the plane was the smell, which reminded me of my time in Turkey. The air swirled with dust, which appeared to be the main product of the nation, with mosquitoes following close behind. The landscape was remarkably flat; a coworker remarked that he could easily have been convinced we were a few miles outside of Phoenix. Everything was the color of sand, even the buildings and rocks, and there were bugs everywhere.

We grabbed our stuff and moved to the building. Our liaisons met us, and we got into the government-issue SUVs for the trek to camp. We were stationed within the Baghdad International Airport (BIAP) complex, and we worked and lived in Camp Slayer. Camp Slayer is a collection of palaces and living quarters formerly used by Saddam's regime and its guests. It's dotted with man-made lakes that held huge fish and, according to rumor, plenty of bodies. After the invasion, Slayer was a logistics and operations base for intelligence teams, including the Iraq Survey Group (ISG), whose duty it was to search for the elusive (nonexistent, as it turned out) weapons of mass destruction. The camp housed a variety of classified operations; personnel from the military, FBI, DIA, and an organization that I am only permitted to refer to as OGA, for Other Government Agency, worked on various projects. The ISG was an interagency task force that was active between June 2003 and April 2005, and it was the primary intelligence force in-country during that time. We arrived just as the ISG was wrapping up; there were no WMDs to find or destroy, so the mission was over. As we settled in, the remaining ISG personnel were taking group pictures and packing up, their mission long since converted from weapons hunting to a variety of counterinsurgency tasks. Our group was intended to be the new in-country intelligence focal point of DIA, the lead intelligence agency for the war, and we were ready to make an impact.

As we made our way down the road after landing, exhausted from the travel and disoriented by the new environment, I marveled at the scenery. Palm trees lined the lakes, and the cars kicked up huge clouds of dust as we raced bumpily through the dark. The air was scorching and impossibly dry, even in March, and sand was omnipresent. More palm trees were sprinkled around the uneven road, but on that initial drive we could see only what the headlights illuminated—which did not include most of the various palaces, lakes, and trailers that populated the site. We could see the sky, though, and it was expansive, like in Montana or some parts of the Southwest.

"Pretty impressive," I observed, looking out the window.

"Yeah, not so much when a missile drops out of it," mumbled a tired colleague. I laughed; he grunted.

Eventually we rolled to a stop in front of a well-lit building. It was the housing coordination trailer, where we picked up a set of sheets and a blanket none of us would ever use. We also got our keys, a pillow, and a point in the direction of our new homes.

The trailers, or hooches, were a quick ride away. They had two doors, one on each side of the front, and four little rooms inside, each with a metal locker, table, lamp, and bunk bed. A hallway connected the four rooms within the trailer. The floors were a light blue linoleum made to look like wood, and despite the fact that I wasn't there for the décor, it was hilariously ugly—light blue linoleum fake wood? Amazing.

The room smelled like dirt, at least until I let loose with the pungent and devastating combination of Right Guard spray deodorant and Febreze. Then it smelled like dirt that somebody tried to cover up with bad air freshener. I took the bottom bunk after debating whether it would be worse to climb up and down or to hit my head while getting out of bed, deciding on the former. I threw on the sheets, tossed my three huge bags of gear into the corner, and collapsed on the bed. It was the delirious end of a very long trip.

Just a few hours later, I woke up and headed to the shower trailer. We had a shower trailer (showers and sinks) and a shitter trailer (toilets and sinks), each about fifty meters from my door. Water pressure, temperature, and cleanliness changed daily, but that first morning, against all odds, everything went smoothly. I showered, went to the other trailer to relieve myself of the bottles of water I'd downed the night before, and stumbled back to the hooch to get dressed. Our leadership had told us that we should wear the uniforms we were issued, which had our last name printed on one side and DOD CIVILIAN on the other. I wanted to fit in as much as possible—no need to accentuate my civilian status by eschewing the uniform—so I put on the blouse, pants, and desert combat boots, making sure I was appropriately buttoned, tucked, and laced. I figured nothing would piss off my military co-horts more than a civilian fucking up the uniform, and I was right: Within days a handful of the sartorially sloppy were, if you'll excuse the pun, dressed down by sharp-eyed soldiers.

We spent the first few days getting identification and badges, filling out paperwork for computer and program access, making sure we had the right keys, and various other boring logistical errands. We also saw where we would be working: the Perfume Palace, the same location as the outgoing ISG. The Perfume Palace, which supposedly got the moniker because Saddam's sons kept a brothel there, was outwardly impressive but, I soon discovered, chaotic inside.

The base's main elements were all within walking distance of one another, so at chow time we strolled to the dining facility (DFAC), which was surprisingly well stocked. Lots of options, most loaded with carbs and calories; it wasn't "good" food, but any lack of quality was overwhelmed by sheer volume, which was much better than starving. I was relatively poor in DC, so I was used to eating as much free food as possible whenever I could, and the fact that it was all free meant I'd probably weigh eight hundred pounds when I got back. Still, in those initial days we were just trying to establish some kind of normalcy, and eating was an easy routine to establish.

In the beginning everybody experienced a weird combination of jet lag and adrenaline, and we were all trying to kick-start our bodies into Iraq mode. NyQuil was basically the desert sleeping pill, with Ambien close behind in popularity. In the morning, there were gallons upon gallons of coffee, augmented by the occasional No-Doz or Provigil. Within a week or so we had mostly shocked our systems into compliance. We saw most of the base through the in-processing system, and it seemed as if basic needs were all pretty well met. Along with the hooches and DFAC, the base had a gym complete with treadmills, elliptical trainers, and free weights; a small movie theater; and a building with two pool and Ping-Pong tables. It also had a swimming pool, basketball court, and volley-ball area.

"Ohh, I'm gonna smoke you at the pool table when we finish this in-processing shit. As soon as we have a free minute, you're toast," we'd taunt each other in those initial days.

"Maybe, but you're dead on the Ping-Pong table. We'll go a dollar a point and I'll shut you out. You'll see, I'll—"

"Sir, there's no gambling on base," our liaison chastised.

They weren't messing around, apparently.

When we arrived, we all figured we'd take advantage of the di-versions, but we ended up working so much that the amenities went largely unused (with the notable exception of the gym). Still, it was nice to know what was there.

Unlike the setting in many war movies, it was hardly a light-hearted environment, especially at the beginning. Virtually every-one was in uniform, and soldiers carried their rifles at all times, either the traditional M16 or the increasingly popular (because it was smaller, and therefore easier to manage inside a car or in urban combat) M4. We were also connected to several other bases that had other names and functions, including Camp Victory, a sprawling mini city that held Multinational Force-Iraq (MNF-I) headquarters and was filled with international personnel, and Camp Cropper, known for its detention center for high-value indi-viduals (HVIs). BIAP was at the heart of Iraq and contained the nucleus of American military operations.

Our initial interactions with the other people on base were uni-formly businesslike, and we quickly got accustomed to the sur-roundings. In some ways, the transition was like going back to college: tiny rooms, cafeteria food, and the camaraderie and an-tagonism that both come from being with the same people twenty-four hours a day, seven days a week. Later we would start to make bets on who would first lose it in public, but the initial days were relatively peaceful.

In those first couple weeks of work it was tough to tell how things would end up. Everything was massively disorganized, but we were willing to be patient. My usual response to stress is to become more insular and focused, so I got a lot done, but the work was pretty rudimentary at the beginning. I used to not understand people who described their work as mostly meetings—it was hard for me to imagine so much talking and so little doing. *What the hell happens at those meetings?* I wondered. After a couple weeks in Baghdad, I knew: Not much. Or, that is, ten minutes' worth of actionable material extended into a sixty-minute conference in which everyone feels compelled to speak regardless of whether their thoughts make an actual contribution. I spent a lot of time hopefully saying things like, "Okay, that all sounds great, good plan . . . ," before somebody started up with a rehash of what we'd discussed twenty minutes before. Then I'd sink back into my seat and wonder how long to wait before making another *This meeting's over, right?* type of statement.

The work did seem interesting, but nearly all potentially appealing tasks could be ruined by several factors, particularly bureaucracy and a lack of collective focus. Still, by nature and by rank I was a shut-the-hell-up-and-do-it kind of guy, so I was confident that I would eventually understand my responsibilities. It was more a question of how many meetings I'd endure in the process.

There was, not surprisingly, a definite atmosphere of War Zone, and it wasn't just the hundreds of military personnel walking around with automatic weapons, not to mention the one strapped to my leg. Physically, we could see some bombed-out buildings, and the security apparatus was extensive; cognitively there was a sense of urgency that isn't present even at the Pentagon. The soldiers overwhelmingly seemed sharp and able, and the civilians, in general, weren't far behind. Unfortunately there was a dearth of specific area and topical expertise, but it's no secret that the most highly educated don't exactly flock to enlist or to join bureaucratic government agencies.

There are some people for whom wartime jobs are a great opportunity for upward mobility from poverty, however: We noticed immediately that the base was filled with third-country nationals, or TCNs (*third-country* meaning "not Iraq or U.S."), who performed a variety of tasks, such as cooking the food, running the laundry system, and cleaning the shower and bathroom trailers. Most of the TCNs were from Southeast Asia, but there were also some Iraqis around. And, of course, the ubiquitous military contractors.

The initial weeks were a whirlwind of activity, and getting adjusted left little time for navel gazing or worrying about the overall situation. I was as close to the front line as I could get without enlisting, and I finally had the chance to make the kind of contribution that I had wanted to for years. I would be able to use my education, experience, and good judgment to support the defense priorities of my country. I would be doing mission-critical intelligence, in the field, in the heart of the most important region in the world for American foreign policy. More specifically, I had the opportunity to help salvage the Iraq project or, failing that, at least move it toward a level of stability that would allow us to begin redeploying American troops. I couldn't wait to get my assignment and throw myself completely into the work.

CHAPTER 4

The first sign of trouble came during the transition from the outgoing personnel to our group, their replacements. For the life of us, we couldn't figure out what the hell they had been doing.

"It's a database, see, with all the names and locations of potential shithead activity in this area, and it's taken a lot of time to develop, and—"

"Okay, okay, but how much actionable material have you produced?"

". . . Actionable?"

The whole point of a counterinsurgency mission is to utilize actionable intelligence, which is basically what it sounds like: intelligence you can act on, either strategically or, more likely, at the tactical level. In-country Defense Department intelligence is heavily weighted toward supporting the shooters, but the group we replaced seemed to be providing a circular function, in that they produced materials for . . . one another. Nothing was broadly important enough to pass up to leadership, and nothing was specific enough to pass down to units.

It became apparent that our assignment was not the counterinsurgency mission we'd anticipated. To some extent we were set up as a new and unique group from DIA. Our leadership told us that we were the largest cohesive DIA group to deploy to Iraq, as previous volunteers had been sent to fill individual slots in a wide variety of operations. We were supposed to be *the* connection between the field and the DIA element in DC, and we had just spent months learning about the history of the insurgency, beneficial and ineffective COIN techniques, and the intricacies of Iraqi tribes, religious groups, militias, and political organizations. This knowledge was supposed to make us a crack team of area experts, able to assist action units in the front and support the Iraq team in the rear (back in Washington). We were geared up to apply social network theory, create a better understanding of the insurgency and its accelerants, use a variety of analytical tools that would help identify insurgents and pinpoint the most crucial members of various groups, and employ our strategic acumen to assist policymakers. We were the heavy hitters, DIA's contribution to the Combined Intelligence Operations Center or CIOC (pronounced *sy-ock*)—the hub for U.S. intelligence in Iraq. But when we settled in, we realized that there was basically no mission for us.

The people who had organized our deployment at DIA had apparently failed to communicate with CIOC leadership, and upon our arrival nobody knew what to do with us. There was already an established CIOC counterinsurgency operation, with groups organized by region of the country. There were also teams dedicated to a few specific issues, such as terrorist groups (whose names were constantly being changed from on high—terrorists, jihadists, al-Qaeda in Iraq, something new every few months) and former Ba'athist organizations. We were not surprised that these efforts already existed, but it meant our ostensible mission was already covered. We could not believe there hadn't been communication between our leadership and the CIOC regarding our role. The top-level supervisors on our team had been given an assignment by their DIA bosses, but those directions were inoperative on the ground.

Our group represented about a quarter of the manpower of the CIOC, and the leaders of various teams all had spots they wanted to fill, so our advance team, we learned, had spent most of its lead time trying to convince the CIOC that we shouldn't be broken up and farmed out. To make the case, our leadership basically had to come up with a mission on the fly. Several of the individuals we replaced were supporting human intelligence operations, and they were having success assisting collectors, the people gathering intelligence in the field. Cinematic exploits notwithstanding, collectors spend most of their time managing sources, leaving little opportunity to keep track of the general issues. Help from analysts with the time and resources to track down information they needed had proven valuable, and our leadership quickly formulated a plan wherein we would become the HUMINT Support Team (HST), working with collectors and sifting through intelligence reports to do real-time collaboration with human operators, military units, and military leaders. Virtually all of our extensive preparation was useless for this new mission, but at least our leaders managed to keep us united.

Even the choice of our leadership was not immune to controversy. There were about two dozen of us on the team, and a friend told me later that Major Jerry Samson, an Army Foreign Area Officer for Eastern Europe, was originally slated to head the group. DIA reportedly felt it would be helpful to have a current military officer lead the group, as virtually all other CIOC leaders were military, and Major Samson was a highly capable manager with extensive intel experience. For reasons that I never understood, however, Major Samson was not part of the advance team; the most senior member of that group was a retired army officer and current China analyst, James McMurphy. McMurphy had no managerial aspirations for the deployment, and was slotted for a senior analytical position until he encountered total disorganization upon his arrival. I had trained with McMurphy during the pre-deployment preparation, and I knew he was an extremely capable leader, able to interact with junior and senior people equally well. His former military status also gave him legitimacy without the formality of being an active-duty officer. He was, however, extremely unhappy to find himself faced with the prospect of six months of ass kissing to keep together a team that he'd never had any intention of heading.

Army Master Sergeant Tony Bloom, who went by the respectful moniker "Top," a term of endearment as the highest-ranking enlisted soldier in our group, was also on the advance team. Top was a grandfatherly presence, kind to a fault but also highly competent and willing to be firm if something needed to be done. He was the transmission that kept all our various operational gears working in concert—the guy who did the logistical work the rest of us wanted to avoid so we could focus on analysis. His towering height was accentuated by a sinewy build, kept up by his daily 0600 runs, and topped by the standard army crew cut. In six months I don't think anybody even tried to argue with Top. Additionally, this was his last assignment before retirement, so he wasn't too worried about sucking up to advance his career. He managed the schedule, car sign-out, housing issues, and a host of other things that made our lives easier.

The advance leadership was rounded out by two individuals who were both unique characters. For vague reasons, Bradley John Gareth, who went by John, was appointed senior intelligence officer (SIO) of our HUMINT Support Team. He was a civilian, and was outranked by several other team members, but when things were set up, he became McMurphy's right-hand man. We suspected it was because he was always willing—even eager—to throw his weight around, both literally and figuratively. Gareth looked like Burl Ives on human growth hormone, and at a bulky six foot four, his brassy personality matched his appearance. He was opinionated, loyal, blustering, and eminently quotable. His attention span was as limited as his patience, and he was always volunteering the group for work that had nothing to do with our assigned duties. He essentially doubled as the team mascot, and you were fond of him as long as you weren't the one he sent on his daily wild-goose chase.

The other leader on the advance team was Major Chris Eckhart, a pint-size Army Ranger and Africa foreign area officer who was endlessly enthusiastic, to the extent that his encouraging monologues sometimes took him so far off track we weren't quite sure what he was getting at. He, too, was earnest and loyal, and as an infantry guy he understood the importance of both discipline and occasional levity. The advance team was rounded out by two junior analysts, both of whom I greatly admired and one of whom, Jose, would end up becoming a good friend over the next year.

By the time the rest of us arrived, things were already in disarray. The CIOC people were pissed that the new bodies couldn't just be split up and allocated the way they wanted, and HST leaders were frustrated that their superiors had failed to properly establish the group with their counterparts in the field. Being split up wouldn't have been so bad, except the jobs that needed to be filled were the ones nobody wanted to do (and no leaders wanted to allocate their people to)—mostly administrative or clerical work.

McMurphy managed to keep us together, though, and the group was divided into three cells: two teams of HUMINT support and the strategic team, which we called Strat. When I was assigned to Strat, I was psyched. Strat covered a few specific issues that I considered both important and overlooked, including kidnapping, assassinations, and insurgent financing. I was astonished that there weren't already teams specifically allocated to these issues—three years into the war!—but the topics were all apparently being worked within the confines of the regional groups. That meant there was no comprehensive tracking of kidnapping or assassinations, and without data or analysis there were no policy prescriptions.

On a daily basis, tactical factors are the most important elements of a war effort: What's happening to whom, where, why, and how? It's the job of leadership and intel to understand the overall factors that influence those tactical realities, and kidnappings, assassinations, and financing are the three most critical tactical elements of the chaos in Iraq. The money generated from kidnappings alone could permanently sustain the insurgency, and targeted assassinations are the single greatest factor in the inexorable exodus of the Iraqi middle class. Further, insurgents require two things: enough support from locals to be able to move relatively freely, and funding. If either of those dries up, so does the insurgency. I was excited to be working on these issues, and Strat was really the only holdover from the original counterinsurgency plan.

Strat was small, just five of us, with a geeky Air Force captain in the lead. We quickly got acquainted by working insanely long hours together from the start. Captain Pete Falley, our team chief, was quick to assert his authority. He called "team meetings" about twice a day, mostly to ask us how work was going and to remind us to wear sunscreen and keep hydrated. These summits were especially comical (and irritating) because there were only five of us, and we all sat within a few feet of one another, but he still insisted we relocate to a nearby conference room for the meetings.

We all thought Captain Falley was a little young to be a team chief; he looked like he could have been in his twenties, and we figured he was in his early thirties at the oldest. We were misled by his youthful appearance and relatively junior rank, however: We soon discovered he was in his early forties, an Air Force Academy graduate, stuck at Captain while his peers rose through the ranks. His failure to advance, we eventually inferred, was a reflection of his lack of leadership ability as well as his constantly voiced frustrations. But it wasn't like the *I'm getting things done through my anger* kind of bitching, more like the *I'm lost and covering it up by becoming irrationally irritable* variety. The five of us who worked for him ranged in age from our twenties to our forties, but we shared a common sense of humor, given to loutish banter and practical jokes—the kind of humor that quickly breeds in the petri dish of proximity, youth, testosterone, and conflict. Such camaraderie can unite a group, but when the boss is out of the loop, it can be a recipe for disaster.

One of the more entertaining and revealing incidents came just a few weeks into the deployment, when Captain Falley had already lost the confidence of his subordinates. The entire HST team sat in parallel rows of desk posts, no walls between computer stations, the people in each row sitting back-to-back with the next line of desks. When we wanted to talk with someone down the row, we'd often just roll our chairs down a few feet to have the conversation and then roll back when we were done. Captain Falley would occasionally get irritated by the chair obstacle course this sometimes created, but it was pretty standard. One afternoon I had rolled my chair down to talk to Jeff, a sharp and sincere analyst who had essentially supplanted the captain as our de facto lead, when Captain Falley returned from his wanderings.

He frowned at me.

"Alex, um, here's a lesson learned."

The captain was big on "lessons learned," from staying out of the sun to remembering to bring your (required) badge to work. Most of these lessons learned came when he had screwed something up, so the rest of the competent team really didn't need such basic wisdom imparted at the cost of twenty minutes of potential work time, but we endured it nonetheless, usually with good humor.

"The lesson learned, Alex, is that when you want to talk to someone, you should get up out of your seat and walk over to them."

"Well, sir, I don't think that's exactly a 'lesson learned,' " I deadpanned, "because it's really fun to wheel down the aisle. Seriously, you should try it." I wasn't being rebellious, just kidding around. Jeff grinned, but Captain Falley wasn't amused, and he squinted at me through his BCGs, the huge army-issue prescription glasses so ugly they're dubbed "Birth Control Glasses."

"Well, how about this," he lisped furiously, his face contorting, "I *order* you to get up out of your chair when you want to talk to somebody!"

The entire aisle erupted in laughter.

"*Oohhhhhhh*, shit!" hooted my friend Renaldo. "He just gave you a direct order!"

Imitations immediately ensued.

"I *order* you!"

"Get up off your chair, son!"

I laughed, as did my colleagues, grateful for the comic relief. It wasn't a banner moment for the chain of command, and it was reflective of the lack of judgment—and lack of control—that our supervisor demonstrated in those first weeks. It was so bad, in fact, that HST leadership quietly told us to ignore Captain Falley and take direction from Jeff instead. This put all of us in a difficult position, secretly reporting to Jeff while giving lip service to our ostensible commander and his increasingly dubious assignments.

There was the "training program" Captain Falley established, wherein once a week we would share with one another what tasks we were working on; we all found emergency projects to work on when those were scheduled, meaning they were always put off until the following week. Then there was the third time he reminded us to stay hydrated, and Kevin, a former college professor and self-styled brainiac of the team, bitingly informed him that we were all pissing clear and didn't need to be reminded that water was a required part of daily life. The discomfort intensified when Falley started sharing his personal life, revealing the blowups at superior officers that had likely kept him at the rank of Captain all those years. We also played jokes on him, as we did one another, especially when he fell asleep at his desk, which was disturbingly often. One day, after he insisted several times that he wasn't falling asleep, we wrote WAKE UP on a piece of paper and slipped it onto his keyboard after he nodded off. When he woke up and saw it, we got a lecture on professionalism. From our dozing boss.

The other two teams, despite having vastly superior leadership, weren't doing much better. We had a crappy team chief but interesting assignments; they had good leaders but ill-defined missions. I can't go into detail about what they were doing, but it was work that we all thought probably could have been done just as effectively from the bowels of the Pentagon. Additionally, the bureaucracy of the CIOC was suffocating. McMurphy, our reluctant but intrepid chief, spent most of his time trying to keep the group together (as dictated by DIA) and much of the rest entertaining VIP guests. As head of HST, he technically also had a leadership position within the CIOC; he therefore had to do the PowerPoint dog-and-pony shows for everybody who showed up to check out the flagship intelligence shop in Iraq. The congressional delegations, or CODELs, were especially a joke. A Senator or Representative would waltz in with an entourage of a dozen or so staffers and guests, all of them heading to the center of the circular room where the seating chart and organizational plan were set up. Most, we figured, just wanted to be able to tell people that they had ventured into the belly of the beast. But even if they were genuinely interested, the trips never lasted more than a few days, not long enough to get a real sense of things.

Analysts could largely avoid the bureaucratic wrangling, but sometimes they jumped into it. About a month into the deployment, Kevin the brainiac told Strat that he was quietly working to get Captain Falley dumped from his leadership position. He had made HST leadership aware of the problems, regarding both analysis and character, and he was lobbying for a change. I can't stress enough how important the chain of command is in a government bureaucracy, and even more so in a military organization. To jump the chain of command risked at best a tongue-lashing (usually from the supervisor whose head you went over), at worst career suicide, with subsequent written evaluations reflecting nebulous detriments such as "poor teamwork" or "immaturity." When there was a problem with leadership, we expressed our concerns to our chain of command and that was that. Going beyond the chain simply was not done. I told my immediate boss, Jeff, as well as Major Samson, that the team was not operating effectively, and that was as far as I was comfortable taking the issue. Kevin, however, was willing to go much higher, and he complained frequently and loudly.

Just weeks into our deployment, rumors of a complete CIOC reorganization began to fly, and many of us hoped that the reorg would put a stop to the bureaucratic wrangling that seemed to constantly cripple our efforts. While leaders fought turf battles, nobody knew what the hell they were supposed to be doing.

The greatest problem was the apparent lack of an overarching counterinsurgency strategy. Most of the CIOC's focus was tactical, supporting units with information and keeping track of events throughout the country. But it was almost exclusively reactive, trying to explain and quantify events after they occurred rather than proactively making recommendations and changes to improve the situation. Reactivity due to lack of a coherent plan from above would prove an unremitting problem for the Iraq project, both in-country and at the Pentagon.

Several weeks into the deployment, the long-rumored reorganization plan finally came down, and McMurphy had come through once again, managing to keep HST united. But it came at a price: We would have to give up one person to another unit, and the Strat team would be integrated into the other two HST groups. We weren't at all shocked to find out that Captain Falley was the designee for transfer, and we appreciated the time-honored bureaucratic tradition of giving up the most useless person when forced to surrender personnel to another organization.

What did surprise us was the complete elimination of the strategic team. As per the new reorganization, we would no longer cover kidnappings, assassinations, or terrorist financing. At least that was the initial order, before the inevitable bureaucratic shitstorm. A young analyst on Strat, preternaturally aged by his receding hairline and youthful marriage, had carved out a niche for himself as a liaison to the embassy's Hostage Working Group, the HWG, a small unit much derided for its manic leader, anarchic atmosphere, and record of abject failure. The analyst, Josh Loumey, had a talent for self-promotion and a willingness to jump the chain of command, which meant that his hyperactive enthusiasm often penetrated to higher levels than it should have. Still, he made a good impression with a few important people, and when he threw a fit after his mission was shifted, it made its way up the chain. All it took was a word from a one-star general at the embassy to overrule the colonel who ran the CIOC, and Loumey was back on the kidnapping beat, albeit on a slightly tighter leash.

Baghdad was replete with such bureaucratic fights and pissing contests, with every niche group wrangling for the cover that came from a general's blessing and support. The diffusion of responsibility also meant constant meetings, reassignments, reorganization, and turnover.

A huge issue with the CIOC, and a crucial problem throughout the intelligence community, is that institutional knowledge on any particular subject or area isn't sufficient to respond to the vast demands of national interest in a time of war. During peacetime, having secret knowledge about a country's leaders, infrastructure, and military capabilities creates the opportunity for advantage. We can both predict and affect events with such information. In wartime, action is the key, and intelligence must be structured around that goal. To be truly useful, intelligence either has to be strategically or politically relevant enough to affect policy, or specific and tactical enough to affect ground operations. Simply deciphering the command-and-control structure of a militia, for example, means nothing if that knowledge isn't used toward some beneficial end. Information is the raw material for power, but that raw material must be *used*.

The favorite description of the CIOC was "a self-licking ice cream cone." While I never especially loved the metaphor, it reflected the frustration of the people who worked in an institution that seemed to exist primarily for its own sake. Products were written . . . and then read by other people in the CIOC. Good analysis was done . . . and never seen by anyone who could do anything about it. We rarely received feedback, and we never had a solid conception of who our customers were or what missions we were serving. There were the "priority requirements," which were supposed to outline mission priorities, but they were broad generalities rather than real guidance, and basically each unit was only as useful as its immediate leadership. Meanwhile, the analysts tried to stay out of the cross fire, struggling to do a good job in the midst of the mayhem.

I was getting my sea legs—or desert legs, in this case—and had mostly adjusted to the environment, pace, and people. The social life, such as it was, kept us sane, and I was getting used to life around the base. I had a new roommate, an Egyptian-born translator who normally lived in Indiana, and we sometimes talked in the evenings about the surreal nature of our surroundings; we also traded stories about why we had volunteered to come to Iraq. Many of my immigrant friends have an especially great appreciation for America, and Adil was no exception. He loved his life in small-town Indiana, and his greatest passion was soccer, which he refereed professionally at home and watched every night in Iraq. Because he had signed up for a year and his hours were somewhat flexible, he bought a satellite dish and a TV, which glowed brightly late into the night.

He told me how happy he was when he moved to Indiana, and talked about the great opportunities for his family there. Adil also told me how he had heard about the shortage of translators for the war, and his subsequent journey through the process of applying and getting cleared for classified work. He was translating the interrogations of some of the most notorious regime leaders, and we talked about various interview techniques. He lamented the interrogators' lack of cultural knowledge, which he felt greatly constrained their ability to make progress with the detainees, and said that he wasn't confident about the value of many of the detainees.

We occasionally talked about home, and he joked about the overwhelming nature of the big East Coast cities while I teased him about living in the boonies. He also mentioned that he'd visited Washington just before heading to Baghdad, and one of the very few times I saw him lose his upbeat outlook was when he described that trip.

"And of course I wanted to see the White House, so I went to the gate on the last day of my visit to see it."

"Oh, I live just a couple blocks from the White House," I told him. "I run past it all the time. What did you think?"

He smiled sadly at me. "I know that I attract some attention because of my appearance, but none of the guards at the other sites or monuments had bothered me, so I figured it would be fine."

"Oh, shit . . ." I knew where this was going, and my heart sank.

"I went up to the gate with my video camera, just by myself. I wanted to get a video of it, but in minutes there were policemen coming up to me."

"What did they say?"

"They asked for identification, wanted to see my papers."

Hearing about officials asking for "papers" is always chilling. It's a particularly international phrasing, and evokes, to me, the specter of totalitarianism, even when it's a benign request.

I smiled grimly. "You were just being a tourist . . . it's a brave new world, isn't it?"

"I tried to explain that I was just taking a video to show my trip before I went to Iraq to work for DoD, but they were very suspicious. And of course, my last name is Hussein, so when they see my license, they are very . . . agitated."

"How long did they hold you up for?"

"They asked me questions for maybe an hour or so before I was allowed to leave. I even showed them paperwork for my deployment training, but then they were worried it was a fake." His good humor returned quickly, however: "Still, it wasn't as bad as anytime I try to get through an airport!" We both chuckled, and he went back to teaching me the finer points of soccer strategy.

As the little time I spent outside of work became increasingly routinized, I awaited the results of the most recent changes at work. When it came down, the reorg affected most of the CIOC, but my general group, the HST, was largely untouched. The disbanding of Strat was the only significant change, and the shift wouldn't take place until leadership figured out where to put us next. Gossip abounded, but we would have to wait for the official word. In the meantime our small Strat crew tried to wrap up the projects we were working on, and we looked forward to whatever would come next. I was cautiously optimistic, and soon that optimism was validated.

CHAPTER 5

After the CIOC reorganization, I once again had a new job, and it appeared that despite my dismay at the disbanding of Strat, I had lucked out. I was joining the Direct Action team, the only unit in the CIOC specifically dedicated to supporting tactical operations. The unofficial motto was "Track 'em and whack 'em." Our group actively sought out targets from within the reams of intelligence products; we researched and developed target packages (files of information on individuals or groups giving our forces all the information they needed to take action against the targets), and when the dossiers were finalized, we passed them to units for operational use. This was as close as any of us could get to the front lines, and I was eager to go after bad guys. It was a small team, just three of us, but the work was interesting and intense.

The responsibility for direct action, especially targeting, was weighty, but I was looking forward to using solid information to help kill or capture insurgents and terrorists. Unlike much of the rest of the CIOC, we would be close enough to the ground to make our work meaningful, and I couldn't wait to train up and get started. Further, it looked like I would have excellent leadership and colleagues in my new assignment.

Captain Falley, my bumbling former leader, was banished to another team in the CIOC—out of HST entirely—and Kevin managed to continue working on a never-ending special project that he invented (and explained, at length, to anyone he could corner). Josh, the irrepressible kidnapping analyst, continued his efforts to run around like a madman every time there was an erroneous report of a kidnapping, which left me and Jeff as the lone unassigned Strat refugees. We were both given over to the Direct Action Cell under the command of Air Force Captain Chris White. Captain White was boyish and charming, the antithesis of Captain Falley in personality and leadership ability, and he was relieved to finally have some help with a growing mission.

"Okay, guys, I know things sucked for you in Strat, but this is a great mission and there's tons of cool stuff to do. We're going to figure out where these shitheads are and then go roll them up." Captain White was earnest, and he punctuated most of his oratory with sweeping hand gestures, as if he were palming two imaginary basketballs and waving them around. He was young, smart, and straightforward, and Jeff and I liked him immediately.

"We're pretty excited to be on board, sir," I told him when we first talked.

"It's going to be a lot of work," he cautioned me, "but it will be way more interesting than the other crap people are doing."

"Yes sir, the CIOC seems to be spinning its wheels a little bit, doesn't it?"

To Captain White's great credit, upon his arrival he took a languishing mission and set to work revitalizing it. He recognized what many, unbelievably, did not: For our work to have an effect, it had to *actually leave the building*. Direct Action had the authority to utilize the intelligence reports we all scrutinized daily, and when we found targets that were viable, we could develop them for other units. Action elements appreciated this mission because they simply did not have the resources or the manpower to do the kind of targeting they wanted to.

The training process and deployment helped correct mistaken or misguided assumptions and perspectives I had on a variety of topics. Learning how to shoot, for example, ruined most of the gunfight scenes in movies for me. Before firing a gun, I had no reason to disbelieve that there really were individuals who could take out four people with two pistols while diving to the ground. It seemed a little dubious, but I figured it was possible. As it turns out, not so much. Similarly, I always assumed that while much of the government is mired in bureaucracy and inefficiency, the military must have great technological and material resources, ample manpower, and a chain-of-command system that cuts through red tape. That movie-driven perception, however, is as mythical as the diving sharpshooter. The units we worked with never had enough people doing intel, constantly had computer problems, didn't have the ability to cross-check intelligence with other elements, and found it increasingly difficult to vet their targets due to uncertain and deceitful sources.

My new team generally had better technological resources than those in the field, making us especially useful. Units on the ground were constantly frustrated by the requirements of working with classified documents, especially Top Secret (TS) information, because they simply did not have the personnel or resources necessary to work with the deluge of such material. Virtually every military member has a Secret clearance; for the most part, a Secret clearance requires a simple criminal background check. Relatively few, however, have TS clearances, which require an extensive and difficult vetting process.

State Department personnel often have similar difficulties, which had caused problems with the embassy-run Hostage Working Group. These organizations and individuals had little access to Top Secret computer systems and phone lines, which the CIOC had in abundance. They also lacked the ability to quickly contact analysts at the Pentagon or even other components in theater. We could, and, even more important, we had direct lines of communication to collectors in the field. Units had their own sources and collection strategies, but they were largely cut off from national-level reporting due to classification and technology issues. We were also removed from ground-level tactical responsibilities, allowing us to devote all our time to research and target prep. Captain White, Jeff, and I threw ourselves into the mission.

I started small, just looking through the pages and pages of intelligence reports, trying to find enough information on groups and individuals for units to want to act on. Basically, if we had a location and a description of the insurgent activity, we would try to put something together. The ideal target package had, broadly speaking, geospatial (satellite) imagery, physical descriptions of the location and individual(s), and information about the misdeeds. Once we passed on the information to the unit in the relevant area of operations (AO), its members could either act or further investigate, and if they did move against the target, they could then gather evidence, interrogate, and determine whether detention was worthwhile.

We sifted through many useless reports, and we argued about the likely validity of some claims.

"There's no way those guys are connected," I would tell Captain White. "One is a Shia religious leader and the other is a secular Ba'athist. If they've ever even met, they hate each other."

"Really? If that's true, why are their cousins, who are Shia and Sunni but apparently secular Baghdadis—"

"Who's your Baghdaddy!" hooted a soldier walking by, loudly quoting the slogan printed on T-shirts sold in the base store.

"—secularists and living in Baghdad, married? Look at this report." Then we'd debate whether two guys who had cousins that married two thousand miles away were likely to conspire together despite disparate backgrounds. Other times the information we got would be completely inconsistent, with nonexistent addresses, outlandish accusations, or names that didn't make sense.

"Sheikh Ali al-Dulaimi? Yeah, right. Ali is a Shia name, Dulaimi is a Sunni tribe. This source is just looking to get paid, and the collector got rolled. No way this is real."

"Yup. Look, this report from the same guy has Omar Haeri"— a Sunni first name paired with a Shia surname. "I wonder if he's purposely messing with us with this shit?"

"Still, you know there's a possibility that they are real people, or that the translator screwed it up, or whatever. Better safe than sorry, right? I'll start the database searches, you check if the regional guys have any record of the names." And we'd continue.

It was as close to full immersion as a civilian could get, and I felt energized by being in the middle of a worthwhile mission. I went to targeting meetings with Captain White once or twice a week, in various locations and with an assortment of units, and saw how operations were planned, executed, and debriefed. I met with collectors, helped craft questions for the sources, and learned how collection really works in the field.

Working with collectors was also a myth-busting experience, as they were nothing like the James Bond or Jason Bourne stereotypes. In reality, collectors often have less knowledge about the greater strategic picture because they need to spend so much time and effort dealing with their sources. They have endless knowledge about specific topics and people, but they need guidance from analysts and supervisors to direct collection toward greater strategic ends. There is a regrettable disconnect in the intelligence community between collectors and analysts, with collectors often viewing analysts as bureaucratic desk jockeys and analysts sometimes seeing collectors as amateurish cowboys. There is some truth to these stereotypes, of course: Good collectors have the ability to brush off the fear and doubt that would disqualify most people from the job, sometimes leading to overconfidence and singular focus, which can be beneficial or harmful. And a good analyst needs to be practical and skeptical about the information he or she is processing, which can frustrate collectors. There can be a similar divide between analysts and action units. These dichotomies are accentuated and reinforced by the physical separation and lack of communication between analysts and action elements, both in intel and in the military, a structural problem that cries out for correction.

Because we worked with collectors, however, many of these problems were mitigated simply by direct communication. Over time, the Direct Action Cell proved itself worthy of trust and cooperation, and we all better understood the self-perpetuating circle of tactical operations and intelligence. Collectors learned what kind of knowledge we needed to create valuable target packages, we figured out how to best research and present that information for successful operational action, and together we worked with the units to effectively exploit those operations to the benefit of the collectors. All over Iraq—and throughout the IC in general—this circle is broken by bureaucracy, leadership mismanagement, and distance (both literal and figurative) among the various parties, but within our small sphere, all parties were trying to make it work. The successes were tentative, but we at least had a blueprint.

We were also enjoying working with one another and, dare I say, having some fun. Jeff, a polite and straitlaced divorcé who didn't drink or curse, was the perfect straight man for me and Captain White. Our friend Renaldo nicknamed him "PG-13" for his abstinence from most sins we could think of, and PG-13 was a good foil and a great sport. Renaldo himself was a character, frequently interrupting the monotony by asking random personal questions that provoked either total indifference or an animated discussion. He also had a temper that, while seldom released, was formidable, and instigated the creation of the "Latinometer," a hand signal we used to represent how pissed off he was and a lighthearted mockery of the Latin stereotype.

All these elements came together in a particularly memorable event a day before a big volleyball game. There was a friendly rivalry between the two main groups within HST, and each team often informed the other how much smarter, more talented, and better-looking it was. We were cheerfully merciless. In the spring, before the temperatures rose to truly unbearable levels, people occasionally hit the volleyball court on Sunday mornings, which by then was usually the only time we had off, and eventually the intra-HST derision began to include individual performances in the volleyball games. After weeks of abortive attempts to schedule a match between the two main HST groups, we finally got one together. Shortly before the contest, Renaldo and I were speculating on what the prize should be.

"Don't you think the shame will be enough? The undying humiliation of being beaten so badly and so publicly?" I made sure to talk loud enough to be heard by the other team, which sat one row over from us.

"I'm not sure," Renaldo mused. "I think we might need something better, more tangible."

"We could make the loser bring us food from the shop, or something. I'm never too fat for more cookies, for example." There wasn't a ton of room for creativity when it came to possible prizes from on the base.

"No, it's gotta be something cool," Renaldo mused.

Suddenly his eyes lit up, a mischievous gleam replacing the usual computer-induced dullness.

"Hey, PG-13," he said to Jeff. "Didn't you say something about your ancient girlfriend doing pottery with her cousin or something?"

Jeff had a history of dating older women, and with him in his early thirties and her pushing forty, it was fair game for teasing. He turned around and rolled his eyes at us. "It was her niece, but yeah, she emailed me that they were doing pottery. I think last time they made a—"

"Listen, listen." Renaldo was on a roll, not about to be sidetracked by Jeff's explanation. "What we need is . . ." He grinned, pausing for dramatic effect. "A *trophy*! We need to get your girlfriend to make a trophy for the winner, an HST championship trophy for our victory. We'll put it up and hail it as representation of our triumph."

"That is exactly what we need," I swiftly concurred, "and your girlfriend is just the one to do it."

Jeff was nonplussed. "I don't think so, guys. I'm not asking her to make a trophy at arts and crafts or whatever."

"Aw, c'mon, tell her to take a break from making ashtrays and construct something brilliant, something epic," I implored. "I'm sure she's an excellent craftsman, and we need something fitting for our win." I was starting to like the idea, and Renaldo certainly wasn't about to let up.

"Yeah, why not? Why won't you ask her?"

"I'm not going to ask her to make us a trophy. That's ridiculous."

We were all cracking up, but Renaldo and I weren't dissuaded.

"Aren't you two dropping L-bombs already?" I asked Jeff. "If she really loves you, she'd be happy to make a trophy. It would confirm her affection."

"Yeah," seconded Renaldo, "it can show how much she cares."

"I'm not doing it."

It took a week, but we finally got him to ask her to make the trophy, and it arrived two weeks later, a brilliant piece of pottery that we treasured and kept in a place of prominence for the rest of the deployment. Even after Jeff's girlfriend dumped him two months before his deployment ended. Deployment wasn't very good for relationships.

In the military wartime environment, notable especially for its lack of women and surfeit of testosterone, virtually no humor was out of bounds, and mordant comedy was especially esteemed. Before anyone went on a convoy, we'd loudly stake claim to his possessions in the event that he didn't return, and we'd mock-seriously argue over who would get the best belongings. We would joke about driving down the base road nicknamed Sniper's Alley for its proximity to a large apartment complex said to house many former regime members, and anyone who made the mistake of flinching when a mortar or rocket shook the building was mocked and imitated. Occasional moments of laughter helped keep morale somewhere north of desperation. They both reflected and resisted the absurdity of many of the people and circumstances in our communal existence. We had little contact with friends and family, being almost completely disconnected from the worlds we'd left behind, and it was hard to process just how easily life went on without us back home. Any psychologist would say that we were simply overcoming discomfort with bravado, and that's probably true, along with the adage, You can either laugh or cry. We preferred the former.

Still, as the weeks and months dragged on, overall morale began to fall, first slowly and then with increasing rapidity. Although most of us had achieved some kind of routine, we couldn't help but see the crushing red tape and turf wars that were debilitating the war effort. Those of us who had studied or worked on Middle East issues for years saw the toxic results of having military intelligence officers with little awareness of area politics or culture try to assess the situation, and given the vacuum of high-level leadership on strategic issues, voids were being filled by people who lacked the experience or education to make improvements. Success stories were the exception, and my teammates and I knew that stagnation was the equivalent of losing.

The HST was doing good work, and we earned praise from CIOC and MNF-I leaders for the relative efficacy of our analytical process and results. We linked collection, analysis, and action, and we had a good combination of high-profile operations (kidnapping support, social network analysis) and low-key but vital undertakings, primarily evaluating intelligence reports and sources. Whether being in Baghdad was a significant benefit to our work was another question, but at least we were a stable group. The rest of the CIOC, conversely, was in constant flux, and the reorganization did little to define a coherent and cohesive mission. Consequently, nobody ever quite knew where assignments came from or to whom they were going, and many of us felt that the CIOC was spinning its wheels. We saw the insurgency adapting and adjusting to events better than we were, and it was impossible to tell if high-level leaders realized this, let alone whether they were taking steps to rectify it.

To be successful, an insurgency doesn't have to "win," it just has to continue to exist. Every day we went to the same morning briefing, which theater commander General George Casey presided over via audio, and we saw the same discouraging trends continue week after week. The problems were widely reported in international media: Oil production was stagnant. Electrical production was stagnant. Water purification was stagnant. There were goals and projections to improve these situations, but every time the deadline for improvement approached unmet, the target dates were simply moved back. Bizarrely, the primary military goal seemed to be fighting "terrorists," generally referred to as jihadists, most of whom were foreign fighters. Press and public Department of Defense reports consistently put the jihadists at between 5 and 10 percent of the overall insurgency, and even that estimate is probably overestimated. Those who did not buy into the jihadist theory of the insurgency largely argued that Ba'athists, or former regime elements (FREs), were driving and even remotely commanding the insurgency.

All the high-level people had theories on the origins and driving force of the insurgency, but they seemed to miss the simple but imperative fact that for an insurgency to survive, it needs support—or at least acquiescence—from the masses. Leadership mostly focused on funding and training programs as the most important elements to defeat our enemies, but the Iraq insurgency is relatively inexpensive and low-tech. The importance of popular support was (and continues to be) underestimated, perhaps because it was the most difficult element for our forces to deal with, due to insufficient manpower and training in nation-building operations. A population without electricity, water, and jobs is much more likely to support violent groups than one with basic services and economic opportunities. Without support from the people, violent groups' tactical abilities decrease, and hostilities cycle down instead of spiraling up. While the debate over jihadists versus Ba'athists raged, the burgeoning nationalistic and rejectionist Sunni movement and anti-U.S. Shia factions consolidated support, power, and violent capabilities, leading to an incipient civil war right under our collective noses.

To be viewed as legitimate by its people, a government must generally be competent in two areas: security and basic services. Iraqis view the United States as the government as much as they view their own elected officials as the government (after all, they reason, an occupying military must control the state, right?), and failure to meet those basic requirements offers insurgents an opportunity to present themselves as able to govern effectively, or at least better. Further, because Iraqis see the U.S. as overwhelmingly powerful and advanced, they think we must be able to provide security and economic opportunity—so if these things do not exist, many believe, it must be because we purposefully fail to provide them. A frequent reference among Iraqis is that the U.S. put people on the moon; how could a nation that can land on the moon not provide electricity?

A young Shia cleric, Moqtada al-Sadr, understood this, and set up his army, the Mahdi Militia, as Iraq's version of Hamas or Hezbollah, attempting to provide for the people what the government can't (or won't) while representing nationalism through armed struggle. Most of us in my group went to Iraq believing that things were improving, if slowly; at that time, spring 2005, there were plans to finalize and ratify a constitution, hold elections that would allow for real sovereignty, and begin transferring security responsibilities from U.S. troops to Iraqi forces. I'd known when I went over that things were bad, but I didn't realize how bad—and crucially, I didn't know that the disaster continued to be perpetuated by failed leadership and the absence of a coherent intelligence or military strategy.

As the months wore on, many of us understood that we were seeing the most authentic and complete picture of the Iraq that American leaders had created, and it was crushingly depressing.

CHAPTER 6

As we increasingly recognized our mission's lack of positive impact, the creeping sense of stagnation intensified, and we sought outlets for our dissatisfaction. For most of the deployment, I tried to avoid sharing bad news with family and friends back home. I did not want to dump my frustrations on them, and I especially didn't want them more worried about me than they already were.

In the midst of the dawning feeling of uselessness, that façade cracked slightly, and I sent home an email that became infamous among my family and friends. It was a combination of honesty and darkness, and I excerpt it here to give a sense of the changing outlook many of us had as we increasingly understood our role in a doomed conflict. It is one thing to explain, in retrospect, my changing perspectives; it is another to be able to show my unedited thoughts from Baghdad.

I stole the format for the update from one of my favorite columnists, the inimitable sportswriter Bill Simmons, by matching song quotes to the descriptions of life in Baghdad. I should admit that I have "bad" taste in music—no cool, hipster stuff for me; I happily enjoy mainstream tunes, including plenty of pop. Never was this more true than in Baghdad, where my work was fueled by steady doses of Evanescence, Linkin Park, Sarah McLachlan, Metallica, the Dixie Chicks, and the like. My favorite, though, and the music that I'll forever remember as my outlet for the difficulties of Baghdad, was Kelly Clarkson. Because I was listening to her music so much—and perhaps because I was losing my mind a little—the email took the format of matching Kelly Clarkson lyrics to my observations. Sadly (or perhaps fortunately, depending on your perspective), the vagaries of permissions law preclude including the specific quotes, but the email's content remains reflective of my real-time impressions.

Hey everybody,

I'm sitting outside my trailer, munching on a cigar, and it's approaching 2200 hours. I imagine there have been times in my life when I was more tired, but I can't remember them. I'm not a big cigar guy, but before leaving DC, I bought enough to have one every other week for as long as I'm here. I figured that we aren't allowed very many vices, and it certainly beat getting addicted to cigarettes. Also, it seemed like a decent way to mark the time. So I'm outside in the canvas chair I bought, typing and puffing away until I either finish the cigar or get eaten to death by mosquitoes.

As is my wont, I have established something of a routine. It is comprehensive and inflexible for two reasons, I think. First, the total lack of control I have at my job irks me and leads me to want control over the few hours a day I'm not at the office. Second, other than the day-to-day insanity at work, there's very little that affects my plans. There's nowhere to go, nothing to do, and no one to see. So I plan, and then I stick to the plan.

Most of that plan, of course, involves my work hours, which are intense. This week I worked 85 hours, Monday through Saturday, and I don't see much sign of it abating. I'm in every morning by 0730, because we have a meeting then and it would be not good to miss it. We have another meeting at 1930, also mandatory, which usually lasts for about half an hour.

So the absolute minimal time at work is 12.5 hours, but if you get in a half hour early to catch up on overnight email, get things set up for the day, etc., and stay a half hour after the nightly meeting to finish up outstanding issues, which is pretty standard, you're up to 13.5 hours a day. And that's assuming that nothing important is going on in the evening, that you don't have any projects that need to be worked on or that there's nothing time-sensitive on your desk.

Well, there's always time-sensitive shit, and there's always stuff coming up in the evening, and projects are constant. There's just no escaping that, so I'm usually at work until between 2130 and 2230 every night, which makes for a 14-ish-hour day.

We each established our own default schedule, with some people finding a way to work reasonable hours and others completely throwing themselves into the job. I was in the latter camp; I wanted to spend as much time as I possibly could in the office, trying to made a positive impact. I thought if I worked hard enough, maybe sheer volume could overcome my increasing doubts.

A directive came down this week that we should limit our hours, and that was a result of two factors. First, leadership is worried about burnout, and I think they're right . . . about some people. Some are obviously not capable of maintaining this pace, but I figure job Darwinism will take care of that. I've worked crazy hours before, particularly during an insane two-month stretch with a law firm, so I know my limits, whereas a lot of people do not.

Secondly, though, is that we do our time-keeping through our home offices, and apparently some administrators back home are giving people shit for working so many hours. Although we're working under a different command here, our salaries, including overtime, apparently come out of the budgets of our home offices. The gall of people in DC questioning the hours of people who volunteered to come to a war zone is, to me, unconscionable. We'll see how it all works out.

One of the good things about being here is that we're allowed time for PT (physical training). After neglecting this opportunity for the first week, I'm now very much on the bandwagon. So at around 1600 on the rare days that I can get away for a few minutes, I head home to change, and I alternate lifting and running. Lifting is in the palace that we turned into a gym, which isn't bad at all, and for running, I cruise around the base in the obscene heat, sweating out roughly 60% of my body weight. I'm doing probably a few miles each time. Escaping for this masochistic exercise is rare, but when I can, it takes the focus away from the crushing monotony of the week.

Sunday offers a respite, usually just a half day in the office, so I wake up as late as possible, which is around 1000 since I'm used to being up so early. After eating and heading over to the computer trailer to check my unclassified email, I go into the office. Before it got too hot, sometimes we'd try to get in a basketball game, but now we can only play at night.

Then, after work, dinner, emails, a little reading, and it's off to bed for what I hope is enough sleep to counterbalance the lack of it for the following six nights. And that's the week. We call it Groundhog Day syndrome, which reflects the fact that every single fucking day feels exactly like the one before it and the one that will follow. I usually don't know what day it is, just whether I'm close to or far from the coming Sunday, which is fine. I like throwing myself into work, never more so than when there's absolutely nothing else to do.

The routine was basically the same for everyone: long days Monday through Saturday, a slight break on Sunday, and then start over. The heat eventually prevented outdoor activity, and there really wasn't much to look forward to, nothing to distract from the office gloom. I hadn't taken a day off in six weeks, and time was an increasingly abstract concept.

It's a little depressing here, and I tried for a while to figure out why, and I'm convinced that it's for two reasons. First, there's nothing to really look forward to, at least nothing unusual. I can't look forward to a nice dinner, or catching up with friends, or heading out to a movie. The walls seems to rise higher and higher every day, and I think the adjustment to having freedom when I get back will be much weirder than having it taken away.

Also, without getting too specific, there's recently been an immediacy of mortality for me, which is not to say that I'm in danger but just that it's important for us to stay focused on the environment, and that's hardly conducive to vivacity. So the things that really make my day (or week or month) are from the outside—emails and letters and whatever, and to a lesser extent, the occasional minute to shoot a game of pool or read a novel.

On one trip to Baghdad, I was riding a bus downtown when a huge explosion rocked the street, sending people scattering for cover. Weapons were cocked, adrenaline pumped, and a coworker and I abandoned the bus, walking back to the relative safety of the embassy compound. Not long after that, a lucky mortar shot landed right outside the main store we all used on an adjacent base, resulting in several casualties. I had been at the store that morning. We quickly shrugged this stuff off; it was nothing compared with what was going on outside the wall, though it was still nerve-racking when it happened.

The work situation is okay. There is simply a TON of politics out here, and I don't mean Republican and Democrat, but rather turf battles and debate over what agencies should be doing tasks and shit like that. Makes me glad those fights are way above my pay grade, but it's difficult to know that at any time we could be reorganized into different jobs or areas or whatever.

In the beginning, I stayed pretty quiet, just watching and figuring things out. By now, though, I'm fully immersed, and getting a lot done; I think avoiding the bureaucratic squabbles at the beginning, making sure I didn't piss anybody off, is paying dividends.

I've had an opportunity to do some traveling recently, and although I can't really elaborate, it was a great break from the usual routine. Some people here refuse to leave the base because they're worried about security, but I can't see not doing whatever

I can to be effective. If that means traveling, I'm up for it, and so far it's been worthwhile.

Taking the helicopter to the Green Zone was a welcome break from Camp Slayer, and I was able to do good work downtown, interacting with collectors, meeting with direct action representatives, and dealing with the Hostage Working Group, among other things. The flights themselves offered great views of the city and were far less dangerous than the IED-laden roads around Baghdad. We flew into the embassy compound on a Black Hawk, often with its doors removed, .50-caliber machine guns sweeping warily on both sides.

The embassy itself was one of Saddam's old ruling palaces, a huge, lavish area that I am sure the Iraqis would like back sooner rather than later. It includes one enormous main building essentially separated into three wings; row upon row of trailers behind this where people live; a warehouse for temporary housing; a pool; and some park-like areas in front and behind. There are a few gaudy statues outside, and the inside is decorated with obscenely intricate detail. My favorite room had a twenty-foot-tall mural of SCUD missiles being launched.

Outside the main compound was a bus station, from which we could travel to various places in the city. On one trip I had some free time between meetings, so a friend and I jumped on a bus downtown. After checking out the al-Rashid hotel, where journalists used to stay, we walked a mile or two down to the Iraqi Tomb of the Unknown Soldier, a huge circular structure with an enormous multicolored spiral at the top. We could see virtually the entire city, including the famous crossed swords, which we walked toward. Weirdly, the downtown was completely deserted. Being in an empty place that was once bustling with life was surreal.

Some of you have emailed me to say, "I could never do that." The thing is, I wouldn't think that the people here are a subset of the population especially suited to working crazy hours, becoming accustomed to frequent sounds of gunfire, or generally working in a wartime environment. But we all manage to do it. The question is not who can do it, though I'm not saying that everybody can. The real difference is who would *choose* to do it, or put him- or herself in a position where it's a possibility, and that is a significant thing.

I received many emails with this sentiment, with several friends asking me: How do you get used to the violence, or the sounds, or the danger? I answered them by drawing an analogy; an imperfect one, to be sure, but it helped them understand. Imagine you lived, I said, in a town that included a prison, and your house was just a few hundred yards from the wall. That would absolutely raise the level of danger in your daily life. Say the prisoners occasionally fought or rioted to the extent that you could hear it. Certainly that would be threatening, but you'd still have the wall in between.

Even if a prisoner or even several prisoners escaped, what would the odds be that they would happen upon your house? The odds that you'd even be home if they did? And although the prisoners would do nearly anything to escape, they'd know that consequences for attempts were severe. You would factor all that in and simply go about your daily life, perhaps with a few more precautions or procedures in case of emergency, noting a level of danger higher than the average person's but not so high that you'd live in your basement all the time.

And that is what we did: figured in all the variables, considered the odds, and lived accordingly. Of course the *situations* are not totally analogous—just how one might deal with them. In Iraq the "prisoners" had mortars and rockets, so the comparison goes only so far, but the danger can still be rationalized down to relatively little, particularly while living it rather than imagining it. While that's obviously not true for the people who are fighting or working out in the open, for the vast majority of us who were combat support, I think that was what happened. It would have been ridiculous to constantly fear the threat, so I compartmentalized and went on with life.

Far more dangerous than my travel, I wrote, were the local

flora and fauna. Not long before I sent the update, I had an uninvited guest, a vicious and sinister insurgent who somehow snuck into my room. I woke, as I normally did, with the alarm blaring for at least half an hour. I threw it on the ground, another common occurrence that I'm sure endeared me to my roommate, and as my eyes tracked their disjointed path across the floor, an unfamiliar sight was transferred to my brain. I blinked. There was a creature on my floor that looked like a spider, except uglier and meaner. What I saw that morning I had never encountered before: a scorpion. Having just awakened, I was understandably nonplussed. I blinked again. My eyes initially told my brain that it was at least eight feet long, which I immediately dismissed as being wrong—it was much larger.

Wait. No it wasn't, it was little! Just a little guy, no more than a couple of inches long, probably an inch and a half . . . with obviously murderous intentions. I idly tried to remember where I had put my gun when I saw it lazily raise its vicious, homicidal tail. This was the perfect opportunity to shoot it, so I reached to my desk . . .

. . . and grabbed my camera. "Nobody will believe this unless I take a picture," I mumbled to the intruder. "Don't move." After a few snapshots, I was satisfied that I had my proof. I then contemplated how I could kill the intruder with no possibility that it could scurry out of sight. I decided upon the good old army boot, desert-style, and with one good *THUMP!* my little friend was no longer of this world.

In a moment of vengeance, I picked him up and placed him on the front step as a warning to other potential intruders. I'm confident that all other scorpions heard of my cruelty and stayed away accordingly. On a related note, I made sure to shake out my boots every morning from then on.

My email had gone through the important updates, but there was one more point I wanted to make, something that bothered me about how I represented the experience of being in Iraq. I was far from the norm, and I wanted to get that across.

I'm very tired and this is very long, but I do want to add one final thing. I think for many of you I am the only person you can associate with this conflict. Before I came, I had no one to associate it with, and that depersonalization is understandable but unfortunate. Without becoming the Baghdad version of Thomas Friedman, I want to share a story about a guy with whom I play basketball who's far more representative of the people here than I am.

Jack is 36 years old, but he looks ten years younger. He's from a southern state, and he is one of the disproportionately high number of Reserve troops serving in-theater. He signed up because the Reserves historically are used only in true emergencies, he said, and although he didn't feel that he would be able to devote enough time to his family if he were on active duty, he wanted to make himself available in a crisis.

He doesn't have a say in how "crisis" is defined.

He's mostly unconcerned with politics because he doesn't have time for it. He's been married 12 years, and his time is fully occupied by his three children, 10, 8, and 6. He owes much to his wife, and praises her as the glue that holds the family together. He would help out more, but it's tough to work full-time, take a full load of classes at school, and be a good dad.

A great regret, he says, is not realizing the importance of college when he was younger. After high school, he bounced around some and eventually began work at a trucking company, first as a driver and then moving up to manager. Meanwhile, his kids got older, and he wanted to make sure they could get an education, which meant saving money, continuing to move up the ladder, being there for them by having consistent hours, and, most of all, he explains, having the moral authority to talk about the value of education. Still working full-time, with his wife also taking classes, he enrolled in the local community college.

Two years later, having demonstrated both talent and interest in geography, he graduated with his associate's degree. This came just after he was accepted with nearly a full scholarship to a local four-year program and promoted at his job in a two-week span, all at the age of 35. Jack lives 45 minutes from where he works because that's as close to the city as he could afford, and he hopes the teachers in his town are as good as those in the closer suburbs. He grinned when he told me that there were few days when he didn't both go for a run in the morning and tuck in his kids in the evening. Three weeks after he received his associate's, his Reserves unit was activated. Three weeks after that he was in Iraq.

His job has been given to someone else now, so he's not sure what he'll do when he gets back, and he has taken a massive pay cut. His wife has had to cut back on the hours of class she takes, and she says it's tough to explain where Daddy is. Still, the kids take pride in what he's doing, Jack says, and the youngest once asked him if the kids in Iraq have the same toys as those in the U.S. Jack laughed with equal parts pride and horror, I think, when I suggested he might have a future philosophy major on his hands.

Jack is just one example, but he's representative of the people here: hardworking, proud, committed, unassuming, and counting down the days until we can get the fuck out. Jack isn't a saint, but there are few people for whom I have more respect.

I know none of you need be reminded about the human capital and the human cost, and I hope this doesn't come across as any kind of lecture. It is just to say I am an anomaly here—well educated, politically aware, and with opportunity and mobility before I left and when I return. Perhaps you'll say to yourself, "Yes, but you're *my* anomaly," and I understand that. But to the extent that you can, when you think of Iraq, think of Jack. I joke about my scorpion and my helicopter trips, and I lament the hours and the phone problems, but I'm under no illusions that this is anything like being in the field. This isn't a rah-rah speech, and many of you will I'm sure take it many different ways, but I haven't talked in much detail about the other people here so I hope you forgive the digression.

Most of the time it's fine out here, sometimes it sucks (usually when I don't get enough sleep, which is, um, always), and it's always good to hear from you guys when you get the chance to write. Don't worry, I'm totally safe, nothing to worry about, and I'll be in touch again soon.

I always lied about the security situation in my emails. I rarely felt like I was in any imminent danger, but usually the mortars and rockets that hit the base came without warning—and therefore no time to wonder whether you'd be okay. There was the huge car bomb explosion during my trip to Baghdad, the time I missed the deadly explosion at the PX by a few hours, and plenty of attacks on the base, which were so common that nobody flinched. The general rule was, if you could hear it, you were too far away to be hurt. Fortunately I avoided the most common attacks, roadside IEDs, by traveling via helicopter, and the base was far safer than being in the field. For the most part we didn't even think about the dangers—they just became part of the wallpaper—but I still wanted to minimize them when talking to friends and family.

Meanwhile, I was pushing to do more for the units I interacted with through the Direct Action Cell, and we slowly built trust and solidarity with the elements we supported. After a while they started asking Captain White, my boss, to assist with post-mission operations, and eventually I joined him. While most of my HST teammates remained dissatisfied with their roles, believing they contributed little to the war effort, I at least felt like I was doing valuable work. Of the hundreds of people in the CIOC, I honestly believed the three-person Direct Action Cell had the best mission. Going after the bad guys, even if it was the equivalent of bailing out the *Titanic* with a thimble, was at least doing more good than harm, I thought. But my optimism was misplaced; I was wrong.

CHAPTER 7

"I'm serious, he's a deaf-mute, not an insurgent!"

"Naw, he's fuckin' faking. I'm sending him to Abu G."

Nerves rubbed raw at the end of a very difficult night, hours past dawn. It was a few months into my deployment, and I was arguing with a senior enlisted interrogator. Captain White and I were working with a brigade to pursue suspected insurgents and facilitators. That night a combination of U.S. and Iraq special forces was hitting targets we had helped identify and research, and the brigade's S2, or head of intelligence, asked us to assist with the detainee in-processing.

The op was a large one, part of the last hurrah of a unit scheduled to rotate out of Iraq soon after. They had been tracking and targeting many groups and individuals in their AO, or area of operations, for months, and were eager to take down some bad guys. Many U.S. operations occur at night, and this was no exception. After working from seven in the morning until ten at night at the CIOC, I drove over to the operation headquarters, where the detainees would arrive. We set up the area, made sure the surroundings were secure, filled out paperwork, and discussed how the evening would go.

"Okay, we're going to bring in these shitheads on that pad over there, and then walk them over to this field. We'll put them on the ground and tag them, take pictures, and do a field debrief. Then they're off to Abu G"—meaning the infamous Abu Ghraib prison—"where they belong." The S2 looked around, apparently satisfied with the setup. Then he continued.

"For those of you who are new at this, it's time to cover the names on your uniform. You don't want these shitheads reading your name and coming after you in twenty years. They'll all be blindfolded, of course, but no reason to take chances. As we in-process, we'll get their names and give them numbers and then move them along." A smart and effective Army Special Forces Captain, the S2 wanted no screwups for the last big operation before he left.

He nodded toward me. "We've got DIA helping us out tonight, so they'll be roaming around. They're cool."

I didn't feel particularly cool, but neither was I nervous. It was finally time to see what eventually happened with all the work I was doing, and I was confident that the targets were bad guys whose removal from Iraqi society would benefit the country and its nascent government.

The S2 walked over to me and my boss. "Just fill in where it looks like we need help," he recommended, "and if there's anything you want to contribute, no problem." It was unusual for a field intel officer to be so accommodating to DIA intel, especially since I was the only civilian in a group of several dozen military guys. But I had worked hard to earn the respect and appreciation of the service members, and the result was this opportunity to see (and contribute to) the endgame of our work.

As we waited, the air swirled with bugs and sand. The spotlights illuminating the field for the operation attracted an impressive, if highly irritating, collection of insects, many of which seemed big enough to carry passengers. They mostly stayed away from my uniform, which I had sprayed liberally with permethrin, the highly toxic, allegedly carcinogenic insecticide. My team chief had his degree in neuroscience, and he vigorously discouraged us from using the stuff due to the neurochemical dangers, but I figured the risk of long-term brain damage was outweighed by the more immediate menace of being eaten to death by mosquitoes the size of Ping-Pong balls.

The bugs shared airspace with sand that was fine but omni-present; you couldn't feel it buffeting your skin, but you could nearly always taste it in your mouth. I had developed a mildly dis-gusting spitting habit from constantly trying to get the dirt out of my teeth.

We got the site ready, and then we waited. Eventually, late that night, the thumping noise of rotors alerted us that the detainees were arriving. We looked around to make sure everything was in place and then moved to our stations. There wasn't the kind of tension you see in movies, just professionals ready to begin a stressful but important wartime job. The special forces guys had done the real work; we were just organizing the aftermath.

"First group coming in!" a young sergeant shouted.

I could see scattered groups of two and three people walking to-ward us, each including a guy in uniform and one or two men in dishdashas, the traditional Arab garb that looks like a long white nightgown. Virtually all the captured men were barefoot, and every one was blindfolded.

The dishdashas billowed in the night breeze as the men were marched to an open area of dirt. Many were straining their necks back and heads up, perhaps to try to peer out the bottom of the blindfolds to see where they were going. At the site they were pushed to the ground, lined up one next to the other facedown, and told to be quiet. Some moaned or whimpered, but most were silent, and I began to notice that most were older than the men we had expected.

One of the soldiers came over to the main table, his face tired but his eyes alert.

"We didn't find the guys we were looking for, but we grabbed some dudes at the targets' houses and then did follow-on ops, too. We've got around forty or fifty coming in," he declared.

This news was alarming. Some of the evidence against our tar-gets was questionable to begin with, and now we had dozens of guys who'd just happened to be in the houses we hit? In an environment filled with bad sources, double-dealings, a lack of knowledge of culture and language, and endless cases of mistaken identity, it was likely that few if any of our detainees were involved in the insurgency, and probably none would have intelligence value. I figured we would have to let most of them go.

"Roger that," the S2 affirmed, disappointed at the failure to hit primary targets but happy with the overall quantity. "Okay, here's what we're doing: We're going to tag them," referring to the Sharpie-written number on each detainee's forehead, "and then take their picture and ask them for their name. After we put all that in the computer, they wait to be debriefed and then we'll decide where they go next."

When most of the captures were on the ground, we started the process of getting pictures and names. Two soldiers would bring the men over to the main table, one at a time, and interpreters, affectionately known as "terps," would ask for their names. I helped transcribe the information, matching it to the respective numbers, and entered it into the computer. To the extent that I could, I also indicated when the name designated a particular tribe membership or likely religion.

The brilliant technique used to test whether the detainees were dissembling about their names was to accuse every third or fourth one of lying. A detainee would stand there and somebody would yell at him that he was lying and that we knew he was lying, and he'd better tell us the truth or else. I don't remember any detainee changing his stated name. We then took off their blindfolds, held their heads toward the camera, and took their pictures, matching each with name and number. It went as smoothly as we could hope, with the exception of one detainee who seemed especially agitated. He kept jerking his head from side to side, leaning forward, and opening and closing his mouth. I exchanged a skeptical glance with a young sergeant sitting with me at the table. I was pretty sure the detainee was retarded.

The terps asked him his name, but there was no response.

"*What* is your *name*!" the translator shouted. The prisoner leaned forward, bent over at the waist. He opened and closed his mouth. Then he did it again.

After a few minutes we had three interpreters screaming in his ear, but the guy's responses were unintelligible. We dubbed him Abu Mohammed, a sarcastic reference to the number of Iraqis who had both of those monikers in their name. One of our biggest problems with identifying people was the name structure, not to mention transliteration. So Abu Mohammed it was, and we sent him stumbling back to the field.

From the very beginning of my time in Iraq, I saw the effects of insurgents on American troops. I was acutely aware of the casualties and the havoc wreaked by Iraqi fighters, and I wanted to see every last insurgent incarcerated or dead, not necessarily in that order. I had no moral qualms about targeting the fighters, and despite intense concern with the politics of the war, I was 100 percent committed to supporting the warfighter and helping to establish a stable civil society. That said, it is a horrible experience to deal with men who have their hands bound behind them and faces covered in dirt from their heads being pushed to the ground. Contrary to oft-spouted bombastic revenge fantasies, to stand before a weeping, terrified, and humiliated man is no power trip, nor is it gratifying. It is particularly distressing if that man is guilty only of being in the wrong place at the wrong time.

As we took names and photos, some of the prisoners cried quietly, and many stared despondently at the ground. Perversely, a few grinned for the photo, a reflexive reaction to the camera that was greeted by many with laughter and jeers. I didn't blame anyone for their denigration of the detainees, and generally everyone was careful to avoid hurting them without provocation, but I preferred stoicism to jocularity. I think people in this situation fell somewhere along a spectrum, from those who were vaguely unhappy to be in total control of the lives of others to those for whom it was a mild thrill. I was squarely in the former camp. I've always disliked bullying, and I found out that day my aversion to causing humiliation extends even to wartime enemies. In the past that was an honorable position; today it's practically seditious.

Still, even those who joked around were not enjoying themselves, I don't think, but dealing with the situation as best they could. The most surprising element was not whether each person was at ease or uncomfortable, but the paradoxical normalcy of the entire process.

The detainees were not allowed to say anything other than their names, and then we took them back to the field.

"Okay," the S2 instructed after we'd processed a good chunk of the detainees, "let's start the debriefs." He meant the initial questioning, interviews that took place right in the field. It is often easiest to get information from people when they are disoriented or shell-shocked, and intelligence information nearly always has a short half-life, useful only if you can get it fast.

Throughout the process, a JAG officer hovered, the requisite legal attendant for such an operation. The military guys said you could always instantly tell a JAG, and this one fit the stereotype. A tall, blond, cigar-chomping presence, he maintained a long string of sarcastic commentary, interrupting himself occasionally to remind us what the minimal requirements were for detention.

"You just need two witness affidavits," he would bark, "so get those papers signed!"

While the troops worked on the paperwork, I headed over to where interrogations were starting. There were a handful of plastic tables set up in a dusty field, with either an Arabic-speaking debriefer or a translator and debriefer sitting at each. After an all-night endeavor of waiting, in-processing, and preparing for debriefs, it was almost morning. The sun was just peeking over the horizon, lifting the early-morning temperature from around seventy degrees to the mid-eighties as the detainees were hauled over one at a time to the debriefing area.

Exhausted and, I imagine, terrified, the detainees stumbled their way toward the tables. The men were blindfolded and cuffed, most without shoes, each one disoriented from fear and fatigue. They were brought over in one of two ways. Many soldiers gripped the prisoners by their elbows, which were secured behind their backs by the plastic cuffs. Some of the escorts slipped an arm in between a detainee's elbow and body, placing a palm on his shoulder. With the prisoner's hands bound behind his back, this position allowed for easy manipulation: Just a slight push down on the upper arm stressed the shoulder socket, immediately causing the detainee to bend over to relieve the pain.

I'm no expert in detainee management, so there may have been good reasons for this posture. Nonetheless, even this relatively minor manhandling made me cringe, especially in the wake of Abu Ghraib. I also was very aware of the deep loathing of humiliation in Arab culture, as well as the psychological impact of such treatment of innocents. If these people didn't hate us before, I thought, they certainly would now. And so would their fathers and sons and brothers and cousins.

This view was compounded by the increasingly erratic behavior of the prisoners. They had been lying facedown in the dirt for hours at this point, long enough for both mental distress and physical deterioration to set in. As they came to the debriefing tables, I noticed that several more had begun to cry, quietly and shamefully weeping at their predicament. Part of me hated them for it, for adding open emotion into an operation that I wanted to treat and view as business. I also, perhaps paradoxically, desperately wanted them to be guilty. We had not found the usual evidence that points to insurgent activity—large amounts of weapons or ammunition, explosive materials, electronic timers, blasting caps, and the like— and I was increasingly concerned that the mission had been unsuccessful. I was further worried that some would believe them guilty regardless of evidence, or lack thereof. It's tough to track people for months, mount an operation, and then admit that it was all useless.

I had no love, of course, for our captives, and I can understand how many found it helpful or necessary to dehumanize the process. My psychology studies came flooding back, with the lessons of Milgram and Zimbardo especially salient. By this time many of the men were showing signs of the strain. There was more crying, and a few began to heave and vomit on the ground or on themselves. I shut out any doubts (and any emotions, really) and refocused on the debriefings.

I remember a few interrogations vividly. My boss and I had relatively free rein, but he was not interested in the debriefings. The S2 invited us to observe or assist the field interviews, so I went over to the closest table. The team was a weathered, solid senior enlisted soldier and a wispy Arab translator. They had worked together for a while, they said, but opined that there wasn't much to accomplish in the initial interviews.

"Why not?" I asked, thinking that the decision of whether to release or incarcerate was a vital one.

"Well, you really can't figure out anything worthwhile in these things," answered the soldier. "We pretty much just get whatever information we can and then send them to the next step."

"What do you mean, the next step?"

"Y'know, Abu G. They get an initial three-month stay, and the debriefers there figure out what happens after that."

"Are you fucking kidding me?" I was, naïvely I suppose, astonished. "But how are we supposed to differentiate between the shitheads and the guys who just happened to be in their fucking houses?" I've always had a bit of a potty mouth, which I blame on my sensitive, kind, and highly profane mother. The military environment wasn't helping this, nor was the realization that the painstaking process of collecting intelligence, vetting it, researching the targets, and finally putting together a target package turned into, in the field, *Anybody who's picked up gets sent to prison.*

"Yeah, well, we'll get affidavits that they all had weapons and resisted detention, and that's enough to lock 'em up for a while. Anyway, if they're off the streets, they're not setting IEDs, right?"

"I guess," I replied. But if they weren't before, they would be when they got out.

A detainee was brought over and told to stand in front of the table. The debriefer went through a list of questions, mostly identification of name, location, tribe, religion, and so forth. The team was a well-oiled machine, with the terp perfectly channeling the speed, volume, and tone of the questioner. It is vital for an interpreter to fully represent not only the words but also the context, physical and lyrical, of the debriefer. This team had the process down.

The questions, however, seemed to lack strategy.

"So what did you do as an insurgent?"

"I haven't done anything, I am innocent."

"I know that you're lying, your whole neighborhood is full of insurgents. You're either one of them or you know something about them. So either tell us who's involved or you go to Abu G."

"I am innocent, I haven't done—"

"Shut the fuck up with that shit!" The questioner lurched forward in his chair. "Are you calling me a liar?"

"I am innocent, I have done nothing wrong," the terp translated.

"You're fucking going to jail, and God only knows when you're getting out. You can save yourself by admitting what you did."

The interview went on and on like this, with aggressive questioning occasionally punctuated by appeals for cooperation. Everything I knew indicated that establishing rapport and trust was the most important element of successful information retrieval. This was clearly not a widely accepted strategy.

"Well, if you're not going to help us, you're going away."

"He wants to know if he can ask a question," the interpreter said.

The debriefer rolled his eyes. "Tell him to ask away."

"He says most of his brothers are here, but he wants to know what happened to his brother who is . . . sick. I think he means he's crazy or retarded, it's difficult to exactly translate what he said."

"Tell him I have no idea. Tell him if he tells me about his insurgent activities I'll find out."

"He still says he is innocent."

"Well then, I can't help him. Tell him he's going away now, for a long time."

The detainee spoke quickly and loudly, his voice breaking.

"What's he saying?"

"He wants to know what he's done. 'Please tell me what my crime is, what I've been accused of,' he asked," explained the terp.

"Somebody said you did something bad," the debriefer sneered.

The interpreter translated, and the detainee trembled with his reply under the heat of the sun and the weight of imminent incarceration.

"Please tell me my crime, tell me what I am accused of? It is false, I promise you, can I not know what I am accused of? What am I accused of?"

I turned away as the interrogator called for an escort to take the prisoner to the holding area for later transport to the prison. No evidence, no charge, no reason. What the hell were we doing? When he was gone, I asked the team if they couldn't have used the intelligence files to ask him about specifics.

"Oh, you mean this file?" The debriefer opened up the folder in front of him, exposing a single sheet of paper with the detainee's name and ID number on the top. "We don't have shit on these guys. They were in a spot with insurgent connections, so they're either insurgents or facilitating insurgents. Fuck it, just send 'em to Abu G and they'll sort it out there."

I thought for a moment. From a purely pragmatic, tactical standpoint, I could see how units might make the decision to simply incarcerate every able-bodied male they came in contact with. From a ground-level perspective, the more men off the streets, the fewer available to participate in attacks. From a strategic viewpoint, however, it was a horrifying approach, one destined for long-term failure.

Considering that the single most vital element in fighting an insurgency is to eliminate popular support for the fighters, rounding up and incarcerating as many people as possible is exceptionally counterproductive. An occupying force can establish a secure environment in one of two ways: Either the citizens must be so fearful of the occupiers that they dare not transgress, or the citizens have to believe the occupying force is better than the alternative.

Ignoring the moral considerations of the former, total repression simply is not possible in the age of mass media, nor does it fit with the long-term U.S. goal of establishing self-determination in Iraq. We also didn't send enough troops to effectively crush all violent dissent. Finally, the kind of infiltration of the population necessary for this kind of strategy is virtually impossible without a broad knowledge of the local language and culture. Unfortunately, the opportunity for Iraqis to view an American presence as a benevolent force was probably lost in the first few weeks of the war, when looters were allowed to run rampant, and certainly crippled by events like Abu Ghraib and Haditha.

The right strategy should not include, obviously, wholesale imprisonment of individuals without probable cause, due process, evidence, access to a legal system, or finite incarceration time. Practically speaking, the United States is creating more insurgents than it is eliminating when it detains or kills innocents. Even if the detainees in front of me had no previous offenses, many of the men may have fought back against the forces that came after them, or could have had more than the legally allowed armaments (in Iraq, every citizen is "allowed" one AK-47 rifle and two clips of ammunition, a rule that is overwhelmingly flouted), but the bottom line was that we were incarcerating these men for no justifiable reason. It's one thing to suspect that we're jailing untold numbers of innocents, but another to witness it and be a cog in the machine that facilitates the process.

As another detainee was brought over to the table, I moved on to a different team. This one paired an English-speaking Iraqi special forces member, who translated, with a young enlisted U.S. soldier. The American was cheerful if somewhat overmatched, and his primary interrogation technique was to describe Abu Ghraib prison, indicating that the only escape was through naming others as insurgents. He also exhorted the detainees to confess to clear their consciences. During a break I spoke to the ISF soldier and asked him what he thought of the process.

"It's not perfect," he said haltingly, "but the insurgents are shit."

From my previous talks with Iraqi forces, I knew that most of them hated the insurgents even more passionately than we did. The Iraqi soldiers virtually all expressed overwhelming disgust for the fighters, with one vital wrinkle: The Shia troops viewed virtually all Sunnis as insurgents, and would regularly refer to Sunnis generally as terrorists; whereas the (rare) Sunni units primarily blamed the fighting on upstart Shia groups and militias. So the armed Iraqis all hated "the insurgents" . . . but they disagreed on who fell into that category.

This soldier was no exception.

"The Sunnis are trying to ruin the country because they cannot stand to be powerless," he charged. "But we will get them."

A new detainee was delivered to the team, and the attempts at manipulation quickly began.

"There is no one left to support your family now, what do you think of that?"

"I am a farmer, look at my feet, I am a farmer," the prisoner pleaded. His feet were callused, though *farmer* and *insurgent* certainly are not mutually exclusive. The debriefer laughed. Then he turned to me.

"You want to ask some questions, mister spy?"

"Okay," I said, thinking quickly. The S2 had given us permission to take part, and although I wasn't going to invite myself into a debrief, neither would I decline the offer.

"What do you think of the insurgents?" I asked. The interpreter frowned at me before translating.

"I hate them," came the answer. "I hate them because they are trying to ruin everything." He looked directly at me; I wondered if he could see me through his blindfold.

"But they made you help them. You had no choice." *Law & Order* reruns and my memories of college psychology classes led me to try the sympathetic approach, rather than a threatening one.

"No! I've done nothing wrong, you have no proof because there could not possibly be any. There is no proof of crimes that did not occur." He had me there, didn't he?

The interview went on, and I inserted the occasional strategic question among tactical queries, never eliciting anything other than denials of wrongdoing and requests to know what the accusations were. Eventually the team decided to end the interview and send him to Abu G.

I moved to another table, where a nineteen-year-old sergeant was working by himself. He looked about fifteen, with wire-rimmed glasses perched high on his nose, just below his buzzed blond hair. Unlike the other two interrogators I observed, he didn't even pretend to try to elicit information beyond the basics. Because he spoke with the detainees in Arabic, I didn't stay long, just enough to get a feel for the rhythm of the interview. As I was about to walk away, however, the sergeant turned toward me, puzzled.

"He's asking if his brother is okay. He says his brother can't speak. What the hell is he talking about?"

"Tell him his brother will be fine." I was sure he was talking about the guy whose name we couldn't determine, but I hadn't seen him since he came in, which had been hours ago.

The sun continued to rise in the early-morning sky, pushing temperatures up toward triple digits. There were scattered patches of vomit, and a few overweight detainees were having trouble breathing, but we were almost done with initial interrogations.

After the sergeant finished, I asked him what he thought of the process.

He sighed. "You know what? I don't think these guys did anything wrong. But I don't get to make that decision, you know?"

It was clearly a structural breakdown, and a massive one: The people in the field thought the prison would decide who needed to stay and who needed to be let go, but those at Abu G thought anybody delivered to them was a guilty shithead.

I wandered back to the second table, where the ISF soldier was shouting in Arabic. The American was looking down, shaking his head, and the detainee swayed on his feet in front of them. As I approached, I saw that it was the possibly retarded detainee whose name we couldn't get during in-processing, and his condition seemed to be deteriorating.

"What's the deal?" I asked the American soldier.

"This guy refuses to answer any questions. Motherfucker."

I looked at the prisoner. He was again bent over at the waist, leaning far in toward the table, with his head cocked like a dog listening to a high-pitched noise. Sweat poured down his face, causing his patchy beard to shine in the increasingly oppressive sun. He looked as if he was attempting to speak, but whenever he opened his mouth, the only thing that emerged was his tongue, which made a motion like he was trying to push something off the roof of his mouth. He uttered a plaintive sound, not unlike a bleating sheep, and leaned closer.

"Guys, I don't think this dude can speak," I said. "I also don't think he can hear you. That would explain your problem here, no?"

"Yeah, but you're wrong. When I went over to get him, he looked up from the ground when I yelled at him. He can hear, and if he's bullshitting about that, he's bullshitting about the talking thing, too."

"I don't think so, man," I countered. "I'm pretty sure you could fire your pistol off behind his goddamn ear and he wouldn't react. At the very least, yelling at him isn't going to get the information out. Plus, a few other of these guys have asked about a retarded guy."

He glared at me. He seemed to consider this, then looked away. I tried again. "I'm serious, he's a deaf-mute, not an insurgent!"

"Naw, he's fuckin' faking. I'm sending him to Abu G."

There was nothing illegal about any of this, as far as I know, nothing against procedure or protocol. I saw no laws being broken, no abuses taking place, and nothing that I would consider outside of the ordinary based on what I have seen, read, and heard about the way we are currently fighting this war. What I did see was broken policy, created and blindly supported by DoD and White House leadership against all rationality and common sense.

I wondered if I should somehow try to affect the situation, but I was far outside my chain of command. I was also just a puke civilian, and a low-ranking one at that. But most important, nothing "wrong" was going on: This was standard operating procedure. I later spoke to my chain of command, emphasizing the fact that this strategy, while executed in good faith, was surely hurting our overall efforts. I have no idea whether this perspective was passed up the chain, but I do know that I'm far from the only one to question U.S. detention practices.

It was nearing noon, and my boss was getting ready to head out; most of the work was completed. I went back to the first interrogation table to sit in on one more debrief. The team was clearly getting tired, but still 100 percent in sync with each other.

"What's your name?"

"Where are you from?"

"What's your religion?"

They went through the list, eventually winding up in the familiar position of trying to get the detainee to confess or identify other insurgents. It wasn't going well, and the detainee, as usual, professed his innocence.

"Don't start with that shit! Don't you start with me!" The debriefer was back to bad cop. The detainee paused, then spoke in a tone that sounded like a question.

"We have a curious group today," the terp observed. "He wants to ask you a question."

"Sure, what does he want?"

The detainee spoke.

"Oh," the interpreter said, "he wants to know if he can say something."

"Be my guest," the debriefer said wryly.

The detainee spoke, and the interpreter paused. He looked into the distance, and translated.

"When you came to our country, we hoped law would return. We still have that hope."

The words were a knife, slicing through the farce. They depicted our failures far more clearly than I could have, and it was a fitting end to the night. In America's Iraq, the burden of proof is on the suspect. Guilty until proven innocent. The action units place the responsibility on the intel crew to sort out the guys they grab, and intel guys figure that the action units bring in only legitimate targets. In that space an innocent individual becomes a prisoner.

Some, perhaps many, detainees are guilty of various crimes. Low-level criminal acts, facilitation of violence, and even actual attacks. But a total lack of evidence, or relying on the word of one questionable individual for incarceration, is the rule rather than the exception. Detention without trial, one after another after another. Press reports put the total number of U.S.-held detainees in Iraq at more than twenty-four thousand, with tens of thousands more being held in Iraqi facilities.* Staying that particular course is a recipe for total disaster.

That day I saw an entire family of brothers sent away—seven in all, I think. One of them was almost certainly retarded, identified by all his other brothers as handicapped, but his interrogator felt otherwise. Off to Abu G he went.

A civilized country and a civilized people cannot presume guilt. Guilt without evidence is anathema to a functioning civil society, and rule of law is vital to win a war that is more about minds than weapons or troops. Pragmatically, a system that incarcerates scores of innocents is a broken one, destined to be fought by those it victimizes. "When you came to our country, we hoped law would return. We still have that hope." I won't soon forget those words.

My boss and I drove back to work. I slowly walked up the steps, dragged myself to my desk, chugged a Red Bull and popped a Provigil, and logged on to my computer. Most of the morning was gone, so I had a lot to catch up on.

---

* Shanker, Thom. "With troop rise: Iraqi detainees soar in number." *New York Times.* 25 Aug. 2007.

CHAPTER 8

The operation was a significant turning point for my view of our presence in Iraq. When we invaded, I believed the war was a bad decision for America's national security, but post-invasion I thought the U.S. presence was preventing a full-scale meltdown. I knew that our presence had created many of the problems that existed, but I thought coalition troops were the dam preventing a flood of sectarian violence and terrorist encampment. The field operation furthered my realization that the U.S. occupation was, long-term, actually making the country less stable. We were arming multiple sides of an incipient civil war, playing whack-a-mole with insurgents, and destroying our moral standing and strategic interests in a vital region. The idea that the most politically and militarily powerful nation in the world could be doing more harm than good was difficult to swallow, but it was something I had to consider. I love my country, and I may love it best for its ability to self-correct; without introspection and improvement, there is no progress, and the American ethos of competition and democratic rule means the government is responsible (and ostensibly responsive) to the people. There's a reason we praise those who admit their mistakes: It combines honesty with an effort to improve in the future. Constant improvement makes America great, and doing the right thing requires periodic reevaluation.

In Iraq that process of review and enhancement seemed to be

missing, especially at the highest levels of leadership. I soon would see firsthand exactly how deficient those leaders were, but while I was in Iraq I could not understand why the overall mission was so disorganized and misdirected.

I occasionally traveled, primarily to the embassy area in downtown Baghdad, which exposed me to a variety of other efforts. Compared with Camp Slayer, the embassy was like another world. I'd never had much love for the State Department, and my opinion was not improved by my interactions with its officials in Baghdad. At Slayer there was an atmosphere of immediacy—you knew you were in a war zone and, the occasional bout of good humor notwithstanding, everyone took the work extremely seriously. There simply did not seem to be the same intensity at the embassy. The embassy pool, a sprawling complex with Ping-Pong tables, pool tables, and a bar, was often packed. The Defense Department prohibition against alcohol consumption wasn't in effect, and many of the pool parties were legendary, devolving into hours-long stretches of drinking, cigar smoking, and mingling.

The embassy's Hostage Working Group, with which I worked in the early months of deployment, was shockingly mismanaged, especially considering the importance of the mission. They ran around like chickens with their heads cut off, but all too frequently in response to yesterday's news. Beyond the incompetent, there was also the weird, like the fact that the U.S. Embassy in Baghdad, perhaps the single most targeted American-controlled land on the planet, was guarded by Nepalese contractors. Not marines, as at most embassies, or special forces troops, or regular army soldiers, but Nepalese Gurkha fighters, contracted to protect the most important American fixture in Iraq. From high-level issues like protection and specialized mission groups down to the byzantine logistical systems for identification, housing, and travel, the embassy seemed out of touch.

Which, of course, it is. The embassy is in the middle of the most tightly controlled area of Iraq, the Green Zone, and it is surrounded by heavily fortified checkpoints that vigorously examine all personnel and vehicles that enter. It is by far the safest part of the country, and although it is only four square miles, it contains virtually all U.S. diplomatic and Iraqi government facilities and personnel. You can walk around in the Green Zone, as evidenced by my sightseeing jaunt, and much of the area is eerily quiet. This isolation, however, seems to create a disconnect for the people who never leave it. The people who only know the Green Zone experience Iraq as a relatively safe place. There are attacks on the Green Zone, but nothing like the surrounding areas of Baghdad, known as the Red Zone. In particular, I think the United States was slow to recognize the grim significance and magnitude of Iraq's sectarian conflict because of this separation. The Green Zone is primarily focused on the political wrangling among Iraq's elites, as well as some general counterinsurgency, but those issues are the hangnail to Iraq's collective heart attack of civil war. To further the medical analogy, political bickering and the insurgency are symptoms, rather than causes, of the overall disease of sectarian conflict and the profound lack of law and order perpetuated by failed—but continuing—U.S. policy.

That is not to say the United States doesn't do good things. I would never denigrate the efforts of the civilians and soldiers who risk life and limb to bring hope to the Iraqi people through public works projects, training, education, and other nation-building efforts. These are the "good news" stories that many war supporters complain aren't told enough, but such criticism mistakes the micro for the macro. That is, building a school in the midst of a civil war is like planting a tree in the midst of a forest fire: a nice gesture, and intrinsically good, but not likely to provide much help overall.

The criticism of media as being overly concerned with the negatives in Iraq belies a greater problem that was widely recognized and ridiculed by many of us while we were there. Most media outlets, for a variety of reasons, cover Iraq minimally and superficially. This is especially true of television news, but it includes most corporate print media as well. The summer of 2005 may have been a new low for television news, and by August many of us in Iraq bitterly joked about it as the "Summer of Sharks and Missing White Chicks." For years I had fulfilled my news-junkie tendencies online; I hadn't watched TV news since high school, and I felt (and continue to feel) that the Internet is by leaps and bounds the best source for news and analysis. But in Iraq, I had to eat, and there was essentially one location to fulfill that basic need: the Camp Slayer DFAC. The DFAC had several TVs, usually split evenly between Fox News and ESPN. At least twice a day I ate at the DFAC, and Fox News was omnipresent. It was jarring to see the shallowness and imprecision of that news, even in the rare instance when worthwhile stories were being discussed. Seeing the breathless reports of missing women and shark attacks, it was disconcerting to labor in a war zone that most mainstream media could not or would not deign to cover appropriately.

The reporting that did exist usually focused on casualties, and while I understand the importance of updating numbers, there was often a striking lack of context—little explanation of how and why the deaths occurred, and virtually no examination of greater trends and themes. In an apparent search for "balance," some media outlets equated the "good" of a school being built with the "bad" of a government that lacked control over its army, for example.

My fellow analysts and I had the benefit of getting information with little or no filter, ground reports from both troops and civilian intelligence collectors; to some extent we ourselves *were* the filter within the government. Those of us with intellectual curiosity and Internet proficiency did an end run around traditional media for useful information by seeking out reporting from independent or international press sources, and we also read blogs, especially a few written by Iraqis in Iraq and by professors who studied the region and its issues for a living. While these news outlets were nontraditional, and at times anecdotal, they were extremely useful. Unfortunately, they were also little used, and in my experience the older the person, the less likely he or she was to use (or even know about) these kinds of resources, so management-level personnel rarely pointed analysts toward those valuable resources.

My teammates and I frequently (if grimly) joked about the deteriorating situation. Or perhaps the situation wasn't deteriorating so much as we were just seeing it more clearly with every passing day. One day Renaldo, who was the senior intelligence analyst on his team, came back from a meeting completely exasperated.

"We just spent another hour talking about what our mission should be, and how to present it to CIOC leadership so they don't break up the team. We're the only ones doing good work, our metrics are great, and while the CIOC wants to split us up, our leadership can't figure out how to explain the benefits of what we're doing. We're going to be . . . here . . . forever," he said, slamming his fist onto the desk as he spat out that last word.

It was yet another laugh-or-cry moment, so of course the entire row burst out laughing as Renaldo fumed. The moment became a sardonic rallying cry. Whenever something particularly stupid happened, we'd look at each other and simply say, "Forever," as in, *We're going to be in this country forever*. Electricity production goals moved back another month? Forever. Mass grave of tortured and murdered Sunnis found in Baghdad? Forever. Vice President Cheney says the insurgency is in its last throes? (An especially incredulous) Forever. Speeches and interviews with administration officials were ripe for ridicule, and we often wondered whether they were dissembling or just clueless. Soon enough my work at the Pentagon would persuade me that it was a little of both, but at the time we had limited access to policymakers and could only speculate.

I clung to the belief that my contribution was a beneficial one, and day to day I was largely unaffected by these larger issues. The Direct Action Cell continued to churn out target packages, and I had gained confidence and trust from my supervisor and from the intelligence contacts working with a variety of coalition units. Some days I worked directly for those units, or supervised other analysts or soldiers in the process of searching for, vetting, and passing along information that would be valuable for operations. At the tactical level the main priority is keeping U.S. troops alive, and I worked tirelessly with that in mind. Whatever my concerns about the strategic level, my job was targeting, and I wanted to be as successful as humanly possible. As far as I was concerned, anyone who attacked U.S. troops was working to subvert the democratic process, and the argument that attacks on the coalition were "legitimate" nationalist acts under an occupation was, I always thought, bullshit. The Iraqi government continued to want a U.S. troop presence, and as long as the United States is in Iraq at the request of Iraq's fairly elected government, there is no such thing as legitimate resistance.

Targeting individuals and groups who attacked Iraqi civilians was gratifying. Having seen the results of insurgent attacks, I had no qualms about going after those loathsome purveyors of carnage. After my experience in the field, I often wondered about the unintended consequences of my work, but that part was out of my control and, to the extent that I could influence my own thoughts, out of my mind. It was often difficult to know the results of our work because feedback was typically infrequent. Most units did not want to take the time to report back about the operations, or even tell us whether they'd used the target packages at all, as they had new things to worry about after each successive maneuver.

While we managed to bridge the gap between units and the national-level intelligence process, there was still a disconnect after our products went out. This was a significant problem, because we were not able to evaluate our process after the fact: Were our sources right? Were the descriptions accurate? Did they get the targets? And above all, what follow-on intelligence was discovered? We weren't able to self-evaluate and improve as much as we would have liked when the information flow dried up. If we got any details back, it was usually just numbers, such as how many captured or how many killed. The information obstacle seems like an easy thing to correct, but due to communications issues and prioritization, it simply did not happen most of the time. Still, generally speaking, my team continued rolling along, getting better and faster as the weeks went on.

One day we got a call that one of the units would be moving on a target package I'd put together. The intelligence coordinator wanted to know if we had any recent information to add, so I ran the searches again, but there were no updates. I stayed late into the night in case there were any last-minute questions, and when none arose, I went to sleep. It wasn't uncommon for us to hear that our packages would be used, and we kept extensive records of the information that did come in, especially as we became more assertive about following up with the units. I went in the next morning and checked for an update. The news was mixed.

"Hey, Alex." Captain White called me over to his desk when I got in, so I wheeled my chair down the row.

"How'd it go, did they move on the target last night?"

"Yeah, and apparently the shitheads were pretty unhappy." *Shithead* was the common moniker for the insurgents, for whatever reason; *hajji* also went in and out of favor.

"Oh?"

"Yeah, there was a little gun battle, we had one seriously wounded and we also killed a couple of them."

One of the nice things about working for the most capable military forces in the history of the world is that they often complete operations perfectly. The United States has the training and technology to be dominant in an operational setting, so when units went after targets, we were cautiously optimistic that our guys would not sustain casualties. But in a country where everybody practically gets an AK-47 at birth, there was always a risk that somebody in the house would get off a few lucky rounds, and apparently that's what had occurred before the targets were subdued.

Not only was there a battle that night, however, but the operation stirred up the neighborhood, and the location was still buzzing with activity, demonstrations, and promises of vengeance. The raid had attracted more insurgents to the site, and with more targets, the unit was going back that night.

"The follow-on operation will be based on the initial package as well as some new intel from the guys they got last night," Captain White explained, "and hopefully we'll be able to get the whole group of them."

The wounded soldier would make it, and although we never got the details on his injury, I was relieved he pulled through.

I came in the next day to a grim expression from my boss. He cut right to the chase.

"We lost two guys in the follow-up last night."

"Aw, *fuck*!"

The fallout from the previous raid had intensified during the evening and into the night, and by the time our troops moved in a sizable crowd had gathered, most with guns locked and loaded. During the operation the locals managed to kill two soldiers before the unit secured the area; a handful of suspected insurgents was also killed. It was a battle not unlike those that occur every night of every day of the war, and compared with the increasing sectarian battles, the casualties were relatively low. The target was good and the operation meticulously planned, but things inevitably go wrong.

Even knowing this, it still affected me. I felt partly responsible for the deaths, not in the sense of being guilty of wrongdoing, but rather that my work led to the operation. Of course, tactical decisions are always made in the field; it's not like I ordered the action or had any part in its preparation. Still, it was a single degree of separation between my work and the deaths of my countrymen, men with lives and futures and hopes and dreams, gone. It sucked. I didn't tell anybody about my reaction, partly because the last thing I wanted to show was any kind of weakness to be exploited (virtually anything was fair game for ridicule), and partly because my personal reaction wasn't something I wanted to dump on anyone else.

People can mourn for others, and feel pain on behalf of actions that are not directly related to them, but it's an entirely different feeling when you're part of it, even tangentially. I imagine the effect is exponentially greater the closer you get to the event, and I do wonder how much a person can understand about the effects of this war without personally knowing someone who's in Iraq, or going to a funeral, or talking to parents—*something* that involves a personal connection. I especially wonder about policymakers who have never had that kind of experience making decisions in the absence of those practical and moral guides.

None of us had the time or emotional energy to ponder these weighty issues, however, so while a variety of events certainly took their personal toll on everyone, I wasn't aware of any discussions about it. If anything, work became the ultimate distraction and outlet for many of us. Homesick? Work more. Disillusioned? Work more. Girlfriend cheating on you while you're in a war zone? Work a lot more. Too tired to work? Spin the roulette wheel of caffeine pills, modafinil, and a never-ending supply of Diet Coke. Work, eat, work, eat, work, sleep; rinse and repeat. Literally.

We all had electronic countdowns on our computers to track the progress of our deployment, and most of us had two or three. In one file, a big circular picture of the desert slowly turned into a beautiful beach scene as the days went by. In another, a beer bottle filled up, with a sidebar counting down by tenths of a second, and in the most popular, what began as sand dunes slowly revealed a bikini-clad model as time progressed. While political and strategic battles raged above us, the analysts of HST kept our noses to the grindstone and looked forward to the ever-closer redeployment date.

CHAPTER 9

I was about two-thirds of the way through the deployment. I would be home in September, right in time for football season and fall foliage, and I couldn't wait. In the office we sometimes talked about what our jobs might be when we returned, and we speculated about what topics we would cover back at the Pentagon. It was, however, too soon to know what was in store.

In our current assignments, things were as disorganized as ever. We were still shifting jobs, hearing rumors about more reorganization, and coming to terms with the everyday inanities and insanities. We were also getting a real taste of the Baghdad heat. Temperatures continued to rise, both figuratively and literally— the highs hovered in the 110s, finally forcing an end to my outdoor runs. People increasingly showed signs of strain, with tempers a little shorter, eye rolls more frequent, and tongues sharper than ever, but at that point it was nothing to be overly concerned about. I still hadn't worked fewer than eighty hours in any given week, and the intensity of the office continued unabated.

Meanwhile, my parents once again endured a terrorist attack in their home city. They had moved to London around the time I'd started working for DIA, and the underground bombings in July, which killed dozens, once again illustrated the zeal of terrorist organizations. This time I seethed, wondering whether the attacks would have occurred had the United States not shifted focus from the global terrorist networks to the Iraq misadventure.

We limped through the developments, taking things in stride. Most of us had readjusted our expectations, so we got an irrational amount of satisfaction and happiness from having the time to watch a movie at night, or hanging out and playing cards, or getting an email from home. Nobody was sitting around bitching or counting down the seconds before we would leave. Minutes, maybe, but not seconds. Mostly.

I was learning a tremendous amount about the intricacies of the insurgency, and the additional knowledge confirmed my general perceptions of the problems. Over the course of my deployment, friends and family would ask about my thoughts on the situation, and while I had to be careful about discussing any classified (or classified-informed) opinions, I could offer general ideas and views.

It was especially confusing at that point because of the mixed messages coming from the administration: Rumsfeld was talking about the insurgency lasting anywhere from five to twelve more years, Cheney claimed it was in its last throes, and the president seemed to think there was no insurgency at all, just some irrelevant "dead-enders." In reality, as I explained in an email in June, the insurgency was strong and, by most relevant measures, getting stronger. More manpower, more attacks, more casualties, and over a greater geographic area. The targets, however, were changing slightly, and that was worth noting: The majority of casualties were Iraqi civilians, not Iraqi or coalition military forces, which raised concern among analysts about burgeoning civil conflict. Attacks on civilians and infrastructure were increasingly prevalent and sophisticated, and May had marked the highest number of IED attacks since we invaded.

The insurgency was not slowing down, but why? There were competing theories, as well as problems with most of them. A critical problem was determining (or agreeing on) motivation. Some people argued that the insurgency is primarily former regime elements (FRE, sometimes referred to as former regime loyalists or FRL), that is, Saddam's old Ba'athist members and sympathizers who have enough money to finance the movement and enough hatred to spend it to either reclaim power or just stick it to the United States. Others maintained that it was fueled principally by foreign fighters, under the guise of al-Qaeda in Iraq (AQI), formerly referred to widely as al-Qaeda in Mesopotamia, or QJBR. Then there were those who blamed the former Iraqi army, which had been summarily disbanded by the provisional government, taking away the livelihood of tens of thousands of armed men who were not necessarily enamored with Saddam but now hated the U.S. for firing them. Armed, trained, and unemployed, this group had motive, opportunity, and ability.

I was never fully persuaded by any of those theories, especially because proponents of each position tended to zealously promote their views, denying the possibility of overlap and denigrating other possibilities. I thought the FRE were mostly old men who had fled to other countries, trying to figure out a way into Yemen or the UAE or wherever else they could spend the money they'd pilfered. Some were involved in financing the insurgency, of course, but money needed somewhere to go, and without manpower these Ba'athists would not be relevant.

The Zarqawi group (AQI/QJBR) never had a huge number of followers, and its influence was (and continues to be) vastly overstated in the press and even among some intelligence officials. The group relies on the support of disgruntled Sunnis for shelter, money, and supplies, and many members are foreign. The jihadists, however, are responsible for much of what gets on television: They perpetrate the suicide bombings that have huge casualties, they carry out the high-profile assassinations, and they either commit most of the kidnappings of Westerners or find a way to buy the captives from whatever group initially took them. These are the guys with whom we will not negotiate . . . because we cannot. They are ideological crazies, and they would love a new Afghanistan but with oil. This goal is virtually impossible, but long odds aren't much of a deterrent. Still, they need significant local support to survive, and they were losing popularity as they continued to kill Iraqi civilians. Even back then, there were scattered press stories about Shia and even some Sunni groups fighting the jihadist elements in certain towns. AQI was dangerous because of its ability to foment wider sectarian war, but it was not then and is not now the heart of the violence.

The former military guys did not have the funding or the ideology to pull off a total insurgency, so it wasn't exclusively them, either.

That's what I thought it was *not*, as I explained to friends; what it *was* amounted to a combination of elements. The insurgency resulted, I believed, from two primary factors. First, and most important, it was a predictable and inevitable result of a nation without legal or civil infrastructure falling into the hands of criminals and local gangs due to a lack of overall security. A large part of the insurgency is for profit, and there is tons of money to be made from kidnappings, theft, intimidation, et cetera.

Around then the *New York Times* ran an excellent piece on kidnapping in Iraq, which I forwarded to friends back home, indicating that several Iraqis are kidnapped every single day. Unlike the Westerners who get beheaded, most Iraqis who are kidnapped will pay a ransom, generally in the mid tens of thousands, and be released. Most of these crimes go unreported, and the perpetrators can make a huge amount of money over the course of just a few days. It's similar to criminal gangs, fighting for power, particularly among the disaffected Sunnis and the poor and dispossessed Shia.

Combine this, then, with the fanatics of AQI, and a religious, anti-occupation face is put on what begins as a collection of local problems. Some people scream when anyone talks about terrorism in law-enforcement terms instead of as a war, but we did not fight the mafia with the army. I don't mean that American criminal procedure should be followed, but the army is a blunt object, great for some things and less good at stuff like this. As I wrote to a friend,

Instead of trying to figure out the One Big Reason for the insurgency, we should be attacking the QJBR elements, stopping the money flow from FRE, and throwing in jail the local leaders of gangs (i.e., "insurgent" groups that are more focused on money or local power than a greater political or ideological goal). The counterproductive sweep operations that are now so prevalent miss these points entirely.

Doing this right also requires other opportunities for the people who would otherwise be shooting at us and robbing others, mostly young males. We need some kind of Tennessee Valley Authority for Iraq, the New Deal for Iraqis—give them productive jobs and a few hundred bucks a month and their collective mood will improve considerably. Remember, many of them are used to getting a certain amount of cash from either the government (thanks to all the oil money) or local tribal and/or religious leaders that allowed them to live comfortably. Many of them aren't used to anything else for the past 40 years. And many of the ones who could get things done are either Sunnis, many of whom we've banned from any meaningful jobs, or professionals, who are getting assassinated at an alarming rate.

When we take a multifaceted approach to a multifaceted problem, instead of talking about black and white and wrong and right, this country will begin to improve.

I also thought the problems were likely to get considerably worse. The rash of kidnappings while I was in Iraq were largely targeted at the middle class, the people most needed in reconstruction and establishing civil society—doctors, teachers, and the like. This caused the middle class to flee, resulting in a crippling brain drain. Moreover, the borders were (and, unbelievably, still are) completely open, allowing a small but constant stream of foreign fighters.

I wrote to a former professor, in response to her question about the likely future of the insurgency, explaining that I was not optimistic:

This is hardly unwinnable, but our current policies are extending, rather than abbreviating, the conflict. "Flypaper," my ass—the war here is creating a whole new generation of trained terrorists, not drawing them here to be knocked off, and there's no coherent goal that we can even aim for to start to get the fuck out. So overall, here's the good, the bad, and the ugly: The good is that there's still hope, and a decent democratic Iraq could be the result. The bad is that the insurgency is strong, and will likely get stronger before it gets weaker. The ugly is that the leaders of the political and military structures, in my humble opinion, don't have a good grasp on what the insurgency is really all about, and therefore don't have a good strategy to combat it.

As I vented my frustrations in emails and at the gym, others increasingly let off steam in the office. What set people off seemed totally random. For some, it was the small but constant irritations, like the three flights of stairs and walk through the 125-degree heat to get to the bathroom because our building had no running water (and drinking liters upon liters of water to stay hydrated necessitated frequent trips). Or the fact that with just two months remaining in our deployment, the entire team was forced to move out of our trailers and into DIA-renovated housing. Virtually everyone had adjusted to the trailers, and being in even closer quarters with coworkers, not to mention the process of lugging all of our stuff across the base in the relentless summer sun, was unpleasant. Then there was the constant sweating, swirling dust, oppressive heat; the monotony and dubious offereings of the DFAC; endless hours and logistical difficulties in the office . . . All these stressors frayed nerves and shortened fuses.

For me, and for some others, the daily irritants weren't as bothersome as the more overarching themes of separation from friends and family, doubt about our mission, and the sense that resources were being drastically misused. The wedding of my cousin Cathy, the first of my familial generation to get married and one of my absolute favorite relatives, exacerbated this feeling of isolation. The day she got married was a tough personal moment, knowing that everybody was celebrating her day as I waited for the email accounts to come in. The night of her wedding, I stayed up until 0400 just so I could call right as the reception began and express my congratulations. We talked for a few minutes, and I was grateful that she took the time to chat, telling me that the traditional Kurdish rug I sent, which I'd picked up from a nearby merchant, had arrived (I was a little worried about the timing); everything had gone well, she added. I glumly ambled back to the hooch, slept for a few hours, and then dragged myself back to work.

And really, I had it easy compared to many of my colleagues, who had spouses and kids back in the real world. Relationships were strained, and some broke; one of the few women on the deployment, married with two kids, was on the phone with her husband just a couple of months in when he told her he wanted a divorce. At least two other team members had serious relationships end during the deployment, and others openly speculated about the faithfulness of their significant others while they were away. Nobody complained about these issues, of course; if anything, they were fodder for more dark humor, but the pressures and difficulties were cumulative.

The few women on the team turned on one another first, and about halfway through the trip, there was a brief but raucous shouting match between two women who, as luck (or inevitability) would have it, lived together. By the end, virtually none of the handful of women there, most of whom lived together, were speaking to one another for anything other than requisite professional dealings. The men got riled up less often, but even the stoics occasionally lashed out. After one of the team was particularly disrespectful to our boss, a midlevel supervisor suggested to the individual that an apology would put the matter to rest. Quickly back came a caustic email with a line that gained instant infamy: "The only people who can tell me to apologize are my mother and my wife."

Many of us tried to release some of the tension through sports, and although our long hours (and the heat) prevented daytime outdoor activity, the basketball court had spotlights on at night. There were regular pickup games, and any energy I might have had for bickering was left on the court. Even the games had a special Iraq wrinkle, of course: In the desert, if you combine cooler evening air—below, say, 110 degrees—with floodlights, the insects gather like a biblical plague. After every game, the court was littered with the corpses of bugs that had ventured into a chaotic combination of sneakers and desert combat boots.

Some people who apparently couldn't decide on an outlet for their particular difficulties simply checked out mentally. This was most common among those whose responsibilities kept changing drastically. It was hard to escape the sense that if a role was assigned but then eliminated two months later, it probably wasn't useful from its inception. People will forgive many, many things in a wartime environment, but feeling useless isn't one of them.

While the overall HST mission stayed relatively consistent, we hoped that as our activity stabilized and progressed we would get feedback and see some results. Because HST essentially established its mission on the fly when we arrived, there was little precedent for the kind of work we were doing. We continued to connect national HUMINT operations with localized units, offer feedback to collectors on reporting and source analysis, and create target packages for action elements, but the effects that we hoped for generally failed to appear.

I am prohibited from being specific about many aspects of my job and HST's mission, but here's how my unclassified performance evaluation describes my first assignment:

Forward deployed to Baghdad, Iraq, to serve as an all-source analyst for the Multi-National Force—Iraq, C2X, HUMINT Support Team operating in the Combined Intelligence Operations Center on Camp Slayer. Conduct in-depth research and analysis on the Iraq insurgency, to include insurgent tactics, techniques and procedures; monitor and assess the role of assassinations and kidnappings in support of the insurgency; and identify significant collection gaps, opportunities, trends, and threads. Support HUMINT operations through source validation and objective evaluation of HUMINT reporting. Provide continuous, direct analytical support to HUMINT collectors through the use of IIR evaluations, SDRs, and HCRs [types of intelligence materials].

Job descriptions are authored at the beginning of an assignment rather than at the end, so a brief summary of the direct action mission was added to mine when the Strat team was disbanded:

Additionally, serve as a member of a three-man Direct Action Cell, which develops actionable intelligence packages for U.S. and Coalition Special Forces to kinetically target insurgents and their enablers.

Most of HST concentrated on the issues described in the latter half of that initial description, but the work seemed to journey into the ether (or ethernet, as it were) without much effect. When people think of themselves as valuable resources working on a matter of great personal and professional import, but begin to suspect that their efforts are being wasted, tremendous cognitive dissonance is created. We all wanted to believe that we were having a beneficial effect. We'd occasionally have rousing political debates, or discuss the general strategy of the work we were doing, but the vast majority of us ended up fairly pessimistic about the overall effort. A new school here, a successful operation there; it didn't distract us from the lawlessness that gripped most of the country. We held on to hope that our daily contributions were worthwhile as long as we could. As people lost that hope and that belief, morale declined precipitously.

During this downturn, the Direct Action Cell continued to plug away. While much of HST was stuck evaluating reports and painstakingly researching sources, we still got to identify and pursue bad guys. Although it was hard to quantify the effects of much of this work, we had enough success to validate it, and there was never any danger of losing the motivation to chase the shitheads who had done the abhorrent things we saw and read about.

As it turned out, although our spirits lasted longer than most, we weren't immune to the arbitrary and capricious nature of the bureaucracy. The Direct Action Cell worked frequently and closely with what my official (unclassified) performance evaluation describes as "a critical Iraqi government source," and many of our successes resulted directly from cooperation with this element. As this relationship developed, our accomplishments began to receive attention from military leadership, specifically a military intelligence component at the embassy. This component supervised our interactions within this unique relationship, and our original supervisor was extremely supportive of our efforts. This overseer was scheduled to redeploy to the United States with a couple of months left in the HST deployment, so we backbriefed his replacement about our mission.

The replacement was intrigued, and he asked dozens of questions about the program. The Direct Action Cell, in concert with collectors and embassy personnel, was able to establish good rapport and trust with this "critical Iraqi government source," and although the interaction was delicate, we considered it vital to both our mission and the long-term success of the Iraqis' own ability to establish security within their country. We felt, with no exaggeration, that the relationship, through mutual education and cooperation, was crucial to the potential for someday turning over security responsibility to the Iraqi government. The replacement, an Army Colonel, agreed, and praised our efforts, indicating support for the program.

The very next day he sent an email to the HUMINT people we worked with saying that none of us could work with the source outside the supervision of a member of his team. Further, any meets had to be planned days in advance, and he discouraged the presence of national-level (DIA) analytical input. In one fell swoop, he put a vital and productive element of the HST (and entire Iraq-based HUMINT) mission in jeopardy. The decision created a small firestorm of controversy, with everyone racing up their respective chains of command, trying to get the support of the highest-ranking official. In a dispute, generally whichever side got the blessing of a higher-ranking officer won. If the highest-level ally you could get was a lieutenant colonel, the other side beat it with their colonel. If you could manage to get some one-star to weigh in for you, that trumped the colonel. And so on. In Iraq, though, many of these bureaucratic battles ended up with one colonel fighting another, and you never knew exactly how it would go.

As the fight slowly made its way up the chains of command, we continued to do as much as we could, but we were furious at the impediment. No tangible reason was ever given, and again the startling ability of people to simply cut off communication was apparent. We devoted our time to other sources and projects while we waited for resolution. As the days turned into weeks, and the end of our deployment drew near, it was increasingly clear that the relationship we had established with the source was crumbling.

The vaunted Direct Action Cell morale crumbled with it, and we despaired of our months of work going down the drain. Like many others on the team, we knew the overall war strategy was doing little to affect the insurgency. Other than a small group of highly capable Iraqi special forces, Iraqi military and police force development continued to stagnate as sectarianism and Islamism grew stronger; the political process languished; rebuilding was stalled. For months we could acknowledge this but still think that our efforts were both valuable and valued, believing that we were helping to turn things around. In the span of those few weeks, that justification took a big hit.

The blow to our spirits would not be the last, however. As our deployment staggered to its conclusion, we began to hear about the team that would replace us, and it wasn't encouraging. We continued to work hard, but the humor was darker and the mumbles of "Forever" became more frequent as we pressed on.

CHAPTER 10

The group's general sentiment was increasingly downtrodden. We were careening toward the end of the deployment, and I finally reached the point where I was really, really ready to head home. It reminded me of *Super Size Me,* the documentary that tracked the rapid health decline of a guy who ate only McDonald's food for an entire month—we joked that a similar documentary could be made about the group's collective mental faculties.

With just over a month before we would head home (plus another week in transit), people were constantly fatigued, nearly always irritable, and quick with tempers. Personally, I wasn't snapping at people or even showing any frustration outwardly, but I felt much less sociable, and I found myself needing to take a quick walk around the office every couple of days to chill out. I didn't really know the proximate causes. The stress, the hours, the people, the mission, the new leadership—it could have been all or none of these, or some combination thereof. I hoped that our new assignments back in DC would provide a boost.

I continued to be amazed by the surroundings, never more so than during a two-day August sandstorm. It shut down Baghdad for days, delaying the then-ongoing constitution proceedings and causing several deaths and hundreds of injuries due to respiratory problems. The weirdest thing was how it looked: Everything was a dull orange, and at its worst the storm reduced visibility to about twenty meters. Everyone on base wore face masks; it was like a SARS outbreak on Mars. The physical feeling was unexpected as well—*sandstorm* is something of a misnomer; it was so fine that it seemed like dust more than sand, and we couldn't feel the sand itself on our skin. I did feel it, however, in my mouth and eyes. My teeth got gritty, and I kept trying to spit out sand while constantly breathing it in. Eyes get irritated and watery, so there was much ridiculing of those who looked like they were about to cry. Outside, and even on the first floor of many buildings (thanks to doors being opened regularly), a thick layer of dust coated everything.

The storm produced a welcome lull in attacks, but the respite was short-lived. Over the summer, attacks increased slightly in frequency but drastically in sophistication and effectiveness. Further, intra-Iraqi hostilities were escalating at an alarming rate. We hoped the political situation, which included scheduled votes on the constitution and plans for a new Iraqi government that fall, would develop constructively, but the idea that the insurgency was focused only against the United States was finally recognized as the dangerous fallacy that it was. Far more Iraqi civilians were being killed than coalition troops, and several of us tried in vain to bring attention to this trend.

Many leaders failed to grasp, even at that late date, the turmoil and dissatisfaction in Iraqi daily life. I wrote to a friend that if you offered the following option to the entire country, the vast majority would take it: You can have electricity, a job, and the ability to travel freely without danger of kidnapping or murder. Your kids can go to school, women can have basic rights, and not a single new bomb will drop from the sky. In return, you will have a dictatorial government, you won't be able to vote, and you can never say anything bad about the ruling party. If you do, you'll be thrown into jail or killed, but if you work hard, tend to your family, and keep your mouth shut, you will be employed and you will be safe. People might not have taken that option while Saddam was in power, or even in 2003, but we had reached the point where Iraqis had no faith in the United States *or* the Iraqi government and would accept the leadership of any group that could provide basic day-to-day security. I was not endorsing the previous regime, of course, just trying to convey how bad things had become. War-lordism, a kind of mafia-style corruption and violence, began to take over.

It baffled me that our chain of command could not recognize the emerging dangers of a population that was at once demoralized and furious. If Iraqis could not take out their frustration on U.S. troops, they would take it out on one another. We were allowing a situation to develop in which not winning was losing, and a third party, beyond the United States and the vast majority of peaceful Iraqis, had control over whether stability or anarchy would reign. That third party, terrorists and/or insurgents, was not about to give up, and we had no plan to remove either the motivation or the means to wreak havoc.

Several weeks before the end of our deployment, an email went around HST, one that apparently had a tendency to flood through groups as their departure date approached, and was hugely resonant within the group for both its humor and its gloom. The following excerpts come unedited from the version I received.

Subject: Signs You've Been in Baghdad Too Long.

You start humming with the Arabic song playing on the radio on the shuttle bus

You start picturing your friends in traditional Arab dress

You realize the contractors have more firepower than the military combat units

You drink the water from the tap because you want to drop 20 pounds in two weeks

Driving around in SUVs with weapons pointed out the windows and forcing cars off the road seems very normal to you

The organization you work for has changed its name more than three times

You're actually excited to get a package that contains 3 pair of socks, 12 bars of soap, and a Victoria's Secret catalog

You've memorized every episode from the 4th season of *Sex and the City*

You see celebratory fire going over the compound at night and think, "Wow, the colors are so pretty" and want to fire back

You're thinking of buying real estate in the green zone

You start ending your rare phone conversations and emails with "out"

You plan on removing all trees and grass in your yard when you get home so it will look more natural

The temp drops down to 102 degrees and you shiver while reaching for your Gore-Tex jacket

You call home and your kids ask, "Who is this?"

You call home and your wife says hello Bill . . . but your name is Sam

When 12 hours is a short workday

When, during the BUA [the daily morning briefing], "DIV asked MNSTC-I for the FRAGO that MNC-I was supposed to publish, but couldn't because MNF-I hadn't weighed in, since they were too inundated with MOD and MOI war-gaming the JCCs within the ISF to square us away!" is a valid comment and generates no questions

The palace catches fire and instead of helping to put it out you grab a bag of marshmallows and start roasting

You step into any office and there are 6 colonels, 12 lieutenant colonels, 15 majors, and 8 captains supervising the work of 1 sergeant

You're ordered to get an air mission together on short notice because it's a "Hot priority" only to have the Major call back once he is in the air to ask "Does anyone know where I am going?"

When the weapon buyback program has become so successful that you have issued the same AK-47 to the Iraqi army three times

You decide that for shits and grins let's take a run around Lost Lake at Camp Victory to see if we can get shot at by the sniper

The highlight of your shopping experience at the PX is to see that they got in a new shipment of Schick Tracer razor blades

You get offended by people wearing clean, pressed DCUs

You make a contest out of seeing who can wear their uniform for
more days before becoming entirely disgusted with themselves

You wonder if the fish served at dinner really was carp caught out
of the Tigris, or if it's mutant fish from Camp Victory's lake

You find it completely acceptable to pick your nose, pick your
teeth, or scratch at your swamp ass while talking to a complete
stranger or member of the opposite sex

A rocket or a mortar really isn't a big deal until the crater it leaves
is big enough to trip over in the dark on the way to the latrine

You go to a social gathering and intermittent gunfire or explosions
don't even cause a pause in the conversation

The call of the jackals is music to your ears

The layer of dust is so thick in your hooch that a sand dune forms

You go to Chapel just for the fresh food at the end of the service

You wake up and think: Baghdad, I am still in friggin Baghdad

My team had fulfilled most of the list's entries, so we considered ourselves officially in Baghdad too long. We felt awful for those who had to stay for a year (or more), including nearly all of the Army soldiers and Marines in-country, as well as those affected by draconian stop-loss policies that prevented them from going home until long after their previous redeployment date. With just weeks left before we were scheduled to go home, we slowly started to deal with the logistics of returning, the out-processing procedures as well as preparing to turn over the mission to our replacements.

By about halfway through our deployment, the team replacing us was established and training back in DC. Despite the extensive evaluations we filled out documenting the irrelevance of our training courses to our actual jobs, the new group was going through the same classes we had endured. A few of us had friends in the group, so we occasionally emailed back and forth about the deployment experience, but mostly we had little contact with them. Not for lack of trying, though; analysts frequently asked our leadership if we could get in touch with our replacements, but we were told that their respective missions had not yet been assigned so we had to wait. In turn, our leadership put pressure on the new group to determine roles so the transition could be facilitated more easily. Within HST, we all agreed that it would be vastly better to start including people back in DC on the correspondence and machinations of our jobs so they could be up to speed when they arrived. We would only have a week or two of overlap with the new group, much of which inevitably would be wasted taking care of logistical issues. If we knew who would be taking over for us, we could simply copy our emails to them, put them on distribution lists, get them involved in the work.

Eventually word filtered through that the new leadership was prohibiting contact between their team and ours. We were stunned. Why on earth would the new team prevent communication to facilitate the transition? When we had a video conference with our replacements, it was dominated by leadership, and on their end some questions and answers were cut off or electronically muted. It was simply bizarre, and the poor communication meant we'd have just a week or two to show the incoming team what had taken us months to establish. As the first iteration of the HST program, we had set up most of the mission and procedures. After months of work, most of the team had finally established relatively stable jobs, and we did not want the new group to have to reinvent the wheel. It would have been so easy to demonstrate most of the assignments via email, and we all agreed there was no better way to learn (and, for us, teach) than by example.

With a month left for most of us, our leaders were about to depart. They had arrived a month before us, in the advance team, and would correspondingly leave a month before we did. When the advance team for the new group arrived, just days prior to our leaders' departure, the reasons for such secrecy quickly became clear. The two heads of the group, Jim and Ben, wanted to completely transform the HST. They arrived declaring that HST needed to return to its COIN origins, with a focus on identifying and analyzing the disparate insurgency groups, without the "tangential" missions of the first group. They also told their team that the first group was ineffective and lazy, insisting that we weren't to be trusted.

Their plan to "return" to a COIN mission reflected their complete lack of situational awareness. According to CIOC leadership, the COIN mission was already covered by other CIOC elements. We knew that an HST effort to do COIN would result in the HST being split up, its members shuttled to open slots in a variety of other organizations within and outside the CIOC. There was no way to convince them of this, however. Jim and Ben, both civilians, had forceful personalities, and they wanted to impose their will regardless of the ground truth. Unfortunately, I would end up working with Ben for months back at the Pentagon, but at the time I just knew him as a volcano of temper, often blowing smoke and occasionally erupting. Jim, a disorganized and disheveled team chief, did not endear himself within the military atmosphere with his unkempt appearance and overbearing nature. Voluble but oblivious to his general effect on people, he was the worst stereotype of intelligence middle management brought to life.

Ben was his alter ego. Tall, aloof, and domineering, Ben ruled by fiat, and his temper tantrums were fearsome and legendary. In his first week at the CIOC, he had a computer problem, so he called the IT folks downstairs and a representative came up to his office. As Ben questioned him, we could hear the technician explaining the problem, telling him that it would take a couple of days to fix. The door slammed shut, but Ben's explosive shouts easily penetrated the flimsy barrier. My teammates and I cringed. First of all, the last thing you ever want to do is piss off the tech people, especially when your computers get screwed up on a daily basis, as ours did. More generally, the environment was a collegial one, in recognition of the fact that we were all contributing to the same goal. Virtually everyone was working hard and doing the best they could, and few would be motivated by verbal harassment.

According to what the original HST leads later told me, Jim and Ben had no interest in talking to them before the original leadership returned home. There was minimal conversation about how the group was organized or run, and Jim and Ben declined most information or advice from the supervisors they replaced. They did not appear to have a set plan, but they knew they didn't want to continue what we were doing. Soon after their arrival, a rumor circulated that both were told by superiors at DIA that they would not be promoted unless they volunteered to deploy. While this was never confirmed, it certainly didn't seem like they were thrilled to be there, and the rumor provided a possible explanation why.

When they arrived, neither one introduced himself to the current team. They didn't join our meetings, didn't let us know what their plan was, and didn't ask for input from our leadership. The responsibility for establishing the teams fell to two other members of their advance team, Adam Fillmore, a civilian who would later become one of my many supervisors at the Pentagon, and Navy lieutenant (equivalent to Captain in the other services) Michelle Elson. Fillmore was highly intelligent and expressed frustration with Jim and Ben, who constantly gave him different directives and then blamed him for not being able to divine their true intent. While it was bad that Jim and Ben didn't talk to the previous HST leadership, it was worse that they did not seem to talk with each other.

In a rigid chain of command, it is often difficult to determine where a communication breakdown has occurred. Since you primarily have contact with the individual directly above or below you, it's impossible to know what happens to any information passed up or down after it ventures beyond your immediate awareness. Problems occur because the chain of command, especially in tough situations, can function like a bad game of telephone. Instructions (and intentions) get altered along the way, but unlike in the game, everybody does not eventually come together to recount the hilarious screwups.

Shortly after the original HST leadership departed, the organizational plan for the new group finally filtered down through the chain of command. The primary mission would be link and social network analysis; eliminated, or at least drastically reduced, were the direct action and kidnapping missions. Captain White and I were tremendously disappointed, and coupled with the blow of embassy interference, this essentially finished our efforts. Whereas our team had three people doing direct action full-time, the new group had one person assigned to the mission, and he would do it part-time. Jim and Ben's changes were not restricted to the mission; travel was encumbered, with approval required far in advance and only granted for "critical" missions. That meant the relationships our group had painstakingly built with units and collectors would be lost as personal interaction was replaced with sporadic email, and it also meant analysts were deprived of the opportunity to see how collectors and units utilized the HST efforts. They created three spreadsheets—three!—that each had to be filled out anytime an analyst left the CIOC, and declared that no more than one person could be at the gym at any given time. They restricted car usage, capped overtime hours, and, in a particularly infantilizing touch, said men and women couldn't be in each other's respective houses after 2300 hours. It was seventh-grade summer camp . . . in a war zone.

It took months for my group to hate Baghdad; the new people were cursing their decision to volunteer within weeks of their arrival. Those of us who were in the final month of our deployment disregarded virtually all these new regulations. What were they going to do, send us home? But the new leadership didn't even care; they just ignored us. After months of hard work and optimism, the original HST personnel slowly came to understand that virtually all of our work was for naught—it would not be utilized, much less continued, and for no apparent reason. It was a sickening realization.

The remaining people on my team started to filter out, and soon there was just a handful of us left, trying to wrap up our respective projects as best we could. We all made last trips down to the embassy, wrapping up professional relationships and cementing friendships that we hoped would endure beyond the deployment. We quietly counseled the new people, who were largely overwhelmed by the disorganization of their leadership and the CIOC, and wished them the best. We were in touch with our former supervisors, now getting themselves established in DIA's Office of Iraq Analysis (OIA) at the Pentagon, and although the news from there wasn't especially promising, I was, perhaps incredibly, still optimistic. A month before my scheduled return date, my boss told me there were two main teams at OIA, counterinsurgency and strategic issues. I sent an email to the major coordinating our return, requesting placement on the strategic team, preferably working governance issues. Although I worked mostly tactical issues in Iraq, I felt that my educational background and interests were a good fit for strategic governmental analysis, and in the midst of out-processing from Baghdad, I received notice that my request had been granted.

I was in the last group to leave, and as the few of us remaining made final preparations, essentially sidelined from the new HST mission, we had neither the time nor the mental energy for reflection. We just wanted to get the fuck out.

With less than a week before our flight back to the United States, the few of us who remained turned in our Iraq-specific security badges, officially ending our time in the CIOC. In just a few days, I would get on a plane, and after about a week in transit (layovers, out-processing, debriefing) I'd be back in DC. I planned to head right back to work at my new job at the Pentagon, which I expected to be high-pressure but also potentially high-reward, as it promised good access to decision makers in the military and the intelligence community. Despite a decidedly mixed experience in Baghdad, I was looking forward to continuing work on Iraq, shifting from the counterinsurgency focus to a strategic one.

We had a few days to get our things together and prepare for departure, and for the first time in months I thought about the overall situation. I was disappointed in the new leadership, but I hoped that the rank and file would keep our work going. I did believe, at that time, that I'd managed to do more good than harm, and I'd certainly learned more in six months there than I would have over years back in DC. I was exposed to all kinds of operational and analytical scenarios, and although I saw the dark sides of the conflict more frequently than the successes, I was encouraged by the intelligence and attitude of many of my colleagues. I don't think anyone ever accomplishes everything he or she wants to on deployment, so I preferred to reserve final judgments until I established some distance. I hoped to use the experience to further what I believed to be rational intelligence collection and analysis, and I was glad I didn't have to stay any longer. I also had nothing but empathy and support for the soldiers who were there for twice as long as I was, in the field and facing down their mortality on a daily basis.

The things I was most looking forward to, other than seeing friends and family, probably seemed weird. Rain topped the list— I hadn't seen rain in more than six months, and I knew I would just stand in it for a while when it first poured down after my return. A bed that could fit my entire body, rather than poking my feet through the bars at the end. Walking without a pistol hanging from my shoulder or thigh. Answering a phone call from family or friends. Two-ply. Food that moved through the body neither too quickly nor too slowly. It was a motley list, but I was looking forward to it all.

Not long before I left, more than a thousand people died in Iraq in the single largest mass-casualty event since we'd invaded. Tragically, the deaths were a consequence of apparently unfounded panic: A stampede resulted from false rumors of a suicide bomber in the midst of a huge group traversing a bridge, heading peacefully to prayer at a holy site near Baghdad. When panic struck, the bridge collapsed, causing deaths from both trampling and drowning. Hundreds more were injured, essentially casualties of the insurgents' ability to incite fear and panic. It was another black eye for the government and coalition forces in the midst of a collapsing political process and Pollyanna-type analysis from the U.S. government and military, and it seemed an appropriate marker for our impending departure.

Because of the limits on describing the end result of my work in Iraq, I will simply reference my (unclassified) performance evaluation. In it, my supervisor described some of what I did:

While serving as a principle [sic] analyst for a critical Iraqi government source, your work was essential to the development of over 140 actionable intelligence packages. Through your mission-first attitude and selfless work ethic, you ensured that the Overt HUMINT Support Team remained customer and operationally focused. . . . You have been performing well above your current grade, in both the quality and quantity of your work. Additionally, you have adapted very well to changes in our mission focus and production requirements. Alex, the intelligence products you produce are consistently professional, comprehensive, well researched, and pertinent. You have received compliments on your work from the HUMINT Support Team Leadership, other analysts within the Combined Intelligence Operations Center, as well as combat units and other governmental agencies.

The "accomplishments" section further detailed my work in the Direct Action Cell.

[Created target packages included] names and descriptions of individuals, imagery, group associations, and locations of target. This intelligence was shared with military action units throughout the theater, resulting in dozens of insurgents being pursued, detained, and incarcerated.

Facilitated the movement and processing of [. . .] detainees suspected of anti-Iraqi forces (AIF) activity. Assisted in organizing the in-processing structure, provided support to direct action units to draft sworn statements to enable detention at long-term facilities, and contributed analytic support to initial detainee screenings and interrogations.

Facilitated feedback process for intelligence gathering before, during, and after direct action operations. Talked with direct action unit individuals, Iraqi special forces operators, collectors, sources, S2 (intelligence) staff, and Judge Advocate General (JAG) officers regarding the intelligence roles and responsibilities in the pre- and post-operation analysis of military action.

Support[ed] Multi-National Force—Iraq, as part of a

HUMINT Support Team, which was responsible for the capture or death of more than 150 key insurgents in Iraq.

I wondered how many coalition and Iraqi soldiers we helped save or protect, and I thought about how many operations were made easier or more effective by our analysis. I also wondered how many soldiers died in actions we helped establish, and how many among those "more than 150 key insurgents" were simply in the wrong place at the wrong time.

The day before my departure, I got my final out-processing signature release and went to a last gathering for the outward-bound. The guy in charge of the redeployment process sat us down and offered us each a "near beer"—what we called the nonalcoholic brew we all choked down occasionally for the sake of nostalgia—and checked our forms.

"Okay," he reassured us, "you all have all the signatures you need. At the end of this meeting I'll sign the last line and you'll be good to go on your flights, whenever they are. Oh, and here's the deal: When you go home, don't beat your wife, and don't kick your dog. Get it? Don't get crazy, and enjoy whatever time off you get."

That was our redeployment briefing. I was pretty sure none of us was in danger of any kind of post-traumatic stress disorder, but I fervently hoped that the actual troops were getting something a little more comprehensive. Given the staggering prevalence of mental illness and disorders in vets from this war, I imagine it's probably hit-or-miss.

Hours later we flew out of Baghdad, again in tactical conditions, and I was relieved once we made it up to cruising altitude. After a few days in Doha, Qatar, and then Germany, I made the transatlantic trip to DC. Nearly six and a half months after I left, I was back home.

I sent a wrap-up email to friends and family soon afterward, telling them I was safe:

Yes, I survived the bloodiest week yet in Baghdad and am back in DC. I'm currently surveying my empty apartment, with television

on, music blaring, air conditioner blasting, shades up, and Internet humming, and I'm already trying to push the last six months
out of my mind. The travel was long and exhausting, and I'm sure
I won't be in the right mental time zone for a while . . . but who
cares? Since I returned I've seen trees, puppies, retail establish-
ments, tank tops, and even a few drops of rain, all for the first
time in six and a half months. Good times! It's great to just see
random people in regular life, walking around with no weapons or
threat, however remote, of impending violence or attack.

I wasted no time in getting back to work; sitting around doing
nothing is not exactly my forte. Iraq was soon being pushed from
my mind, at least to some extent, and I reflected only briefly upon
my return. My deployment had certainly taught me a ton about intelligence processes and procedures, foreign policy, and government work, and exposed me to some great people. On the other
hand, it laid bare many of the gross deficiencies in intel, government, and leadership within the ranks of public service.

Iraq was, to some extent, already a failure even then. I knew
from my time there that any discussion of "fighting until victory"
was absurd: The new goal was apparently to set up a secular, pro-
Western (or at least not anti-West), representative government that
keeps a single Iraqi sovereignty and respects the rights of minori-
ties. The further, original goal was to demonstrate to other Middle
East nations that the United States would use force to protect itself
against threats not only immediate, but also prospective. Finally, it
was thought that a democratic government, responsible to the
people, would prevent and discourage terrorism within and outside its borders, also demonstrating that the problems of the Middle East are the fault of their own governments, not the U.S.

After being in Baghdad, I knew that virtually all of those goals
were no longer attainable under any reasonable scenario. They
may never have been in the first place. The objectives constantly
evolved, of course, but we had moved the goalposts. Attempting to
make Iraq reasonably safe for the average citizen, establish a functioning infrastructure, and chaperone in a representative (essen-

tially parliamentary) democracy were goals that were supposed to fall into place, not take years, hundreds of billions of American dollars, and, most important, thousands of lives. In an email summarizing my time in Baghdad, I wrote,

Let's look back on the original goals: The government will not be secular, and the constitution does not encourage secularism in public government or private life. Virtually every significant party in Iraq is virulently anti-U.S., anti-coalition, and arguably anti-West. The nation still has single sovereignty, but that is precarious at best with a federalist system that may allow the Kurds (in the north) and the Shia (in the south) to establish virtual mini states, leaving the Sunnis in the middle, where there is no oil wealth, to fend for themselves. There are no minority rights, and Islamist groups have sprung up as local governments and self-appointed religious police. Women inarguably have fewer rights protected under the new constitution than they did under Saddam.

The oil industry is in shambles, partly due to lack of security and partly due to rampant corruption and theft. Wolfowitz's prediction that Iraqi oil revenue would pay for the war has been rendered beyond ridiculous. There is no infrastructure (most cities have power for a handful of hours per day, according to news reports, and the water situation reportedly isn't much better) to speak of, and security is precarious with skyrocketing numbers of assassinations and kidnappings, which are far more prevalent than even the common suicide bombings, primarily targeted at the Shia. The government is increasingly connected with (and perhaps dependent upon) Iran, which will spark fears of a greater Shia–Sunni conflict in the Middle East and weaken our position in any kind of diplomatic or military crisis with Iran.

Most important for American security, nations across the world now believe that we are virtually incapable of launching a significant military operation at this time. Whether that is true or not, the belief is pervasive and crippling to many foreign policy goals. We're stretched too thin, the cost is crippling the economy both long-term and short-term, and *democracy* is now a dirty word in the Middle East. All a dictator has to do to discourage reform is say, "Look at Iraq. There's democracy for you. Is that what you want?"

Once again, all problems in the Middle East will be blamed upon the U.S., just louder now. Iraq may become a terrorist haven and training ground, with the next generation of terrorists ready to be exported just as the Afghanistan mujahideen were after the Soviets left (see: bin Laden, Osama). We are less safe, not more safe, and the worst thing is that it was predictable, or should have been. To put it another way, it takes a special kind of idiot to push an egg off a table and then blame the egg for exploding into a mess.

All is not lost, of course. We'll learn, and perhaps the security situation will improve enough so that we can declare victory and leave—probably when we put infrastructure and individual security at the top of the priority list. Eventually I think there will be an Iraqi government that is accountable to its people, but whether these accomplishments were worth the cost is another question. It's also worth noting that setting timetables for a staggered withdrawal would likely help the situation, not make it worse as some argue.

It is certainly our duty to continue trying to establish civil infrastructure, and at the very least prevent set-piece battles from breaking out (set-piece being shorthand for "traditional" battles, with hundreds or thousands of people fighting each other for territory). We're still better than anybody else in the history of the world at that, and just a few fighter jets can prevent set-piece battles and keep training camps from cropping up (again, a straightforward job for the Air Force). This role does not necessitate a huge number of ground troops, however, which is consistent with my above-stated proclivity for a staggered and planned withdrawal. But continuing upon our current course would be both dangerous and ineffective.

Freedom is a noble thing. I'm in favor of Iraqis having self-government and autonomy. And you know what? I'm in favor of all 6 billion people in the world having "freedom" (again, as generally defined as a government responsible to the people through elections and other democratic processes). However. It doesn't mean I'm going to pay for all of them to have it, and it also doesn't mean I'm willing to die for their freedom. I'm no isolationist: Disliking stupid intervention is different from disliking all intervention. The war on terrorists (and not "terrorism," which is a tactic, not a target) should be real, not a feel-good gesture for public relations purposes.

So . . . I saw and did some good things, and I saw and did some bad things. Overall, I'm glad I went, but I'm not in any hurry to go back.

I arrived home in the early-morning hours of a Saturday, and Monday morning I went to work. DoD gave us a week off and a week of half days to readjust, but I wanted to save that time for when I could use it to visit family and friends. I wasn't interested in wasting time; there was more work to do, and I was ready to do it. Like many of my teammates, I felt no urgent need to analyze my experience right when I got back. If anything, I was ready for some distance from all things Baghdad.

That Monday I was still on Baghdad time, so the 0500 wakeup to be at my new office by 0630 was easy. I arrived excited about the new assignment, ready to work. As I walked up the Pentagon Metro escalator, I saw the war protestors who came to the Pentagon every Monday, and I read their signs as I walked toward the security checkpoint. Jose, my old friend from the Baghdad advance team, met me outside. It was time to start my new assignment.

CHAPTER 12

I gave Jose a big hug when he met me outside the Pentagon, which earned us a few stares. I hadn't seen him in several weeks, since he'd redeployed, and I asked him how things were at the new office.

He rolled his eyes.

"We gotta get you a badge and computer access. That should take, oh, about a month. Welcome to the Pentagon."

"Awesome." I smiled knowingly.

I had no idea what to expect from the office; despite being aware for months that we were coming, leadership had not given the redeploying group any information. Not where we'd be working, not how to get to the office, not a start date. I'd emailed my putative boss to let him know that I'd be coming right in after my return, but never heard anything back, so I'd made sure Jose could meet me when I arrived. We headed inside.

"So is our office in South Carolina, or what?" We had been walking for a while. I sometimes wondered whether the Pentagon was specifically designed so that people could only figure out where they were going and nothing else, and we had taken more turns than I could ever remember. I should have brought bread crumbs.

"Well, we're in crisis space still."

This was the first in a litany of bad initial signs. *Crisis space* essentially means temporary space, which usually does not bode well for the office setup. I couldn't understand why the main office for intelligence for a three-year-long war was in temporary space.

We went up a ramp, around a corner, down two flights of stairs, around another corner, through the hall, through various security stations, up some stairs, past several sets of doors, and finally arrived at a sign that said OFFICE OF IRAQ ANALYSIS. Jose was also assigned to the Strategic Issues Division, or Strat, and as we walked, he told me that my placement was fortunate.

"Strat," he said, "is way better than COIN"—the other main team in the office. "Major Lewis, who heads up the COIN shop, is pretty crazy. I'm sure you've heard about the push-ups."

I had. Major Lewis thought it was funny to make people do push-ups in the office for various offenses, such as tardiness. He viewed it as a team-building experience.

"And right now Major Vollmer is our boss, but he's heading out in just a few days. Major Nimick is taking over, which is actually really good news."

I knew Major Nimick from his work on the pre-deployment process, and people generally thought him a fair and effective manager. He had the ability to lead, delegate, and then mostly stay out of the way of his analysts. In an agency where micromanaging was the rule, this approach earned him respect and loyalty. Within the structure of a team, the team leader performed most administrative tasks, and the senior intelligence analyst (or officer) oversaw the analytical process. There was some overlap, and it sometimes became a problem when a team chief and senior intel person both thought themselves the final authority on analytical issues. Jose predicted that this wouldn't be a problem with Major Nimick and Evan Gruber, our senior intelligence officer.

When we finally got to the office, it was not the standard DIA cubicle farm, but rather rows of desk stations, similar to what we'd had in Baghdad. It looked like a Wall Street trading floor, with lines of computer screens and everybody next to one another. Oddly, the stations were minimally adorned; missing were the usual pictures of kids and family, the quotes and cartoons that personalize a work space.

Jose introduced me to Major Vollmer, the departing team chief.

"Oh, I, uh, didn't know you'd be in today," he mumbled.

"Yes sir, I emailed you a couple of times before I headed back stateside, and I've also been in touch with Major Nimick, who told me I'd be on the Strat governance team."

"Well, we don't really have a desk for you," Major Vollmer admitted, "but there's a couple people out sick today, so first let's get you the right paperwork and then you can jump on whatever empty desk you can find."

"There aren't open desks for the incoming people, sir? I mean, I'm one of the first to report back"—because I hadn't taken the usual vacation time upon returning—"and there are many more of us coming in the next couple weeks."

"Yeah . . ." He trailed off, looking awkwardly at the ground. "We have a little bit of a space crunch." That would turn out to be an understatement.

"We're technically in J2 spaces," Major Vollmer elaborated, "and we do a lot of their current intel requirements, but we're also tasked to DI," the DIA's Directorate for Analysis. "So basically, when either DI or J2 needs something, they task us with it, but when *we* need something, the J2 says it's DI's responsibility and DI says it's J2's responsibility."

"Sounds pretty much like the usual," I commiserated.

Military intelligence has a convoluted structure for several reasons. Crucially, it occupies the unusual position of being responsible for both tactical and strategic intelligence gathering and analysis. While other agencies do have some tactical roles, the armed forces have by far the greatest interest in tactical, ground-level information. The military is also involved, however, at the highest levels of strategic decision making, so the issues covered by the Defense Intelligence Agency run the gamut from specifically micro to broadly macro. Consequently, there are multiple tracks of authority over DIA. On the one hand, DIA employees are ultimately responsible to the head of DIA, and they also report up the chain to combatant commanders of the various commands, such as Central Command (CENTCOM) or Strategic Command (STRATCOM). On the other, DIA also informs advisers, like the Joint Chiefs of Staff, and policymakers, such as the Office of the Secretary of Defense (OSD). The Joint Chiefs and OSD both have their own large staffs under their respective headings, but DIA is tasked with providing strategic intel to all of these disparate entities.

Within the Joint Chiefs of Staff, like most military structures, there are different divisions for various topics: J4 covers logistics, for instance, while J3 is operations and J2 is intelligence. When we talked about the J2, we were referring to Rear Admiral David Dorsett, the principal adviser to the chairman of the Joint Chiefs on matters of intelligence. The chairman, of course, directly advises the president. Similarly, DIA has significant input into the SecDef's daily briefing, and we constantly responded to assignments from DI (which went up through the normal DIA chain of command) and J2, with SecDef taskings coming somewhat less frequently. We also took on projects from specific military organizations. With so many bosses, it didn't surprise me that things were somewhat complex. But the biggest issue in our office was the tug-of-war between J2 and DI, which reflected the difficulty of having the same issue-based team do both immediate and long-term analysis. While in theory it was good to have all the experts in Baghdad counterinsurgency together, by not separating the team into current and strategic sections the long-term issues were inevitably overtaken by day-to-day matters.

The Strat team tried to resist that trend, and my new boss laid out the general plan of attack.

"Juan, this is Alex; Alex, Juan," Jose introduced. "Juan is the governance team lead within the Strategic Issues Division." We shook hands and I tried to make sure I had the hierarchy right.

"Okay, so it goes, from top to bottom, *Office* of Iraq Analysis, Strategic Issues *Division*, and governance *team*, right?" I thought I had a handle on the order and appellations, but I wanted to make sure.

"Yup," laughed Juan, "and the other teams within Strat, besides our governance team, are Shia, Sunni, and Kurd. We all consult with each other a lot, obviously, and you'll meet those guys today. In the meantime, let me introduce you to the rest of governance." Juan, I would learn, was always reassuringly calm, and his ability to combine a relaxed temperament with an intense focus on the mission was rare in DoD. As we met, a couple of people nearby turned around from their desks.

"This is Kate," Juan said, nodding his head toward the woman sitting to his left.

"Hey, I'm Alex." We shook hands.

"Hi! Welcome back!" Kate beamed enthusiastically. She was a contractor, one of many in the office.

"Next to Kate is Andrew," who was also a contractor, "and that's the team: you, me, Jose here, and Kate and Andrew." Juan surveyed his charges approvingly.

"We have our daily morning meeting in just a few minutes," he told me before turning toward Jose, "so why don't you take him over to Shawn to get some paperwork started?"

I glanced at my new teammates before we walked away.

Kate, a pretty brunette with an animated disposition and a quick smile, looked young enough to be part of the youth brigade of the office. Andrew was a little older and, I noticed, wore a wedding ring, as did Juan. Andrew was a little disheveled, his tie draped, untied, around his collar, below about three days' worth of black stubble on his face. Andrew and Juan were both former Army officers, Jose's father was a career enlisted soldier, and Kate was dating a former Marine. All of us had worked in Iraq (with the exception of Kate, who nonetheless had plenty of experience working abroad), we were all under thirty-five, and we all knew the substantive issues as well as the culture of the agency we worked for. It looked like a solid group.

Jose brought me to Shawn, the go-to guy in the office for administrative issues. Shawn was dubbed "Frozone," I later learned, because he bore a striking resemblance to the Samuel L. Jackson–voiced character in *The Incredibles* and moved at glacial speed whenever anyone needed his help. Jose told him I needed a badge and computer access, the standard new-person stuff.

"Well," Frozone frowned, "it's going to take some time."

It was sometimes hard to tell whether inefficiency was the fault of bureaucracy or individual laziness, so we were used to giving a little nudge to the administrative people.

"You guys have known that I was coming for six months, right? I mean, everybody who deployed signed up knowing that a commitment to this office upon our return was part of the deal, and we were in Iraq for six months, so the office knew for at least that long that we'd be coming. Why is this such a surprise that we're starting to filter in? If everything was going to take this long, why couldn't we have filed the paperwork weeks ago, either by fax or email or whatever?"

"Nobody told *me* about it, so we'll just do it now. And don't bug me about it. I'll let you know when it all comes through."

"Okay," I sighed, resigned to having no computer access for the moment. A nudge was one thing, but fighting with people whom you needed to get things done for you was nearly always counter-productive. Especially tech people. Support staff in government can be vindictive, and nobody wanted to incur their wrath. In the meantime, because I lacked an updated badge, I needed an escort to go anywhere outside the immediate area. Which meant, for example, that anytime I had to go to the restroom, somebody had to come along and stand outside. I made a mental note: Any bathroom trip requiring more than thirty seconds I'd take care of at home.

By the time I finished writing my name, address, Social Security number, phone number, and emergency contact information a dozen times on various forms, it was time for the morning meeting. Every day around 0800 the Strat team gathered to do a quick update from the night before and update the plan for the coming day. The morning meeting was not the first event of the day—most of us arrived in the office around 0630—but it set the agenda and coordinated our efforts. There was only one conference room in the entire office, so everybody in Strat gathered in an open space between two rows of desks, creating a makeshift circle with some sitting, others standing, and a few in between, leaning heavily on the short walls up around the ends of the rows. That last contingent tended to grow as the week went on, but on this Monday it was a small delegation.

"Okay, good morning, everybody." Evan, our senior intelligence officer, began the meeting. "We have some new blood today: This is Alex, and he's going to be on governance. Alex, I'm Evan. Happy to have you."

"Thank you, sir. Happy to be here."

"Okay, so what do we have for production today?"

We went around the circle, each person briefly talking about what he or she was working on, and everyone providing updates on anything new in their specific areas. A few people said, "NSTR"—nothing significant to report—or simply "Nothing new," while the rest mentioned the written products in progress or taskers from a variety of customers. I could never figure out why assignments were called "taskers" rather than simply "tasks" (or in the singular, "I got a tasker" instead of "I got a task"). The projects sounded interesting, and the focus seemed to be on the kind of political issues that I thought would, long-term, have greater effect on the war effort than the tactical stuff, despite the personal and immediate gratification of targeting intel and ops. Especially for an administration led by a man who as late as 2003 reportedly didn't know the difference between Shia and Sunni, our analysis of internal dynamics in Iraq was, I figured, invaluable.

Generally, there were two categories of projects: PowerPoint slides and written products. Slides were for the daily J2 briefing, while written products could go to a variety of customers. Every morning at 0515 the J2 received a briefing on the day's current intelligence, which he vetted and then took to the chairman of the Joint Chiefs later that morning. Slides included a heading describing the issue, a bulletized summary of the intelligence, and a brief analytical assessment at the bottom. The assessment was the crucial element, and the section the J2 generally spent the most time changing, but it was usually just two or three lines. Before slides got to the J2, they had to make their way through a byzantine approval process, so it was crucial to get a consensus among Strat before anything moved up the chain. Strat's morning meeting helped flesh out (or "flush out," as my old boss in Iraq would say) our thoughts. The slides usually had a short turnaround time, just a day or two, as they were intended to be current intelligence updates. Although longer-term slides also ran, they were less frequent. The written products could take either days or weeks, depending on the topic, length, and review process, and there were several types of papers, all of which went to different sets of people. Some projects originated with the analysts, others were directed from above, but virtually all, regardless of how important the intended recipient, were crafted by the analysts (rather than by our bosses).

The morning meeting came to an end, and I wandered over to my temporary desk. I wondered what would happen when the rest of my deployment group came back if there wasn't even a single open desk for me, but I knew I was the only person from the Baghdad team going to Strat; maybe the COIN section had more space and it wouldn't be a problem. In any case, I figured leadership would find a spot for me as things settled down. I spent most of the day making phone calls to figure out how to do more paperwork, for closing out Iraq matters as well as in-processing at the Pentagon. Everybody ate at their desks, so around noon I unpacked my lunch and scarfed my usual sandwich and yogurt while perusing a book on Shia politics that I picked up off the desk. Real work would have to wait until Frozone got me my log-in and password information.

In the afternoon, before I left, I talked briefly with James Mc-Murphy, the former HST chief, whom I hadn't seen since he'd redeployed from Baghdad with the rest of the initial advance team. A longtime China expert, his extensive analytical expertise was being wasted in the Iraq office.

"I was a manager in Iraq," he frowned, "not an analyst. I kept up with the traffic, sure, but the longer I go without looking at China, the harder it will be to get back into the swing of things. I've been doing China for twenty years! I mean c'mon, I'm just taking up space here."

The initial information on our commitment when we volunteered had been sketchy, and while I understood it to be a yearlong rotation to the Iraq team, with six months in Baghdad followed by six months at the Pentagon, others were told that the six months in the rear would be abbreviated or waived.

"When do you think they'll let you go back to your old office?"

"I don't know. First they said it would be a few weeks but now they're saying a few months. They have me doing *special projects* here, which is code for 'We have no idea what to do with you.' "

A China expert isn't much help in an Iraq office, especially when everybody knows his presence is transitory, and there were several others in a similar position, biding their time at OIA before they could get back to their permanent assignments. For the deployment, DIA had wanted anybody willing to volunteer, since there weren't enough Middle East experts to fill the group (and most of the ones who existed had already done a deployment or two) and because they figured the COIN mission would be universally new, so they'd train everybody up. Back in the Iraq office, however, the majority had either educational or work backgrounds in the country or region, so it wasn't easy to find a place for the transients. I was looking forward to being in OIA, and already thinking about staying permanently, but there were plenty who did not share that goal, and they would be in limbo for a while.

"Yeah, that sucks," I sympathized, "but hopefully they'll realize soon that you're more valuable in your home office and let you go back." Who exactly could reach that determination, and then make it actually happen, was a question nobody seemed able to answer. As that first afternoon went on, I talked a little more with the rest of the governance team, chatting about their respective projects and topics, and eventually wrapped things up.

"Hey, Juan, do you need anything else from me today?" I asked. "I'm fixing to head out pretty soon."

"No, go ahead. We'll start to get you up to speed tomorrow and see if we can't find some projects for you to work on. Have a good night."

After getting detailed directions for how the hell to get out of the building, I headed home. It was a good group of people, I thought, especially my immediate supervisors, and I was encouraged. After the stressful and often disquieting analytical experience of Iraq, I had renewed hope that I could contribute to making good policy, both with intel and at a government level. Despite the disorganization of the first day, I was, like a lab rat that keeps getting shocked in a dogged pursuit for food, hopeful.

CHAPTER 13

Over the next few weeks I gradually readjusted to being home. The little things made the biggest difference—being able to leave my apartment and just go for a walk, the marvel of food delivery, grass, rain. I caught up with friends, picked up my car, cleaned my apartment top to bottom, and got reacquainted with normal life.

It was weird to try to pick up where I had left off six months before. People kept asking me if I had nightmares, or if I was jumpy or whatever, but I wasn't. I was fortunate that my deployment was relatively safe and did not involve many of the scarring experiences that troops in the field go through. I was happy not to hear and feel explosions and gunfire on a regular basis (insert your own DC crime joke here), and I sought normalcy. If I had any issues about the deployment, I wasn't about to sort them out while I tried to transition to another job; if I've repressed something bad and it comes out when I'm fifty, I'll (hopefully) be in a better position to pay the shrink bills then anyway. The joy of going to read a book in Dupont Circle, a small park near my apartment, outweighed the benefits of trying to Make Sense Of It All.

Having said that, it is a profoundly weird experience to reenter regular life after six months of being on a tightly controlled military base with few options for food, travel, privacy, or communication. While the restrictions are limiting, the routine eventually becomes automatic, and it's something we all came to rely on. Many people in my group quietly mentioned having a difficult time readjusting, with several talking about wanting to go back. For some it was the distance from the front line—they no longer felt like a real part of the war effort and wanted to be back in the thick of it. For others, the shift back from virtually no choices to total freedom was overwhelming. My initial prediction that the culture shock would be worse from the return than upon arrival proved correct.

Still, thoughts about being back were not openly discussed, and we instead favored swapping stories about how we spent the money we'd saved while deployed. Clothes, restaurants, and weekend getaways were the favorite; none of us got rich from the experience, but many who lived paycheck-to-paycheck before the deployment had some savings—especially the younger crew, virtually all of whom had sublet their apartments and, unlike the older folks, didn't have to keep paying a mortgage. In the first couple of weeks of our return, the deployment group stuck together, reminiscing about the especially memorable events of the deployment, but it didn't take us long to throw ourselves into our new assignments.

DIA's Office of Iraq Analysis, we discovered, had a veneer of control, under which minor anarchy reigned. Right as I joined OIA, the office chief, a caustic and reticent Navy captain (equivalent to a Colonel in the other services), left to lead another office. A rumor quickly spread that he'd been fired on the spot by the J2 during an argument over OIA analysis. Supposedly the debate wasn't even particularly specific; the J2 just wasn't satisfied that the Captain knew what the hell he was talking about. This was not especially surprising. The Captain was infamous for being detached from the rest of the office, not having a good handle on either analytical or administrative issues, and generally displaying the kind of dictatorial tendencies of a stereotypical high-ranking Navy officer. The diminutive and amiable office deputy, a civilian named Roger Amato, became acting chief. Roger was an Iraq lifer, and he loved to tell stories about being on the Iraq team during the Gulf War.

I spent my initial time at the office doing research, reading intelligence traffic and open-source (unclassified) materials to make sure I fully understood Iraq's internal political dynamics. There was a big difference, I knew, between knowing regional politics and understanding internal affairs. It wasn't enough, for example, to comprehend the differences among Shia, Sunni, and Kurd; I had to know the political parties and the major players in each group. As the weeks progressed, I slowly managed to complete all the administrative requirements, usually by going around Frozone to circumvent his sluggish pace and loud objections to status check requests, and I gained access to the requisite programs and facilities. I read, attended meetings, read, helped edit other people's products, read, talked with my teammates about our analytical approach, and read some more. I learned fast, and soon I was contributing to written materials and participating in briefings.

While I got spun up on the analytical issues, I was also trying to figure out how the office functioned. It's impossible to navigate a bureaucracy without first understanding it, and I preferred to learn by observation rather than the (more common) trial-and-error method. As best as I could understand, there were basically three levels within OIA. The analysts, who made up the preponderance of office employees, were one group, and we were a collection of military (both enlisted and officers), government civilian employees, and civilian contractors. Some offices delegate specific tasks to contractors, usually more tedious jobs, but our contractors were usually treated just like the government employees.

Virtually all the analysts were younger, from their early twenties to their midthirties. Many had graduate degrees, and a high number had experience in the field through either civilian deployment or military rotations. Men outnumbered women—though not by as much as in Baghdad—and we came from widely varying regional, political, and educational backgrounds. Collectively, however, we were a clean-cut, all-American, and slightly nerdy crowd, as one might expect from people who can pass the rigorous background investigation required to earn a Top Secret security clearance. Nary a shaggy haircut among the men, or creative attire among the women, or really any of the relatively minor expressions of individuality (or eccentricity) of our generational peers. Due to DIA's focus on generalists, however, the latest recruits were often drawn from liberal arts programs, so many analysts were well socialized from their college experience, and given the political focus of our office, we didn't have the hard-core science and technology intellectuals on whom many offices relied. Within the analytical group, there were leaders (primarily team chiefs and senior intelligence analysts, or SIAs), but they supervised a small number of people and had more of a peer relationship with analysts.

Above the analysts in the office pyramid was division-level leadership. The Strategic Issues and COIN segments each had division chiefs and deputies, as well as division senior intelligence officers. SIOs sometimes overlapped divisions, but Strat had one primary division SIO, the aforementioned Evan Gruber. Evan was a contractor whose default expression was one of contemplation, his brows constantly furrowed between thinning hair and wire-framed glasses. He spoke softly and deliberately, and because of his reserved demeanor, I was always surprised by his sense of humor, which ranged from bitingly witty to frat-boy clowning. Evan was a fair analyst and arbiter, but he had the unenviable task of facilitating communication and assignments between division and office personnel.

Our division chief, Army Lieutenant Colonel Jerry Hepler, was an excellent manager and one of the kindest men I've ever encountered. He ministered to an active congregation in Virginia and was a devoted family man. I never knew exactly how old he was, but he looked like he could have been anywhere from midthirties to midfifties. He was in great shape, had a full (if tightly cropped) head of hair, and spoke like a man accustomed to attention and respect. Lieutenant Colonel Hepler also would not accept profanity or bawdy commentary in his presence, and all it took was a raised eyebrow to stop an offender midsentence.

"Sorry, sir," we'd say guiltily, and we truly felt chastened (right up until we forgot ourselves in his presence the next time).

Major Nimick became the deputy division chief, and he was the day-to-day manager of Strat. Whereas Lieutenant Colonel Hepler dealt with the office leadership and kept the Strat trains running on time, so to speak, Major Nimick took care of administrative issues and oversaw analytical efforts. My new colleagues seemed satisfied with our division-level supervisors.

At the office level, the top of our chain of command within the immediate surroundings, things were more complicated. Roger, the former deputy chief, took over as chief, leaving the deputy position open. Below him there were several office analytical leads. We called them office SIOs, but to differentiate them from the division SIOs, I'll call them office intelligence officers, or OIOs. When I arrived, there were three or four people who could, at any time, insert themselves as OIO authorities. They were all constantly in and out of the office, doing congressional or military briefings, attending conferences, reporting to J2 directives, and generally being the "public" (within the confines of the intelligence community) faces of the Department of Defense's Iraq shop.

Army Colonel Arnold Kerik, an OIO, was politically the best-connected person in the office. He has been described in the media as the DIA senior intelligence officer for Iraq and was one of just fifteen current U.S. military officials to advise the Iraq Study Group (aka Baker-Hamilton commission). He was also one of the first and most vocal proponents of the Ba'athist insurgency theory: While others downplayed the existence of an emerging insurgency in the months following our invasion, Colonel Kerik was trying to convince influential military and DoD leaders that Sunnis loyal to Saddam, especially those disenfranchised by Paul Bremer's atrocious decision to disband the Iraqi military, were organizing for a national anti-coalition effort. Because he was ahead of the curve on the insurgency, and as a vital player in the early intelligence game, he had extensive connections to journalists, pundits, think tanks, politicians, and prominent neoconservatives in DoD.

Colonel Kerik was a tornado of activity, constantly interrupting meetings to weigh in with his personal analysis, and we always worried we'd be the target of one of his random tasks, usually pet projects wholly unrelated to our usual assignments. Colonel Kerik was a polarizing figure, and his ideological followers within the office defended his every statement. The rest of us thought he was increasingly crazy, partly for his analytical dogmatism and partly because he was abrasive and condescending. He was famously dyspeptic, even when trying to garner support. In attempting to convince Andrew, my Strat teammate, of a particular point, Kerik insisted, "I need support from the bottom feeders like you, Andrew!" He was retiring soon, and we hoped he'd go to a think tank or defense contractor. We wouldn't be so lucky.

Elaine Oyle was, by all appearances, the anti-Kerik. She was the rising star of the office, a young OIO who'd mastered the wheeling and dealing of DoD bureaucracy by employing a sweet façade that masked a manipulative approach to office politics. Some resented her quick rise through the ranks, some begrudged her connections to powerful officials within DIA, but most of us simply objected to her "kiss up, kick down" method of management. An admired boss would defend his people to leadership but chew them out in private if necessary; a hated boss complimented his people until they were criticized by his bosses, at which point he would sell out his underlings in a flash. Elaine was the latter. Her exact title and mission were never quite clear to us, and leadership constantly offered conflicting and mystifying explanations. What we did know was that a paper could go through several people with minor edits and then hit her computer and get completely rewritten depending on her personal views on the matter at hand. My new colleagues recommended submitting products for OIO review when she was gone from the office.

Depending on the day and the staffing situation, there were others who had OIO review privileges, but when I arrived the office-level leadership essentially included Colonel Kerik and Elaine, as well as Roger, the OIA chief. We didn't have a deputy chief, and we were a little understaffed at the OIO spot because Colonel Kerik was frequently out of the office, but SIOs picked up the slack. That's what we had to work with, so we did it, and soon more OIOs would arrive to further complicate the process.

For a product to be "published"—made widely available to the intelligence community—there was a nebulous procedure that I struggled to understand (and everyone struggled to keep up with changes to). For a written paper, either an analyst would come up with a topic from reading traffic, which we called "initiative" products, or a superior would assign a subject. The analyst would research the issue for an appropriate time, ranging from hours to weeks; once the paper was complete, it would make its way up the chain for approval. When I completed a paper, for example, it would first go to Juan, my team chief, who made edits and comments and sent it back to me to incorporate the new elements. I then sent it to the rest of the governance team, giving Kate, Andrew, and Jose the next edit. Once I'd incorporated their changes, the product went to all of Strat, so the Shia, Sunni, and Kurd teams could take a look. After they approved the draft and made suggestions and changes, I edited it again and sent it to the Strat senior intelligence analyst and the Strat deputy team chief—Major Nimick when I first started—and they'd kick it back down to me. Through this stage the comments and suggestions were generally considered "optional," in that if I disagreed, I could discuss the suggestion or, if it was a minor thing, disregard it.

Following all of these levels of editing, the paper would go to Strat leadership: the Strat OIO (Evan) and division chief (Lieutenant Colonel Hepler). At that level, I had to really weigh whether I wanted to push back against comments or suggestions, but it was still possible to disagree without risking a professional reckoning. Once I made adjustments and got their approval, the product moved to office-level personnel. I would send the paper to all the office leadership, both managerial and analytical people. This step was a little unusual in that while any OIO could approve the product for release, each could also preclude publication. Up to the office level, you had to get approval from all of the individuals in the chain of command; conversely, once it got to OIOs, if any of them authorized publication, a product was good to go. They would often ask us to check with other OIOs, so it was hit or miss, but which OIO read your product first often dictated how much further editing would be required at that late stage.

At any point in the progression, edits could be bounced back and forth between analyst and editor multiple times until both sides were satisfied. Some products required the approval of the OIA chief, but most just needed OIO authorization and then could go out. The process was extensive and often convoluted. Much as with judges or baseball umpires, people were ostensibly adhering to the same conventions, but their interpretations and personal preconceptions could greatly affect both the pace and direction of a product in the editing phase. Sometimes people would skim a product and give it the stamp of approval, or they could tear it apart—it was impossible to predict—but by the time most products were published, at least a dozen people had had the opportunity to edit or comment on them. The process could take as little as a few days or as long as several weeks. If someone disagreed with the analytical conclusions of a paper, the easiest way to kill it was to delay editing it until it was considered OBE, overtaken by events, the DoD expression for "old news." This was kind of like a DoD pocket veto. Slides that went to the morning J2 briefing went through a similar editing process, but they were usually turned around in a day or two, so there were daily meetings to get everybody in the same room to plan the slides and hash out any disagreement.

Not surprisingly, this process continually broke down. It was problematic for a variety of reasons that I would later discover, but in the beginning it was a moral victory just to figure out who needed to see what and when. My Strat colleagues, especially my team chief, Juan, were extremely helpful in advising me how to best navigate the system—if you knew the tendencies of the supervisors, it was much easier to get analysis through the process.

"If you're writing something critical of Ba'athists, try to get Kerik to read it first—he's always focused on them, and he'll be in your corner," Jose explained. "But if it's on Shia stuff, send it to the OIOs on a night when Elaine is working 'cause if Kerik reads it he'll rant and rave that we're ignoring the Sunni angles. Get it?"

"No. What the hell does it matter who reads it when?" I didn't yet have enough experience with the process to understand the biases at the top and how they affected the analysis.

Jose sighed. "You'll figure it out as you go along. It's a disaster, but if you do it right, you can get some useful information through without too much interference."

And in fact I did figure it out fast, mostly because I quickly became one of the more prolific producers in the office. I had the background to understand the greater strategic issues, as well as field experience that taught me about the specific players, both group and individual. Still, that combination was not unusual: Most of my coworkers had much more experience working the issues than I, and many had served, either as civilians or in the military, in Iraq. What made me unique, I found, was an ability to complete projects quickly and without need for extensive editing, a skill resulting from two factors. When we wrote papers, we often needed to read dozens, sometimes hundreds, of pages of information (and just to make it especially fun, most intelligence reports came through in ALL CAPS). My bookish youth, which gave me little athletic proficiency and a pallid skin tone, did leave me able to read very quickly. I could burn through the intelligence reports faster than most people in the office, allowing me to either read more material in a finite amount of time or to read a given set of reports faster than others. Added to this was a writing-intensive education at a liberal arts college that emphasized grammar and logical construction.

That combination allowed me to finish assignments fast, and my bosses knew they wouldn't get bogged down trying to make my papers readable. In most offices this would have been nice but not necessarily invaluable; in OIA there were so many time-limited tasks that the combination of fast reading and a precise writing style was a tremendous asset. Early on my boss assigned me a few quick-turnaround projects for high-profile customers because I was aggressive about wanting to work on valuable projects; once I proved myself, I earned the trust of my leadership to do high-visibility tasks and the leeway to pick and choose my own initiative projects. I had a good eye for predictive analysis, and working with talented and insightful colleagues helped me along.

Within the first couple of months I was writing pieces for some of the top officials in DIA and DoD, as well as regularly briefing foreign delegations, high-ranking officers at home and in-theater, and the J2 himself. I don't flatter myself that my opportunities were a result of pure talent, of course; I was on a team and in a system that made significant contributions from junior analysts a necessity, and my immediate bosses encouraged analytical participation in briefings. I also wanted to do as much work as I possibly could, and on the important issues. Further, the governance team was constantly busy, and my initial time there included a national referendum on the newly drafted Iraqi constitution as well as, just two months later, the first full-term national elections. So my quick ascent in the office reflected a confluence of determination on my part, supportive leadership by my superiors, and a fast-moving political situation in Iraq.

Of course, I still didn't have a desk, and as the rest of my Baghdad companions began to filter in, space and resources got even tighter. Of the tons of problems with the office and with the analytical process in general, including fairly shocking examples of analytical modification, terrible human resources, and atrocious morale, the thing that bothered many of us most frequently was the lack of material resources in the office. We simply could not believe that three years into a major war, the most significant military and foreign policy effort in decades, and with American soldiers dying on a daily basis, the main Department of Defense Iraq intelligence shop was in temporary office space without the resources we needed to succeed.

The office was budgeted for roughly a hundred people, and due to deployments, rotations, and a backlog of candidates for open slots, we actually had about eighty. For those eighty, we had approximately sixty computer stations. At any given time, there were people who simply could not do their jobs because we didn't have enough computers, and the ones we did have were undersupplied. The systems used by the different intelligence agencies vary (another infuriating problem), but within DIA there are three distinct networks that analysts use to do their missions correctly, and all three are vital for comprehensive, complete, and accurate analysis. Those three include two classified systems, which I'll call ClassA and ClassB, as well as the unclassified Internet, or Unclass. Nearly all the computers had ClassA, which we used for our primary classified interoffice email, so about fifty-five of sixty stations were ClassA-connected. But the other two systems, both crucial, were sparsely allocated. It was impossible to get a straight answer from Frozone about what our system capabilities were, and to this day I'm not sure whether he just didn't care enough to find out or if he refused to tell people because the answer was so embarrassing. I sometimes asked him about the issue, and the conversation always went something like this:

"Hey, Shawn, are we ever going to get more ClassB and Unclass machines in here?"

"I'm working on it, man, I'm working on it."

"Oh yeah? How?"

"Well, we're talking to J2 about getting more, but they say it's DI's responsibility to supply you guys." Frozone viewed himself as above it all, so the office was always *you*, not *we*.

"Okay, we've got roughly eighty people in the office, right? How many ClassB systems do we have?"

"Why do you want to know?"

"So when I tell my leadership how we're losing the war because of lack of computers I can give them exact numbers," I explained calmly. His efforts to avoid the question were infuriating. "How many do we have?"

"Leadership is already aware of the problem."

"Yeah, I know, but it's been three years, so maybe it would help them along to have a little numerical reminder. How many ClassBs do we have for the sixty computer stations for eighty people in the office?"

"You don't have to worry about that."

"I know I don't *have* to, but I *am* worried about it. We can't do our job on a day-to-day basis because somebody's screwing us, and all I want is information I'd be shocked if you didn't have. Do you know what our system figures are? You're in charge of that stuff, right?"

"Yup."

"Yup you know what they are, or yup you're in charge of it?"

"Yup."

"So how many?"

"Don't worry about it."

We had this conversation, or a variant thereof, probably twice a month. I finally went around the office and did a rough count. Other than office-level leadership—virtually all office management had all three networks—we had about fifteen ClassB and a dozen Unclass machines for sixty computer screens, eighty people actually tasked to the office, and more than a hundred personnel spots within OIA. To add insult to injury, the room adjacent to OIA, visible from the Strat area, was filled with empty cubicles, most of which had two or three of the systems already set up. There were probably an additional seventy cubes in that space, and they were nearly always empty, with the exception of one or two occasions when a small group used the space for a few days and then moved out.

When we asked management why we couldn't use the unused workstations in the adjacent room, leadership told us that they were J3 spaces. The operations (J3) staff, that is, had control over allocation of the desks.

"We're already in J3 space as it is," Roger would say. "We can't use that room."

"But sir, it's empty—nobody uses it!" We were reduced to making sure he knew the definition of *empty*.

"We're working on the space issue."

"Sir, you know that we're doing shift work because of space, right? From 0600 to 1500 and 1100 to 2000?" To alleviate the overlap, most of the office used some version of an early shift and a late shift. It wasn't that we needed to constantly be staffed—the office already had a 24/7 crew, and everyone was on call around the clock because of the nature of our assignment—we just had too many bodies for too few computers.

"I know, we're working on it. It's in progress."

"Yes sir. When do you think there might be some kind of resolution?"

"Hopefully soon. We'll keep you posted."

The adjacent space had been empty for months before I arrived; it remained so throughout the time I spent at OIA, and, according to friends still in the office, it's unoccupied as of this writing. There still aren't the computer resources we needed to do our job properly, and leaders are still telling personnel that it's "in progress." I suppose it's not surprising that DoD and administration leadership who failed to provide proper armor for troops and transportation in Iraq would neglect the intelligence operation driving the war effort, but one despairs despite the predictability. I wonder how many operations we could have helped, how many better predictions we could have made, and, most important, how many lives might not have been lost if we just had the same number of computers and desks as people.

Obviously being understaffed and undersupplied is not an atypical situation in an office environment, especially within the government. Plenty of agencies, departments, and offices have similar problems, and I wasn't so naïve as to think we were alone in our deficiencies. I was, however, idealistic enough to believe that the administration meant it when they claimed that Iraq was our nation's top priority. The failure to properly equip the people working on the war had a significant deleterious effect upon events on the ground, and I don't think it's unreasonable to expect the Department of Defense's main Iraq team to have what it needs to do its job.

Of course, the office did have about a dozen enormous flat-screen TVs blaring Fox News nonstop from the walls, so if we ever wanted our noses rubbed in the idiocy of DoD priorities, we needed only to look up.

CHAPTER 14

Despite the common feeling among analysts that the office was not appropriately prioritized or resourced, we all understood the importance of the mission and our work, even if it sometimes seemed our higher leadership did not. Those of us working strategic issues were especially earnest because we knew the other military intelligence organizations and teams were mainly focused on the insurgency, making our small group the primary shop for governance issues.

Under most circumstances, the CIA is at the forefront of government-level intelligence. Military intelligence isn't usually a focal point for broad political issues and assessments, and traditionally DIA is a distant second to CIA (and, sometimes, NSA) in that arena. During wartime, however, DIA takes the lead on many issues that CIA would otherwise control. When "political" becomes "political-military," DoD understandably plays a larger role. More broadly, both the Global War on Terror (GWOT) and Secretary Rumsfeld's extended stay in the president's inner circle have greatly increased the power and influence of intelligence agencies controlled by the Department of Defense. Due to the methods of movement, planning, and communications favored by transnational terrorist groups, the GWOT has made DIA and NSA, which is also overseen by the Pentagon, increasingly influential, much more so than the National Geospatial-Intelligence

Agency and the National Reconnaissance Office, both fixtures of Cold War satellite preeminence.

Much is made of Secretary Rumsfeld's efforts and power in consolidating U.S. intelligence, and his influence is difficult to overstate. In Washington whoever holds the purse strings has the power, and with the Pentagon controlling a reported 80 to 85 percent* of the American budget for intelligence, the SecDef has great latitude to affect the processes of intelligence. Further, Secretary Rumsfeld had the trust, confidence, and attention of President Bush for several years.

We were all aware of the amplified importance and access of our office to decision makers. It was increasingly clear that the CIA's influence was waning as CIA and executive sources continued to trade accusations of blame over the Iraq WMD debacle (and further demonstrated by the ungainly and hasty "resignation" of CIA director—and political hack—Porter Goss). The State Department, while headed by Bush confidante Secretary Rice, has a relatively small intelligence agency and is distrusted by influential neoconservatives in the White House and vice president's office. Secretary Rumsfeld's creation of a new position, undersecretary of defense for intelligence, in March 2003 further advanced his goal of greater Pentagon (and personal) control over not just tactical military intelligence but also strategic national intel. Stephen Cambone, a friend of Secretary Rumsfeld, filled that new position, and press reports widely indicated that he set to work advancing the secretary's objectives for national intelligence. The feeling around the office, therefore, was that DIA had more power and authority than ever before, and the analysts in my office were eager to put forth accurate and valuable assessments. Unfortunately, these efforts were often met with resistance.

Not long after I started at OIA, however, I began to witness the process through which intelligence was inappropriately altered and adjusted as it made its way up the chain of command. As I did

* Sappenfield, Mark. "Pentagon's intelligence role rising." *The Christian Science Monitor.* 18 May 2006; Ackerman, Spencer. "Rumsfeld's intelligence takeover: Power grab." *The New Republic.* 21 June 04.

more high-profile work, I increasingly saw and experienced the issues that so many observers of the intelligence community, both expert and lay, correctly identify as major problems. These included difficulties in vetting analysis within agencies as well as with the handling of those assessments by advisers and policymakers.

When I returned from Baghdad, it was just a few months prior to a hugely significant event for U.S. policy and Iraq's political development: the first national vote for a full-term Iraqi government, in December 2005. The previous election, in January 2005, resulted in a victory for Shia Islamist parties, and the biggest winner was the United Iraqi Alliance (UIA), a coalition of major Shia groups. Secularists had a particularly disappointing showing. The two major Kurdish parties managed to join together despite enmity that erupted into civil war in the late 1990s, and their list had just over half as many seats as the UIA. Sunni parties had largely boycotted the January election, leaving them with little voice as the constitution was drafted; elite Sunnis, appearing to recognize this error, were gearing up to be a force in the December contest.

The dismal secularist showing greatly concerned the Bush administration, which had installed former exile and neoconservative darling Ayad Allawi as the new Iraq's first prime minister under the initial temporary government. Allawi was a Westernized, secular Shia whom U.S. officials believed would have credibility with Sunnis, Shia, and Kurds. American press widely reported that Allawi had connections to and perhaps funding from the CIA, and his party's poor performance in January 2005 was a tremendous disappointment to many of the original architects of the war.

The other on-again, off-again neoconservative favorite was Ahmed Chalabi, a shifty, opportunistic former exile who was allegedly slated to be installed as Iraq's post-invasion leader until Iraq's religious leadership foiled this plan by insisting on elections. Chalabi knows how to talk to Western audiences, and he speaks of a silent majority of Iraqi secularists that is music to the ears of those who felt they could turn Iraq into a nation friendly to Western governments and business, tolerant of Israel, and a force for change in the greater Middle East. The dark side of Chalabi, however, includes a conviction (in absentia) for the theft of hundreds of millions of dollars in Jordan and a widely reported rumor that he turned over secret U.S. materials to his connections in Iranian intelligence.

After the January elections, the winning Islamist parties shunned these secular Western favorites, instead tapping as prime minister Ibrahim Jafari, a deeply religious party leader who spent much of his time in exile in Iran and whom observers frequently derided as indecisive and taciturn during his tenure in office.

Before the December 2005 elections, American officials, including President Bush and Ambassador Khalilzad, began making statements indicating the importance of the elections as a turning point, repeatedly saying that the end of Sunni electoral boycotts would lead to a "national unity government" that would propel Iraq into stability. My office, however, was convinced that Islamists were on track for another sizable victory. Young democracies often "vote identity"—that is, citizens frequently vote with the party representing the demographic with which they most strongly identify. In Iraq that demographic is, generally speaking, religion for the Arabs (Shia and Sunni) and ethnicity for the Kurds.

The parliamentary system further allows for (and to some extent exacerbates) this. In the United States, identity voting is mitigated by the existence of two major parties and, more important, winner-take-all congressional elections: Regardless of the national vote, whichever candidate gets the most votes in his or her district takes the seat. This creates a strong incentive to vote for one of the two major parties, as it is highly unlikely that a minor party (or minor-party candidate) will win. In Iraq's parliamentary system, conversely, seats were originally allocated based on national percentages; in the December elections that was scaled back only slightly, so that seats were awarded based on provincial percentages. In the United States, a party that wins 20 percent of the overall vote is nothing more than a potential spoiler; in Iraq, roughly speaking, that party gains 20 percent of the seats in Parliament.

The challenge is then for major parties to establish a coalition that has the parliamentary numbers to elect a prime minister and avoid votes of no confidence that would require new elections. Identity voting is therefore a crucial force in Iraq, and U.S. officials hoping for and expecting victorious "consensus" candidates grossly misunderstood both Iraqi priorities and the electoral system.

When Iraq's civil society broke down after the U.S. invasion, the political infrastructure was nonexistent. Saddam's regime cracked down on any political activity outside of his Sunni-dominated Ba'ath party, and after the invasion Ba'athists were banned from political activity, much like de-Nazification in post-war Germany. In the absence of established political parties, there were two categories of groups most ready to fill Iraq's void: religious leaders and sectarian militias. The secularists simply had no political infrastructure, and with ethnic and religious tensions rising through 2004 and 2005, few voters trusted "consensus" candidates. Leading up to the December elections, despite the grossly corrupt and largely ineffective Jafari administration, my colleagues and I were confident that Iraqis would not turn to "centrist" leaders who were at best seen as insufficiently loyal to their sectarian group and at worst viewed as U.S. pawns.

When we presented this analysis to leadership in OIA, however, we were severely admonished for being "too pessimistic." At first I thought the disagreements were simply analytical in nature. Analysts are sometimes overruled by leadership, which can be both appropriate and necessary, as senior leadership often has a combination of expertise and experience that analysts lack. Junior analysts are often the driving force behind assessments because of their specific focus and expertise, but good leadership will include honest disagreement.

It is an oft-repeated adage in Washington that the country is run by twenty-five-year-olds, because of the legions of congressional staffers who help administer the legislative process. Similarly, because of the time and focus that junior analysts put into their specific areas, it is often the workers at the bottom of the intelligence community, not the top, who have the best insight into a variety of issues. For this reason, when assessments are made by analysts and approved by their analytical supervisors (the SIAs, SIOs, and OIOs), it is—and should be—unusual for their bosses to fundamentally alter the basic conclusions. As the elections approached, however, these kinds of adjustments occurred with alarming frequency.

"You're being too pessimistic. [The secularists] are gaining strength."

"There's no way Iraqis will vote for [those in power] again. We can't pass this up the chain."

"[Other agencies] are predicting something totally different, and we need to make sure we're not too far off message with this."

We heard variations on these lines repeatedly. Disturbingly, the critiques were frequently leveled as accusations of poor analytical tradecraft rather than by engaging the substantive issues. Ad hominem attacks were substituted for analytic discussion, and analysts were generally powerless to resist pressure from above. This was partly because office leadership would directly engage analysts rather than talking to our superiors: When an office-level supervisor tells an analyst to do something, it is not up for debate. Whereas our supervisors might have been able to push back against this kind of interference, for analysts the power imbalance was so significant that we had few options.

During the fall, new OIOs arrived. Ben, the screamer from Baghdad, had come home early from his deployment. Just a couple of months into the mission, he was out of Baghdad. When I talked to my friends who were in Iraq, they said that the analysts had no notice or warning that he was departing; they just woke up one day and he was gone. Upon his return, he had not lost any of his bluster.

Roger immediately made Ben the senior analyst in OIA, and the hierarchy at the top of the office shuffled somewhat. Ben technically outranked Elaine, but Roger clearly trusted Elaine more than anyone else despite her relative inexperience. Colonel Kerik was, for the moment, frequently out of the office, dealing with his retirement from the Army, and we fervently hoped he would find a job somewhere in the Eastern Hemisphere, though we heard he would soon rejoin the office as a civilian.

We also had another OIO arrive, Eric Furbent, a rotund lifer with extensive Middle East experience and an outspoken affection for the Bush administration. Eric bobbed his head when he talked, often wringing his hands, and his demeanor was so awkward that it was often difficult to talk to him. It was quite a group of senior leaders, and as much as we could, the analysts left Evan and Major Nimick with the unpleasant job of dealing with them. But the power imbalance between OIOs and analysts was exacerbated by the trend, led by Ben, of OIOs directly engaging analysts, bypassing our superiors. Jumping the chain going up is a big no-no, but senior people routinely bypassed the chain going down, and we had little ability to defend our assessments against someone who was several steps above us on the ladder.

It didn't help that our OIOs were not exactly encouraging discussion.

"Did you write this shit?"

"Yes sir, do you have edits for me?"

"This is too pessimistic. Again! Why are you guys always off message?"

"Sir . . . is there something analytically wrong with the paper? Did I miss something in the reports?" We would often at least try to steer the criticism toward substantive discussion.

"Yeah, you did. Change this, and this, and this"—pointing to the paper—"and get it to me again. And it better be halfway decent this time."

Analysts could raise the issue with our immediate leadership, but then we were complaining to our bosses about their bosses, and this had its own difficulties. When we had supervisors who were willing to address these issues with office leadership, our bosses were ignored or criticized by their superiors; when our supervisors were not willing to challenge the orthodoxy, they rebuked us for questioning authority. The process was extraordinarily frustrating, and morale steadily declined as the pattern continued.

There is nothing wrong with analytical disagreement, and in fact the intelligence community could probably use more internal debate rather than less. When my fellow analysts and I talked to our supervisors about it, they sometimes reminded us that discussion is good for the final product and said not to worry about it. But there are major differences between healthy discussion and what passed for dialogue in DIA's Iraq office.

Two crucial elements differentiated the intelligence manipulation from healthy debate. First, while we analysts supported our assessments with reams of documentary evidence and citations of related previous accuracies, our leadership generally failed to engage us on the issues, instead questioning our analytical rigor and proffering the ubiquitous "too pessimistic" accusation and making appeals for "balance." Second, the changes were *virtually always* in the same direction: toward a more favorable evaluation of what Bush administration officials were hoping for.

The analysts in Strat began to openly kid one another about the "too pessimistic" mantra. We also quietly discussed the irrationality of such a statement; for something to be too pessimistic, there had to be a baseline against which our assessments were being measured, we reasoned. That is, pessimistic for whom, or compared with what? If we had been told that our assessments were simply wrong, that something else was going to happen, it would have at least been less obvious that there was a bias at the top levels of our analytical leadership. As it was, the criticism was unattached to any analytical insight, alternative scenario, or even substantive disagreement.

The pressure to be "more optimistic" was so pervasive that it became a running joke in the office. The problem was ridiculed so openly that we created a "Wall of Optimism," an area of the wall in our section where we taped up cartoons and statements that called for cheeriness and bliss. The Wall of Optimism stayed up for weeks, perhaps months, and we constantly jokingly referenced it whenever someone made an assessment that was contrary to Bush administration goals or statements. In an event of exquisite irony, the Wall of Optimism met an ignoble end when one analyst, furious with yet again being told that his assessment was too gloomy, tore down the dozens of posted items.

Discussion of this problem was hardly limited to analysts, and a couple of the more courageous supervisors attempted to raise the issue with their bosses. This is an email exchange, edited slightly to make it unclassified (and with my emphasis added), with comments from the office's lead intelligence analyst, Ben, and the response from Major Nimick:

Colleagues,
See highlighted portion of [. . .] comments on [Secretary] Rice. There's quite a bit of evidence (gleaned from feedback from customers of this brief) that [our analysts are wrong]. What this means for us is that we will have to be carefully tuned to the effects of our (U.S.) policy nudges and pressures . . . and track developments in our products. Bottom line: we cannot afford to summarily rule out scenarios we haven't forecast, or previously thought are low probability. *Some form of [result in line with Bush administration goals] is likely to emerge, but not on its own.* We have to be cognizant of this and not 1.) ignore its prospects, or 2.) work in a vacuum assuming it can't happen because Iraqis [won't make it happen] . . . the current mix is far more complex.

The response from Strat's chief, Major Nimick:

At the risk of being contrary. . . .
1. I would submit to you that I haven't met the analyst in SID [Strategic Issues Division] that ignores potential prospects or works in a vacuum based upon unfounded assumptions. Indeed, a review of our assessments over the past several months would reveal that our analysts were generally correct where

others from other agencies were less than correct. I think we owe these analysts kudos in lieu of your suggestion that they are not performing their analysis in a professional manner. I have the opportunity on a daily basis to witness the exchange amongst the analysts, and it is rife with alternative assessments and "what ifs" [. . .]

2. *I would further suggest that we should NOT be cognizant of any of the administration's policies or initiatives when it comes to shaping our intelligence assessments, as your note seems to suggest.* We owe them, in the words of the Chairman [of the Joint Chiefs of Staff], "our best assessment of the facts." Whether we are on or off message should not be taken into consideration. We are failing the leadership if our assessments are shaped by policy initiatives.

3. I think we would be well served to *not* ignore the prospect that [what the analysts believe is actually true]. We should seriously consider the very real notion that it is [what analysts think it is], and we should articulate that very real possibility to policymakers in forums such as yesterday's. *I'm frankly somewhat amazed that the State leadership is presented [with] an intelligence briefing on Iraq and their answer is to try to figure out ways to change the truth, rather than to deal with it.* [. . .]

Unfortunately, this kind of honest and direct response to analytical manipulation was exceptionally rare. Further, this supervisor, who was overwhelmingly valued and respected by those of us who worked for him, was punished for this and other similar "disobedience." Within months of sending this email, he was stripped of his leadership position and put in an out-of-the-way administrative post. That demonstrated to the rest of us the danger of speaking truth to power.

It is indescribably demoralizing to an organization when a huge number of experts believe that their leaders—both in the office and high in the administration—are either lying or oblivious. Within the office, the attempts to maneuver our analysis into more optimistic predictions meant that either our leaders were clueless about both the ground truth and the likely course of future events, or they were being mendacious. Neither was a particularly encouraging option. High up in the administration, of course, it was even worse, and analysts were aghast at some of the public comments by President Bush, Vice President Cheney, Secretary Rumsfeld, and others. We would sometimes get advance copies of executive speeches to "review" and would pass a copy around the office, circling the lies. Analysts would point out these inaccuracies to our supervisors, but information flow has a peculiar feature of which we were all aware: For information to reach the top, every single person in the chain of command has to tell the next person until it goes all the way up; for it *not* to reach the top, it takes only one person to kill the transmission. And you never know who that person might be.

While we impotently watched the administration distort and/or misunderstand the situation, and chafed under unpredictable and unhelpful leadership, things in Iraq continued to deteriorate. We tried to defuse our collective dissatisfaction with dark humor and Sisyphean effort, but many of us felt the weight of the fact that people were dying in dizzying numbers. We saw the stark and heartbreaking effects on millions of people, including tens of thousands of American soldiers who placed their faith in their civilian leaders, trusting that those leaders would employ sound judgment, have concern for their welfare, and prosecute the war in a reality-based fashion. Meanwhile, we circled the lies in speeches.

Analytical manipulation regarding Iraq's December elections was just one aspect of the larger problems, but those pressures brought the issue into stark relief in the office, especially at the analytical level. A particularly memorable day was the eve of the vote, when a senior official from the State Department's intelligence agency, the Bureau of Intelligence and Research, came to the office and spoke to our office leadership about State's view that a certain secular candidate was surging as the election drew near. Not wanting to be an outlier from this "emerging" position, Roger

Amato, our office chief, directed us to create a slide indicating that the Islamist parties were increasingly worried about gains made by this candidate.

Virtually everyone in the Strategic Issues Division vehemently protested, indicating our collective view that such an assessment was misguided and misleading. Several weeks earlier I had written a detailed and extensive prediction of the elections that directly opposed such an estimation of secularist success, and my teammates and supervisors were confident that my earlier predictions remained accurate. The battle over the slide that day was heated and protracted, but in the end a powerful few forced their view upon the analysts, and we submitted a slide that *none* of us felt was an accurate representation of our analytical judgments. The morning of the election, the chairman of the Joint Chiefs of Staff and the secretary of defense, and perhaps the president, were told that this candidate, an administration favorite, was rapidly gaining ground. Within days, it was clear that the candidate had performed miserably.

From inside the situation, having our assessments changed was such a common occurrence that most analysts didn't think anything of it, didn't realize how badly the process was being perverted. But even those of us who thought it was a serious problem had little recourse. Not only did we have little ability to question higher authority, but the problem went all the way up the chain.

Not surprisingly, strategic assessments of Iraq were forefront in the minds of senior policymakers and advisers. There are essentially two top advisers to the president within the Department of Defense—the chairman of the Joint Chiefs of Staff and the secretary of defense—and we regularly provided products to both. The Joint Chiefs are served by a variety of high-ranking officers who report on specific aspects of the military, and the J2, whom we always referred to by rank rather than name, is in charge of advising the chairman of the Joint Chiefs on intelligence matters.

The morning J2 briefing begins just after 0500 hours; Power-

Point slides are presented on the most vital issues of the day. There are usually no more than a handful of slides, and the briefing covers issues around the world. Iraq slides are a mainstay of the briefings, and when I began work at OIA, analysts would brief the slides ourselves, supported by the presence of analytical supervisors. Analysts briefed the slides because we were generally more knowledgeable about the specifics than was leadership, and when we briefed, we arrived in the middle of the night, between 0100 and 0200, to make sure nothing had changed and to go through a variety of vetting meetings. During those overnight meetings, the slides were viewed, edited, and approved up the chain of command.

One of the most colorful—and reviled—characters in the process of briefing the J2 was Colonel Suloney, a delightfully clueless intel careerist with an authoritarian streak to go along with his obliviousness. The day after an important vote in Iraq, I told him the turnout percentages for various constituencies and regions.

"Okay," he said, clearly disappointed and hoping for a way to redeem the results. "Well, what's the margin of error for those turnout percentages?"

"Sir," I replied slowly, "they're *turnout percentages,* not polls . . . so, um, the numbers are firm."

Still, the myopia with far greater impact involved the details of the war, and any remaining respect for Colonel Suloney was lost when he asked an analyst if Shia militias had ever attacked coalition forces . . . a question he posed in February 2006. He, too, of course, believed that we analysts were far too downbeat in our assessments. Perhaps he was simply unaware of any attacks at all.

Charges of pessimism were not limited to my office leadership, as the J2 himself, an intense and fiery Navy Rear Admiral, was notorious for berating Iraq analysts for "gloomy" judgments. At one briefing that became infamous in the office, I was explaining a major event that we believed had left a prominent Iraqi leader politically weak. The slide indicated that assessment, and the J2 asked me to explain our view. The following is the conversation we had, transcribed from an email report I sent to my supervisors that morning, edited to make it unclassified:

"Explain to me why you think [he] is weakened by this."

"Sir, [they] wanted a consensus candidate rather than a divisive vote, but they weren't able to agree. Then they wanted a private vote, but this result was made public. Finally, a large victory for one candidate or the other would have at least shown strength within the party, but instead, [they present] a fractured public image and a leader who doesn't have the full support of his own party." I was pretty satisfied I had explained things adequately, if slightly haltingly.

"Well, I don't see how that weakens him. Can you tell me facts that show he's weakened by this?"

"Yes sir, [he] is already being challenged publicly, which is both unusual and damaging."

The J2 glared at me. "No. This is good. I think this strengthens [him]."

"Um . . . sir?"

"I think that this shows that you can have a debate in Iraqi politics, and have a disagreement and still get to a solution. If everybody had decided to walk out, then he would have been weakened."

"Yes, uh, yes sir, that's true, but no leader wants to [have split support], especially when that result is made public, and—"

"A week ago we didn't even think he'd [win], and now he has. That's not weakness, is it?"

"That's true, sir, but—"

"I think [they] will all line up behind him when this is all over, they'll all come back together."

Horrified, wondering if the J2 ever read anything we wrote, I replied, "Sir, [they are] fairly divided—"

"How are they divided? Do you have facts to support that?"

I knew I had already gone past the line of acceptable analytical disagreement, and was well on my way to a public smackdown if

I didn't relent. We quickly learned the limits, and even in this brief exchange I had exceeded them.

"Yes sir, we'll change the bullet and keep an eye on things."

When I recounted the exchange to my coworkers later that afternoon, they were stunned. It was another huge blow to morale, the idea that a solid and cohesive judgment of the entire office would be summarily reversed with no analytical basis. In the assessment, he turned a weak politician into an ostensibly strong one, thereby making the government seem much more secure than it actually was. Just a few months later, this "strong" leader was pushed out of his post, a major—and "unpredicted"—event. It was difficult to keep producing intelligence products that we knew would just be altered or killed, and many of us began to talk about how to best couch our analysis so it would be less prone to manipulation. The J2 had the stereotypical iron fist of a Navy officer, and spouted spirit-lifting encouragement such as, "I don't mean to be an asshole, but you're not listening" and "The next time I have to tell someone to put things in chronological order, someone's going to get *fired*."

It is also worth noting that this J2 does not have an analytical background in Iraq or even the Middle East. He came to the Joint Chiefs staff from a background of Pacific-theater command, and it appeared that his interest and expertise were along those lines. He seemed to have an excellent command of Pacific and Asian issues, but it was a constant struggle to explain and re-explain the cultural and political issues of Iraq and the region. Why we would not have a commander with a Middle East background in charge of advising the chairman of the Joint Chiefs of Staff on worldwide intelligence during a time of war in the Middle East is simply beyond me, and this kind of questionable allocation of personnel plagues the intelligence community.

I cannot say for sure why our analysis was constantly changed toward a sunnier outlook for Iraq; only those who made the changes can truly know why they established that pattern and that culture. I do know the circumstances around the behavior, however, and I can see two obvious possibilities. One option is that these leaders honestly believed that the evidence repeatedly pointed to conclusions different from the ones to which the analysts came. Perhaps the leaders, despite all evidence and historical indications to the contrary, believed that analysts were misinterpreting the data, and always in a way that made things seem bleaker than they really were. During my time in the office, at least, DIA's Iraq political section was uniquely prescient within the intelligence community, but perhaps even after consistently accurate predictions and assessments, leaders were genuinely convinced that we were incorrect in most of our pieces. If that is the case, I have serious concerns about how senior analytic and managerial positions are awarded and maintained.

It is also possible, however, that the environment the Bush administration has created, in which loyalty is the ultimate virtue and officials at all levels are afraid to report unwelcome information up the chain of command, has infected the intelligence community. If approval depends upon telling supervisors what they want to hear, or if careers rely on giving "good" news, then the culture of corruption and atmosphere of fear created by the Bush administration has crippled our intelligence efforts. Similarly, if intelligence is adjusted due to ideological considerations—because some officials place loyalty to their political allies over loyalty to the facts and reasoned assessments—that, too, would cripple the intelligence process. If those elements of conscious or unwitting intelligence manipulation were the cause of the unremitting adjustments to analysis in my office, I have even more serious concerns about how senior analytic and managerial positions are awarded and maintained.

This kind of behavior and atmosphere begins at the top, and many in the office blamed an administration that disdains accountability and rewards ineptitude. While this administration has a limited amount of time to wreak havoc, however, the current and future leaders in the intelligence community will be around for decades to come. The IC is internalizing these harmful behaviors, and although they started from pressures outside the agencies, they are now being perpetuated by forces within. The bad habits created during the lead-up to Iraq were being reinforced rather than corrected, causing great potential harm to America's security and the U.S. intelligence community. I started to wonder whether my very presence represented tacit approval of a system that I recognized as broken.

CHAPTER 15

D espite the growing concerns and frustrations about the office, I remained dedicated to the tasks at hand. After Iraq's winter elections, the results validated the predictions contained in the paper I'd written in the fall. It created something of a stir because the paper turned out to be remarkably accurate, far more so than the forecasts of other agencies and departments. Before the election occurred, a high-ranking official requested a follow-up evaluation of our assessments, and I wrote a memo that described our precision. The memo made its way up through the chain, and a few days later the office got a note from Stephen Cambone, the Undersecretary of Defense for Intelligence, praising both the prediction and the self-evaluation. Among other things, his note included a proclamation that we would jokingly quote when somebody in the office did something well: "Good on you!" Dr. Cambone then asked for another memo that explained the methods we used to predict the outcome with such accuracy. Ben called it "quite a feather in your cap," and my boss said it would put me on track for a DIA bonus.

I began to write the explanation of our methodology, and I tried to resist the temptation to criticize other agencies while explaining how and why we did things differently. State, in particular, was very sensitive about their screwup, and I didn't want to piss anybody off.

"Sir, can't I just say that I copied and pasted Juan Cole?" I joked with my boss, referring to the University of Michigan professor and blogger whose analysis many of us frequently read. "Or how about just saying that I waited to see State's assessments and then predicted the opposite?"

"Consult the Wall of Optimism," he jested, "and you'll find the answers to all your questions."

But it turned out that the methodology paper would be controversial even with my lighthearted approach. I talked about why we dismissed intelligence indicators that other agencies relied upon, and indicated in particular that it wasn't helpful to listen to a candidate's *supporters* to determine the actual level of support. I also said that mainstream Western reporters had little knowledge of internal Iraqi politics and were often seduced by Westernized, English-speaking Iraqis, thereby overlooking candidates with the most domestic backing and legitimacy. When the people at State's intel shop saw the paper, they made their irritation clear in a strongly worded challenge of the findings. They accused OIA of criticizing a fellow intelligence agency, regardless of the fact that comparison with other forecasts was only a very minor element of the overall discussion of our own predictive methodology. Their retort indicated that agencies should support one another—demonstrating that even *after* an event, groupthink was an active force. Not only shouldn't we disagree on our predictions, State seemed to be saying, but we should minimize those differences after the fact. Especially in light of Secretary Rice's later claim that the entire intelligence community had failed to predict the Hamas victory in Palestinian elections, the indignation over an accurate assessment was ridiculous.

Through the fall, up until the December elections, Strat was insanely busy, but within itself the team ran like a well-oiled machine, especially the governance section. Every random assignment from above that did not have a specific connection to the other groups came to us, and we rolled with the punches that came from being the catchall group for taskers. Juan delegated nimbly, Major Nimick ran interference with office leadership, and Evan was constantly reviewing and augmenting governance products. Under-staffed and undersupplied, the analysts took it as a challenge; like a sports team that bonds over a collective feeling of disrespect, we sublimated our irritation through nonstop effort.

As we increasingly demonstrated knowledge and prescience, other offices and departments increasingly called for our input or opinion. The entertaining/horrifying side effect of this was getting to see how little many policymakers and advisers really knew about Iraq, especially the political process. When Iraqis voted on their constitution, we repeatedly had to explain that three provinces needed to vote it down by a two-thirds margin for it to fail, a fact widely reported in the press; officials had all kinds of ridiculous notions about the rules of the vote. The subsequent national elections prompted even more questions, and trying to explain a parliamentary system of government to people who barely understand the U.S. political apparatus was a challenge. One day a high-ranking official from J5, the directorate responsible for strategic plans and policy, called to ask how many seats there were in Iraq's parliament. For a layperson, this kind of information is inconsequential, but for people active in the effort to create a functional government to not know its structural basics was alarming and depressing. It was clear that the rhetoric of democracy promotion was much loftier than the actual efforts, and even interest in the process, of many of our leaders.

Meanwhile, despite a general lack of attention to strategic issues (due partly to the focus on counterinsurgency, among other things), leadership continued to criticize analysis for being "off message." We tried to talk about, for example, the rising number of displaced Iraqis being an indicator of sectarian violence—in other words, a civil war gauge—but we were told the dislocation "isn't that bad." It was a catch-22: If we wanted to warn of impending problems, we were told they weren't problems yet, and if we focused on a problem that was occurring, some said we should be predictive instead of focusing on things that could not be changed. The aftermath of the elections was especially tough because we told our supervisors that the government would take several months to form, meaning that there would be no functioning government until the spring. This directly contradicted administration rhetoric at the time, which lauded Iraq's electoral process and promised that a "national unity government" would be quickly established and promptly effective. We even got questions about what would be accomplished during the first hundred days of whatever administration was established. We all had a good laugh over that—considering the pace of politics in the Middle East, we knew we'd be lucky if the parliament met more than a handful of times in that period.

Email was an easy way to blow off steam, and we occasionally sent notes back and forth about the events that confirmed our general view that things in Iraq were going to shit. In the midst of public reassurances about the growing capabilities of Iraqi soldiers, for example, a graduation ceremony for newly trained troops was a total debacle. Soldiers had publicly protested immediately after their commencement when they discovered they had been lied to about the location of their assignment. They were Sunni soldiers, and the United States was especially eager to bring Sunnis into the Iraqi army, but hundreds of the troops quit on the spot. Not only did it demonstrate incompetence in planning, it meant there were now hundreds of angry Sunnis with newly issued military weapons and uniforms. Yikes.

A good friend on the Sunni team, Aaron, sent out an email with the story included, commenting,

Is ANYONE surprised at this? We can build all the slides in the world, the principals can lean on their talking points all day long, and we can continue to convince ourselves that all will end well in a harmonious hand-holding session of kumbaya. This is the security reality, the challenges that these ISF [Iraqi Security Forces] trainers face every day. The analogy of trying to fit a square peg in a round hole seems to fit.

We weren't a policy shop. It was not our job to suggest courses of action, but rather to explain the facts on the ground and indicate what would happen in the future based on what was actually occurring. But that doesn't mean we didn't understand the policy (and politics) of it, and we all knew that "stay the course," a ridiculous notion when the course is heading over a cliff at the horizon, wasn't going to cut it.

Another office entertainment was an occasional caption contest, in which someone would email a picture and invite the recipients to come up with a pithy description. Most of them were obscure joking references to Middle East politics (the best caption contests were always group pictures of Arab leaders pretending to be interested in cooperating), but sometimes they referenced domestic affairs. The runaway winner from a picture of Secretary Rumsfeld with his hands up and in front of him was, "When one of my generals starts to disagree with me, I grab him around the [neck] and shake vigorously, like THIS!! That usually results in them sitting in a rather lobotomized state . . ." The perception that leaders ignored the judgments of the people paid to deliver such analysis was pervasive. Even people who were not politicians, whom we figured should know better, fell into the trap of overestimating progress.

A spring *USA Today* article revealed massive problems in reconstruction projects, saying in part, "The $21 billion U.S. rebuilding campaign in Iraq has made 'substantial progress' but will leave a legacy of unbuilt projects and unfulfilled promises, says a report issued today by the U.S. reconstruction watchdog." Aaron alertly recognized the program as something we had just discussed in a recent conference. Even as a steadfast conservative with goals of getting into Republican politics, he opined:

An interesting article concerning reconstruction concerns. Besides the reality that anyone that was directly involved with this aspect of the war could predict this due to poor management and accountability of funds, and horrifyingly bad standard contract procedures, I note the highlight discussing Operation Shield. Not 45 days ago many of us sat in a three-day conference sponsored by [an intelligence agency] and the Army LTC that commanded this operation spoke to the attendees. He spoke of the overwhelming success of this very program and highlighted the efficiency of their accountability procedures.

At the time some of us that have seen this "force" in action questioned the validity of the claims. Now reports are surfacing demonstrating that things were not as rosy as reported. It highlights the importance of objective [intelligence] reporting and how those that are closest to the information may not always see it for what it really is. There are so many other influences in place when it comes to intelligence it is a good thing sometimes when not everyone is on the same page and tough questions have to be asked to reconcile those differences.

The fact that people felt compelled to voice these points, when the ideas should have been understood by every single person in the office, spoke volumes about the environment for analysts in the Department of Defense's Iraq shop. As winter turned into spring, the fights between office and division leadership continued, and analysts were often caught in the middle. Rather than dealing with each other about disagreements, SIOs and OIOs would simply go right to the analyst and demand changes. OIOs would come over to our stations, insist that we were interpreting data incorrectly, and suggest the "proper" assessment. We would adjust it—they're the boss, after all—and then our SIO would see it on its way up the chain again and change it to something else, often prompting another OIO hissy fit.

The specific ideological perspectives of office leadership also became clearer as the disagreements persisted. All the analysts could predict the edits and suggestions of each OIO, and by the spring we were up to five supervisors who all had the ability to release products from the office (and therefore also the right to basically make any changes they wanted in a product): Ben the Shouter, Elaine the Upstart, Awkward Eric, and the chief and deputy of the office. Roger, the chief, was taking a more active role in reviewing documents, wanting to get back to his analytical roots, and the office finally replaced his old deputy position. The new second in

command was none other than Arnold Kerik, working as a civilian and back with a vengeance from his retirement. He was now
more involved than ever, running around the office and asking
people what they were working on so he could add his opinion
(that is, inject his ideology) to everything—whether related to the
office or not. He would launch into tirades over minor analytical
disagreements, once telling an analyst, in all seriousness, "Well, it's
clear I need to do more micromanaging here!"

One of his more infamous acts occurred during the national immigration demonstrations, of which one of the largest took place
in DC. He was watching the television broadcast, looking perturbed, and later, while talking to Jose, he seemed curious to get
the perspective of someone he assumed had a vested interest in the
issue.

"So, Jose, what do you think about these immigration pro-
tests?"

"Ummm . . . sir, uh, what do you mean?"

"Well, it just seems like these are the kind of people that want
statues of César Chávez and Che Guevara put up, who don't want
to assimilate or join American culture and values."

"I, uh, think they're mostly trying to avoid getting thrown in
jail, with this new bill in Congress."

"But don't you think they're going about it the wrong way? I
mean, look at you: You've clearly adapted and assimilated."
Colonel Kerik smiled condescendingly. Once he got going, there
was no stopping him, even when he was talking himself over a
cliff. Jose, as we all knew, was of Puerto Rican descent, and of
course since Puerto Rico is an American territory, Puerto Ricans
are not immigrants. And even if Jose was an immigrant, it was
hardly Kerik's place to congratulate Jose on his putative assimila-
tion. But Colonel Kerik wasn't done shoving his foot down his
throat.

"And you speak English so well!"

Jose was speechless, in both his (fluent) languages. It wasn't as
if he had an accent, or any lack of command of English in speaking or writing; although he had a Hispanic name and appearance,

he'd been born and raised in Texas, just like millions of others who were born in the United States and now face the kind of foolishness demonstrated by comments like "You speak English so well." When the story made its way around the office, people laughed so hard they cried. For weeks, when Jose would say something, somebody would ask him to repeat it in his good English, or compliment his diction.

All five office-level managers had a say in production, and each could bounce a product back and forth with an analyst before it got published. We could usually predict what their respective changes were before even reading the new version, but it was difficult to specifically tailor a product because we never knew to whom it would go. Roger would say we were being too pessimistic, and he'd tell us to check and see what CIA was saying. Roger never wanted to be too off track from our big brother (no pun intended). Ben would initially say it was fine, make some minor changes, and then tell us it was fine as long as Elaine said it was okay. Elaine did by far the most extensive editing, and she made tons of what we called "happy to glad" changes: She would insist that a part of the paper was terribly wrong only to change it to something nearly exactly the same. *Happy* became *glad, likely* became *probable,* and so on and so forth, with specific words as well as general assessments.

Eric did not edit Strat products as often as the others, but when he did, he always asked why there wasn't a greater focus on Shia militias and Iranian influence. Conversely, Kerik would lose it if we wrote a paper that didn't blame the insurgency on Ba'athist conspirators. As far as I could tell, although these principals talked on a regular basis, they never addressed their fundamental analytical disagreements, all of which affected our analysis as it went through the chain. They fought proxy wars for their particular biases and ideologies through the analysts, and there was little we could do about it.

To add insult to injury, in the spring the J2 decided that his morning briefing was no longer acceptable in its extant form. For years the briefers were analysts, the subject matter experts on whatever issue was being briefed on a particular slide. The daily briefing was often combative (the J2 was not afraid to steamroll the experts, making note of his seniority by warning, "You're digging yourself a hole, mister junior analyst," or by simply dismissing analysis that displeased him: "I quit reading when I see stupidity in reporting"), but the morning brief was one of the rare times when analysts communicated directly with senior leadership and could offer unadulterated assessments. It seemed, however, that analysts told him what he didn't want to hear one too many times, and he demanded a designated briefing team.

Rather than having the subject matter experts from each relevant office available for briefings, the new group was a handful of people pulled from various places and put onto a team that needed staffing around the clock. It was practically a suicide mission; we knew the group would be berated constantly by the J2, and they wouldn't have the time to review all the traffic necessary to make fully informed assessments. What used to be a job for hundreds of analysts working to put slides together, with dozens of them briefing at different times, was made into a duty for about fifteen people. It was a terrifying prospect due to the hours, vague job description, and inevitability of burnout. Not surprisingly, there were not enough volunteers to fully staff the new team, so offices were told to figure out whom they would send, involuntarily, to the new team.

A favorite in Strat was Christopher Jiminez, an exceptionally capable and good-natured analyst whom we were confident was on the fast track to a leadership position. Christopher was barely thirty, but many analysts looked to him for input and editing when we needed help. Most important, he was willing to stand up for our assessments, and was one of the few senior intelligence analysts who wouldn't back down from OIO intimidation. As the year progressed he became increasingly disillusioned with the process, and correspondingly outspoken. He was the one who sent the joking email about Rumsfeld strangling his generals, for example, and we wondered how long he would last, considering his evident disappointment with mounting office interference.

We didn't have to wait for him to decide to leave, however:

When the J2 told offices to form the briefing team whether people wanted to join it or not, OIA leadership transferred Christopher. Many of the analysts saw it as a punishment: He was going from a position he liked, with regular hours and a subject area he knew completely, to a new unit that had a brutal schedule and little ability to do long-term analysis, which he was focused on. We thought that Roger, who supposedly made the decision, liked Christopher, but we couldn't help noticing that defenders of analysts were being jettisoned.

Christopher, who was higher up the chain than most of us, vocalized analytical concerns about the adjustment of assessments and he was shot down repeatedly. He didn't give up, though, and kept identifying the problems in analysis and structure within the office, slowly but surely falling out of favor with many of the senior leaders. When they told him he'd be switching to the briefing team, it sent a chilling message to the rest of us: Challenge the status quo and your career is in danger. I don't know if this was done purposely or was simply a by-product of normal office activities, but it was part of a trend that many of us recognized and talked about openly. If we were honest about the facts, would we be the next ones out the door?

Christopher wasn't the only one, of course. After Major Nimick sent the email insisting that analysts should not be focused on administration rhetoric, his relationship with office leaders deteriorated to the point that they reassigned him from the supervisory position at which he excelled to a "special project" where he worked alone, on a menial administrative task, until he requested a transfer to another office. Apparently the new definition of *insubordinate* was "telling the truth to a civilian supervisor and then getting yelled at," the result of which was the revocation of a leadership position and interference with one's career path.

The Wall of Optimism. Major Nimick being transferred. Christopher being transferred. The rest of us being badgered into submission, worried about our assessments and our careers.

"Alex, you can't criticize the Iraqi constitution. State put a lot of work into that!"

Roger was exasperated, trying to convince me, once again, that my predictions were "too pessimistic." He claimed that things were better than I thought, and he was especially pissed about my description of the Iraqi constitution as "hastily written." He insisted that I could not "criticize" it because doing so might offend the State Department, which had largely authored the document.

"Sir," I replied cautiously, "that's the nicest thing I could think of to say about it. The Iraqi constitution is a piece of shit, sir, and it's causing all kinds of problems." Needless to say, Roger prevailed, with political considerations triumphing once again. The Iraqi constitution, in addition to indeed being hastily written, is the source of much of Iraq's political conflict. Pretending otherwise was detrimental to understanding the situation on the ground.

For the first time I began to wonder whether I could really make a career in the intelligence business. At virtually every stage of my development at DIA I had been hopeful, only to have reality come crashing down. I talked with friends and family to gain their perspectives, but it was hard to communicate just how discouraging the situation had become.

"I'm willing to stick with it as long as I think we're doing more good than harm," I told my friend Jena, further lowering the bar of expectations, "but I'm really not sure if we are." Jena was also working in the bowels of the government, toiling in the Manhattan district attorney's office on child abuse cases. As we talked, I told her I was worried that perhaps my concerns were no more than the kind of common (and cyclical) dissatisfaction that many people, especially young people, occasionally have with their jobs. She was no stranger to bureaucracy and frustration, and as she compared my experiences with those of others who were sometimes perturbed by their jobs, she made a good point.

"The important thing is that you feel right about what you're doing," she said, "and it's not like you're unhappy because you don't like your boss or you're doing poorly. You get along with your coworkers, you're doing really well, and you believe in the mission. You're frustrated because you're not sure if the system you're in is actually doing good. In all my time at the DA, even when things were bad, I was mad that we weren't doing *enough* good, not that we were actually having an actively negative effect. Whether you decide to be there or not reflects, to some extent, whether you believe in what you're doing."

I reluctantly considered whether I still did. Meanwhile, I increasingly leaned on friends and my then-girlfriend, Sadie, a brilliant and fun southerner who had to endure my growing uncertainty about the job. Some days I didn't want to talk or think about work at all; other times I felt I was blabbering on about it. The creeping self-doubt and insecurity were neither attractive nor pleasant, for myself or those around me.

Finally, at one point, Justin, my candid Texan friend, told me to recommit myself.

"Look, stop worrying about it and do the best job you can," he reasoned. "This is something you've wanted to do for a long time, something that took a ton of effort, and you're passionate about it. You *volunteered* to go to Iraq. I mean, c'mon. Stop letting it affect you and make whatever impact you can in the office."

He helped jolt me out of my vacillation, and I resolved to continue to work hard and hope that there would soon be a light at the end of the tunnel.

For many analysts, the preferred approach was to just lie low and try to ride out the problems. Self-preservation is a powerful urge, and having been in that kind of situation, it is easy for me to imagine how many of the great failures in intelligence occur. It's not easy to oppose an insidious influence, especially when it's treated by leadership as standard operating procedure. You begin to rationalize it, telling yourself that your long-term contribution will outweigh any benefit of speaking up right now. You wonder if it would even make a difference, and if not, what's the point of putting yourself out there? And what if, God forbid, you're wrong? A rational assessment of the evidence supports your position, but they're so very *sure* of themselves; perhaps you're the one missing something. Better to just let them win this battle and keep your powder dry for the next one. When something really, really important comes up, then it'll be time to take a stand.

It's easy for this to happen. To avoid it, you have to be sure of yourself and willing to face and disagree with people who can harm your career and reputation—something that's not looked upon favorably in any work environment, let alone a government bureaucracy. I don't blame my colleagues for feeling like they could do little to stop the runaway train of mismanagement, but personally, despite deciding to keep focused, I was growing ever more uncomfortable with the methods of the office. My unhappiness with the leadership, and our collective view that leadership wouldn't stand for dissent, was further solidified with the selection of Strat's new boss.

CHAPTER 16

With Major Nimick banished to administrative duty, and the Strat chief, Lieutenant Colonel Hepler, being tapped for duty with another unit, we had a vacancy at the top. Around the same time, the entire office was in flux because a long-rumored reorganization was (yet again) about to occur. The reorg was supposed to be the salve that would alleviate many of our problems, in terms of both office procedures and the analytical structure. It was in the works for months, and rumors abounded about how it would all shake out. There were meetings, debates, deliberations, and plenty of gossip, but the actual decision was a closely guarded secret among the office-level leaders. We kept hearing, though, that many of the issues (including space, resource allocation, and office standard operating procedure) would be addressed and resolved.

In terms of morale, it's nice to be able to put up some pictures and know that you can start working right away when you get in. More important, it is difficult to do your job when you don't have a file cabinet or a permanent phone number or know which systems you'll have access to on any given day. In the midst of a years-long war, nobody in my office even had voice mail. It just did not exist on our phones, for whatever reason, so messages were always getting screwed up or lost or otherwise bungled. It's also tough to be a good colleague when every morning is a competition for computers.

When leadership finally implemented the reorganization, many of the analysts were stunned. Instead of getting more resources or space, we were getting more people, making an already tight situation even worse. Further, the allocation of office personnel didn't make any sense: There was now overlap among many of the teams, with the same regional categories that many of us saw falter and then collapse at the CIOC in Baghdad.

In addition to an entirely new structure, Strat got a new leader, Air Force Major Eddie Sebelius, who was a recent returnee from a Baghdad rotation. Again, we were disappointed and discouraged. Our previous leader was confident and assertive, but Major Sebelius had a backbone like cooked spaghetti and a work ethic about as robust—after a month or so on the job he threw a tantrum over his responsibilities as the head of Strat, declaring, "I'm not doing the work schedule anymore. It's too hard! I gave it to the team chiefs." Some supervisors, such as Major Nimick and Lieutenant Colonel Hepler, are straightforward with their own leaders and tough but fair with their charges. Some are good with their leaders but not with those they lead, or vice versa. Some are bad at both. Major Sebelius was so unsure of himself that he commanded the respect of no one. Not those above him, and certainly not those below him, and his aversion to confrontation made him conciliatory at all times. From the start everybody walked all over him, and the fights between analysts and OIOs immediately became more caustic due to the lack of a legitimate intermediary.

In short, the much-heralded reorganization of the Office of Iraq Analysis gave us no additional space, an even worse organizational structure, and a leader in whom nobody had faith. In a further indignity, the OIA itself received a demotion from "office" to "division," meaning that we all now had another layer (or two or three) of supervision, having been subsumed into another larger office that was not even based in the Pentagon. All the products that formerly required office-level approval before publication would now have to go through all the same people as before *and* the editor and head of the new overall office. Most of the Strat team was broken up and parceled out to the new subunits, with the notable exception of the governance section, which remained intact. I breathed a sigh of relief that Juan was still my boss. Still, it was a thin silver lining to the cloud of continued problems.

In the midst of this turmoil, an email went out that reflected many of our frustrations and indicated that they were not limited to my office.

One of the smartest, most interesting senior intelligence individuals I met during my tenure was Rick MacKenzie, a DISL (defense intelligence senior level, a very high rank) in the J2's office who reviewed J2 documents and often put together an informal overnight update of worldly events and developments, called Nightwatch. Many of us read those updates religiously for the insight and perspectives of Mr. MacKenzie, and we were sad to hear about his impending retirement. He'd spent decades in the community, and was sharp in both mind and word. Many of us viewed him as an institution, someone to look up to; he was a senior leader who had the respect of the analysts and policymakers alike. Before he left, he sent out a widely read missive that expressed a damning and incisive view of the U.S. intelligence community. I did not agree with it all, but it showed that the deep frustrations were not limited to the analytical level:

> This [Nightwatch email] is the last I shall write as a J2 DISL.
>
> In the reviews of intelligence performance since Pearl Harbor, one salient finding links them all. The problem of intelligence failure is a problem of analysis. The analyst screwed up. The normative response by the U.S. intelligence overseers has been to add layers of management, to reorganize and add collection technology. Never mind that none of those were ever found to be causal in intelligence failures. People do what they know how to do. Americans know how to reorganize, to manage, and to make gadgets.
>
> Thus after all three major intelligence failures since 1941, the intelligence agencies have done the same things over and over and expected a different result. In every and all 12-step programs

that is the definition of insanity. The postmortem reviews of the 9–11 attack and the Iraq WMD issues have showcased once again the underlying insanity of our intelligence agencies. The problems were problems of analysis and analysts, but layering, reorganization, and technology have been slavered liberally, true to form.

We have more layers with more on the way. In the past two years we have experienced nonstop reorganization and that is not finished. DIA has been reorganized so that it is no longer recognizable to this 38-years veteran of DIA. Communications and collection have been enhanced or are in the process of being enhanced. We are drowning in classified message traffic even without consulting the Internet. Fixes are in motion for everything except analysis.

Something remains fundamentally wrong with analysis. Predictive accuracy scores for this year are down to 53% for all DI directorates. One must sense a crisis in analysis, in the management of analysis, in the training of analysts and in the intellectual curiosity of analysts about their real profession—not area expert, but aide to national security problem solving. As near as I have been able to judge, the pathology affects all agencies. So take some comfort from the company of others.

In the J2 we began to make progress in improving predictive skills when we unified warning with current intelligence between 1999 and August 2005. All analysts were warning and area experts. This works because the start of wisdom in analysis lies in recognizing that the phenomenology of national security affairs is very limited, despite the proliferation of countries and functional specialties. U.S. intelligence has ever written only about five kinds of warfare and nine kinds of instability.

The second part of wisdom lies in recognizing the hidden architecture of human behavior. If people are involved, events must be predictable. [. . .] Life requires predictability. State processes have beginnings, middles, and end states. They are the basis for making sound predictions. It is not rocket science, but it is science, far more than art. And behavior is always predictable to a very high degree of precision. Apply the scientific method before you publish.

The third part of wisdom is in recognizing how alien American life and culture is to those parts of the world that threaten us most. In the third world, the kids kick balls of rags when they play soccer. American biases are accountable for most intelligence failures in the past 58 years.

A fourth point is to be true to the intelligence evidence. The indicators never are wrong. As an attorney I assure you that the lawyers do not win cases, the evidence wins it.

A final point on methods. Analysis is not the same as synthesis, diagnosis, or prognosis, but all four constitute the core cognitive processes that we demand of our analysts. All four require separate but linked training courses and education. And all four are governed in practice by the requirements of critical evaluation. I wonder how many analysts have had any training in critical evaluation techniques. Do we have any methodologists? [. . .]

Intelligence analysis is a profession in its own right. It is not the same as academic graduate work, though it draws on that type of learning. It is not journalism, though it also draws on that profession. Our task is less to understand the world as it is than to solve the way ahead in keeping this Republic safe. You do not need to know the laws of thermodynamics to use an automobile. You just need to know how to drive and you must know how to read the future to drive safely.

One of my first introductions to analysis used the metaphor that we are like people in a rowboat, using where we have gone to guide our way ahead. Long ago I found that to be fatuous. We are in a motorboat moving at great speed and if we cannot guide it looking forward, looking backwards will not save us. The challenge of intelligence success always lies in future time.

Good luck.

The crucial message of MacKenzie's email is that the intelligence community has not just lost its way, but is continuing down a path that has been disastrous in the past. Not only are we repeating earlier mistakes, but we are institutionalizing processes that make future failures a near inevitability. The scale of those failures is indeterminate, but considering the effects of 9/11 and the Iraq war, we cannot afford to let this pattern continue.

Unfortunately, it is easier to succumb to an environment and its trends than it is to resist. Especially for careerists, there is little choice but to acquiesce to the atmosphere imposed by leadership and management. The character of a work environment is set by the boss. In our case, the ultimate bosses were the Secretary of Defense and the Commander in Chief, and it's no secret that they, along with their respective inner circles, do not appreciate dissent. When analysts talked about assessments that would displease our leadership, we occasionally joked that Cheney would come down and scream at us if we didn't make it more palatable. At the time it was funny, just a quick laugh about the widely held belief that top leadership routinely micromanaged the intelligence process; in retrospect, the very fact that this view was widely held demonstrates how broken the intelligence system really is. The good news is, I think, that this feeling is a relatively new development in the IC, as longtime DIA employees generally viewed the changes as a post-9/11 phenomenon. The bad news, conversely, is that it has taken but a few years to politicize the process and create massive morale problems within the IC, the first line of defense in the protection of the United States and its people.

With the growing dysfunction of the office, both structural and analytical, I increasingly wondered whether I was contributing to my nation's security . . . or helping to provide a fig leaf of cover for high-level leaders and politicians to implement ideological policies regardless of input from those paid to present analysis and advice to decision makers. Was I making a beneficial contribution, or helping maintain a façade of normalcy for a crippled and corrupt process?

When people asked me, as they often did, whether I was glad I went to Iraq, I usually said that I thought I had done more good than harm, and if that was true, it was worth it. As long as I was making things better for American security and foreign policy, however minimally, I was satisfied that I was doing the right thing. But as the weeks and months progressed, I continued to ask myself if that was still true, or if my presence was helping validate the broken system. The individual ideologies and the desire to please (or fear of aggravating) superiors in the chain of command were insidious forces, and they were not only perpetuating the errors of the past, but in fact reinforcing them.

A process that inhibits analysts' ability to do their job correctly, and that hurts the ability of decision makers to see and act on accurate, unadulterated assessments, is crippling to the safety and security of Americans and to a capable and effective foreign policy. When the process is broken, errors (and their effects) are often cumulative, perhaps exponential. The J2 didn't like the "too pessimistic" material we produced, so he created his own briefing team from scratch, grossly narrowing the perspectives he received; my office jettisoned two capable leaders and replaced the Strat chief with a compliant flunky; assessments were repeatedly criticized and changed for being "off message"; administration leaders made statements we all knew did not reflect the intelligence reports we were sending up the chain. The list went on and on, and I was not sure if I could, in good conscience, continue to be part of such a dubious enterprise.

"Julio? Is Julio here?" Strat's new team chief, Major Sebelius, looked around expectantly. We had a running debate going over whether he was racist or just stupid because of his inability to remember Jose's name. He had worked with Jose for weeks, maybe even months, and still screwed it up. It was especially amusing when he mixed up Jose and Juan, calling them by each other's name, but the latest was to say *Julio* instead of *Jose*. The "stupid" votes far outnumbered the ones for "racist," but everybody acknowledged that the sheer number of Hispanic-sounding names that Major Sebelius could accidentally come up with was impressive. Of course, we all started calling Jose by the major's misnomers. Even better, this Hispanic-specific brain fart wasn't limited to Major Sebelius; Colonel Kerik also couldn't seem to make the effort to learn the correct names of Jose and Juan, and his most frequent error was calling Jose "Juarez."

But leadership never seemed particularly concerned with people's names, or even knowing who worked in the office at any given time. Ben was especially infamous for introducing himself repeatedly to analysts, until he had met them half a dozen times. Not that we really cared that much, and I suppose it's not vital for supervisors to know the names of the people who work for them, but it cast doubt upon both their intellect and their interest in running a functional office. The name thing really jumped the shark, though, when the SIA who was booted to the briefing team, Christopher Jiminez, sent several of us this email:

> Dude, my new [briefing team] boss just called me "Juan." Um, I'm not even Latino. Have I reached the Julio Pantheon yet?

Jose quickly fired back a sarcastic reply.

> Mr. Kerik will now want a slide on why you speak English "so well." Remember to spell-check it—you wouldn't want to embarrass yourself.
>
> Regards,
> Julio.
>
> PS. What a turd.

Morale continued to unravel. If the problems weren't analytical, they were structural; if they weren't structural, they were with leadership; if they weren't with leadership, they were analytical. In particular, the nascent briefing team created a new level of stress for analysts and our SIOs. We were still assigned the task of creating the daily slides, but briefing team members could make any adjustments they wanted immediately before the daily J2 presentation. So we would create a slide and send it through layer after layer of editing up the chain of command, only to have it completely changed at the last minute. Christopher, whom we all liked, was doing his best to mediate between his old and new offices, but the relationship was fast deteriorating.

It got to the point that we would arrive in the morning only to find that our slide was completely changed from what we had submitted the night before. Sometimes it was the J2 who modified it, but usually it was someone on the briefing team. Perhaps it was too much to ask for the same person to take abuse from the J2 for weeks at a time, or maybe the individuals who briefed Iraq issues were part of the *everything is great—just clap harder!* crowd, but many of us felt the developments with the briefing team signaled the death knell for the office's beneficial contributions to current intel. We would spend hours or days on a slide, dozens of us working together to try to determine an accurate and useful assessment, and then one person could (and would) unilaterally alter it at the eleventh hour. The problem was one of analytical process: For our assessment to go to the J2 the judgment had to go through a rigorous review process in our office, getting approval at several stages on the way up the chain of command. The idea that the assessment of an entire office could be overturned by a single individual, in the middle of the night and with no real oversight, was jarring.

Once again analysts, team chiefs, and SIOs persistently raised the issue with office leadership, and once again we saw no appreciable change. It went on for weeks, with emails exchanged, arguments instigated, and bureaucratic battles waged, all rising in intensity. After a particularly egregious alteration, Evan, the Strat analytical supervisor, sent an email to much of the office, including high-level leadership.

> Yesterday, we pushed back hard against this slide going forward. I personally talked to [a member of the briefing team]. I especially noted the assessment, especially the last line in which all of us in Strat disagreed. Ben agreed with our concerns. I personally told [the briefer] the assessment had to go. Our analysts worked hard and fast to offer corrections to this slide, which we received for review at the last minute. This slide was put together on [briefing team] initiative with virtually no time to review before it went to J2 afternoon review. Our review remarks were ignored.
>
> We don't stand by the slide. We refute it. This process is unacceptable.

"This process is unacceptable." Evan was right, but nobody stepped up to fix it.

Yet another slide that had gone to the chairman of the Joint Chiefs of Staff and the Secretary of Defense contained an assessment that the entire Strategic team knew was false, and even our

SIOs were now involved in heated exchanges. We all thought this problem could be resolved with just a little bit of assertive leadership: Get all the significant players in the same room and talk about it! There were really only half a dozen or so people who had control over most of the various issues, and it seemed like they simply refused to communicate. Our office leadership, the OIOs, had no problem telling us what to do, so why was it such a problem for them to resolve issues at their level?

As our efficacy plunged, so did our spirits. It was nearly impossible to walk around the room and not see the "DIA vacancies" website up on a computer, or five or ten. Virtually everyone under the age of thirty was looking to leave the office in the near future, and many wanted to flee the intelligence community altogether. Ironically, the only office with a reputation worse than OIA among analysts was the counterterrorism task force, so the two offices with the most vital missions were also the least desirable to work for. Analysts were looking at defense contractors, think tanks, and a variety of nonprofit and nongovernmental organizations, hoping that something attractive would come up. At one point an email went around that described an opening working as an intelligence analyst for Disney, to research and assess threats to its theme parks. Although I have no idea how many people actually applied, several people said they were going to. When national intelligence agencies are on the verge of losing their most vital analysts to Disneyland, there's a problem.

Still, those who did leave were loath to publicly explain why, as most were moving to another intelligence or military job, and they knew if they were lucky enough to escape our office, there was no reason to risk their future by being open about their reasons for departure. It wouldn't do any good anyway, people rationalized, and it wasn't as if the office didn't already know about the rampant analytical dissatisfaction. We all talked about what we would do next, and the general consensus was that people either needed way more money to make the work worth it (many defense contractors offered six-figure starting pay for employees with a Top

Secret clearance, versus the roughly thirty-eight-thousand-dollar salary most of us started at) or would simply move on to something they actually enjoyed.

Even in the most difficult days of Baghdad, I clung to the hope that I was a benefit to my country's security, to its future, and I couldn't stomach the thought of leaving such an important agency. My memories of 9/11 and the lead-up to the Iraq war heavily influenced my continued desire to stay and try to improve the system from within. Slowly but surely, though, I began to think seriously about leaving. I joked about it in the office, telling people that the next time Major Sebelius called Jose "Julio" I would quit. Then I told them that I would give my two-week notice on the spot the next time Elaine told us to change our assessment because it was too pessimistic. Or the next time I had to use three computers in one day because of resource shortages. All these things happened, of course, but I continued working.

I went to a National Intelligence Council (NIC)–sponsored meeting to create a paper that would outline the indicators of a potential Iraqi civil war, but the gathering careened into a debate over whether we could use the term *civil war* to describe what was already happening. I sat with representatives from CIA, State, military commands, and the NIC, and watched sadly as they battled over semantics. All the while, violence in Iraq, against both coalition forces and Iraqi civilians, continued to rise. DIA added more people to the J2's briefing team; violence continued to rise. Administration officials repeatedly claimed that the United States had turned a corner; violence continued to rise. And so did my uncertainty about whether I wanted to continue to be part of the process.

I saw other people, many of whom had far more to lose than I, speaking out against the war and its practitioners, and I felt increasingly guilty for facilitating a bankrupt process. Wasn't my presence an implicit endorsement, not necessarily of policy, but of the system? I read articles about the Dixie Chicks, whose music I loved, and how their lives had been turned upside down simply because they expressed embarrassment about our president, and I admired their fortitude in continuing to speak out for what they believed. Individuals and groups who challenged the war and the assumptions behind it were an inspiration, and that kind of courage helped me find the nerve to be honest with myself about my role in the continued deception of the American public.

Every Monday there are protestors outside the Pentagon: They stand behind metal barriers right by the Metro escalators. There are usually about a dozen, with more around the holidays and fewer in inclement weather. Some hold signs, some just stand there, and one old Asian guy usually beats a slow cadence on a small drum. Nobody usually pays them much attention, except for the Pentagon police, and I doubt most people think much about them. I had mixed feelings about the protestors: On the one hand, I respected their convictions and their persistence in coming every week; on the other, I didn't agree with most of their signs and positions. I'm certainly not a pacifist, and sometimes war *is* the answer. Much of their focus, however, was on mistakes by leadership, especially Abu Ghraib, and I think any sane person recognizes those kinds of events as reprehensible atrocities.

One day was different. In the midst of my doubts about the job, I came up the escalator, tired from a long, intense week and looking forward to the weekend respite. It was Good Friday. I was startled when I got to the top of the escalators; there was a big group behind the barriers. I hadn't thought about the holiday protest crowd. As I made my way toward the first security checkpoint, I saw an extremely unusual scene. One of the protestors had on an orange jumpsuit and a burlap bag tied over his head, as in the pictures of Abu Ghraib. While that image alone is disquieting, this orange-clad and bagged individual was tied to an enormous cross. It was an extremely unsettling juxtaposition, the imagery of Easter and Christ with the evil of torture and its cover-up, and I stared as I walked by. I'm not an overly religious person, but neither am I immune to appeals using the profundity of faith, and the image stayed with me for days.

On a lighter side, even a satirical movie about a Washington spinmeister, *Thank You for Smoking*, pinged away at my conscience. In it, the antihero protagonist is asked why he lobbies for cigarette companies, and he usually answers that he has rent to pay. At one point a voice-over observes that paying the mortgage is "the yuppie Nuremberg defense." While I certainly didn't think of myself (or my colleagues) in that light, it made me realize that at some point during my months at the Pentagon, my reason for being there had shifted from wanting to be part of the process to fear of the unknown of leaving. I didn't want to stay, but I wondered if I could just stick it out for a few more weeks . . . or months . . . or years . . . perhaps things would improve, it might be worth it again. As the weeks dragged on, however, I was more and more uncomfortable, chastened by my fear of leaving and my implicit endorsement of policies and actions I believed were antithetical to our overall goals in intelligence and national security.

From the beginning of my employment, and for most of my life, I had believed in the system, the government, and the goodness of civil servants, especially those paid to keep us safe. Most of all, I believed that it was better to be a part of the system, even if it was an uphill climb against all the ills of the bureaucracy, than to criticize it from the outside. I generally believe in solving problems quietly and efficiently, and the idea of taking a public stand on principle did not appeal to me. But I also knew that I might have an opportunity, however small, to affect some of the worst elements of the office simply by leaving it. It was no longer a question of whether I wanted to stay, but rather whether I would have the courage to depart.

They say the definition of insanity is doing the same thing over and over and expecting the results to be different, and that's basically what I was doing: trying to do a good job, hoping that my work would not be manipulated or ignored, in the face of overwhelming evidence that the intelligence effort—and the war in general—was grossly mismanaged and politicized. With that realization, I wondered if I could, perversely, do more good by leaving than by staying. If I left the office and, more important, told leadership *why* I was leaving, maybe it would be a wake-up call. Most of the people who left didn't want to make waves, so they cited all kinds of reasons for their departure other than the real one: that

STILL BROKEN | 187

they hated the office and did not want to stay. If I was willing to be honest about why I and many others wanted to get out, maybe the office leadership would actually take useful steps to rectify the problems.

As I was trying to decide whether to leave, and what to do next if I did, I was still writing about the issues that I thought were most important in Iraq. I felt somewhat freed from the constraints of trying to benefit my long-term career prospects, so I was increasingly taking on more controversial issues. I tried to write about civil war indicators, but the paper was killed. Apparently that was not a priority. Then I wrote a comprehensive assessment of increased Shia dissatisfaction with the United States; after weeks of work that, too, was shelved, and I was told that the ruling Shia would "come around." Again there was no analytical disagreement or discussion, just orders from above to stop writing on those topics. Good thing civil war and conflict with Shia leadership never became problems.

Right around then, our chief, Roger, told us that his new supervisor, who was based off-site at DIA's headquarters, wanted to come and meet individually with his new charges. The boss, Clark Yates, was an unknown, but the rumor mill described him as a manager type (rather than an analyst) who was quiet and fair to his people. He was also a little corny, evidenced in part by the "shareholder" jar that he kept for people to submit pennies in order to "buy in" to the office. One coworker mused about pissing in the jar.

The first day of meetings included Jose and Juan, among others, and I had a session planned for the following week. The morning of the day Jose and Juan were scheduled to meet with Clark, Jose wandered over to the computer I was able to grab that day, looking dazed.

"You're not going to believe what just happened," he murmured.

"What, somebody call you Juanita?" The joke just never got old.

"No." He grimaced. "Even better. Something that perfectly sums up how screwed up this place is."

"Oh? What happened?"

"Juan and I were in a meeting with Kerik, and when it was over, he asked us to stay for a minute. He goes, 'So you guys are meeting with Clark today. What are you going to say about the office?' "

"No way. That's ridiculous." Bosses trying to find out what we were going to say in private meetings with their supervisor: always a classy move.

"Oh, that's not even close to the best part." Jose leaned in and lowered his voice. "We basically said that we hadn't thought much about it, but that we would tell him what we thought was good and what we thought was bad, basically just avoiding the question. Then he nodded, and he looked at us and proceeded to tell us what he wanted us to say."

"No . . . *way.*"

"Yeah, he was like, 'You guys know that the only problem here is that we don't have enough people, right? We just need more billets,' "—the government term for a funded job position. "He goes, 'Tell him that we need more personnel and more billets, and that's the only problem. Because the leadership and the structure we have is exactly what we need. It's great. And Roger is a great leader. Roger is a great leader. Roger is a great leader.' Then he just stared at us."

"He said 'Roger is a great leader' three times? And told you that billets are the only problem you should talk about? Really?" I was incredulous. This was so dishonorable that I thought Jose might be kidding.

"Yup. He just went on and on about how great the office is, how the leadership is so good, and how we should really tell Clark that. The only problem, he said, is that we just need more people."

Of course, we already had more people than computers and more billets than people—the office simply couldn't hold on to its employees—so that was ridiculous. Far worse was pressuring analysts about what to discuss with a supervisor who was looking for honest input, good and bad, about his new division. Jose was right: It really did sum up the office.

"So what did you say?"

"I was like, okay, and I told him that I'd tell Clark that a lot of things were good but that there was room for improvement. Then he let us go."

Within the day every analyst had heard the story. But nobody said anything to leadership, and so once again wrongdoing went unaddressed. For the time being.

I can't say that there was one specific moment that made me decide to leave; my departure was the result of many events over a long period of time. I could give people the benefit of the doubt for some of the occurrences. I could try to convince myself that they had good intentions but were misguided, or that they just made the wrong decision in a difficult environment. But Jose's story epitomized the many incidents for which there was no excuse, no possible justification, and while it wasn't the straw that broke the camel's back, it was definitely a big push toward the door.

Later that afternoon Clark met with Jose, who reported to us afterward.

"He just asked basic questions—what I liked about the office and what I didn't, what I would change if I was in charge for a day, and how things might be improved. Stuff like that. It went about half an hour."

"So what did you say about what was bad?"

"I told him . . . I told him that there were some structural issues, that sometimes it was hard to know exactly how the chain of command worked. I said that leadership was sometimes inconsistent and that we could use more resources."

The rest of the analyst crew was disappointed, but we understood. It was hard to tell the higher-ups about the problems. We all had respect for the chain of command, and most of the analysts were not confrontational by nature. Even those who wanted to talk about what was going on in the office often did it in an indirect or euphemistic way. "Leadership improperly changes our analysis" turned into "Sometimes there are disagreements with leadership that may not be based entirely in disagreements over the facts." "After three years we don't have enough goddamn desks or computers" became "The shift-work schedule that we've gone to has created some stress upon the general workforce." We all played the euphemism game at some point. Through this oblique communication, analysts believe that they have explained the problem without being impolitic, and the supervisor can say that the problems were never clearly expressed. Adding to the general reluctance to criticize was the fact that you never knew what would get back to your boss even when it was supposed to be confidential, and nobody was willing to risk his or her job.

Except, eventually, me.

"I'm going to tell him everything," I said to the other young analysts after Jose told us about the meeting. "Why not? I'm not going to be here for the rest of my life, and if he knows what's actually going on around here maybe he can do something about it. The only reason all this shit still goes on is because everybody is silent about it. I'm gonna tell him."

"Yeah, right," Kate scoffed. "You say you will, but you won't."

The other analysts knew me as mild-mannered because of my good relationships with all our supervisors and my willingness to endure the constant corrections without getting emotional. Sure, I'd joke around and bitch about things with fellow analysts, but I didn't always seem like I was on the verge of a nervous breakdown, as did many others in the office. They didn't know, therefore, that I would do exactly what I said because I thought it was right. There is nothing more dangerous to a controlling and manipulative structure than somebody who finds his or her conscience and resolve, and I had found mine. My internal debate over what to do was nearly resolved, and I had come down on the side of speaking truth to power.

The next week I went into the meeting with Clark believing that I would be leaving soon, and I felt liberated. I could be totally honest, and at worst they'd only be able to make me miserable for whatever short time I had left. I wanted to finish up a few projects I was working on, so I hadn't yet told my boss I'd be leaving, but I knew it was just a matter of time. I walked into the meeting. Clark and I shook hands.

"So, Alex, what do you do here?"

"Well, sir, I'm on the Strat team in the governance section, so I look at overall Iraqi political and strategic issues. I broadly cover all the ethno-sectarian groups, and I've become the resident expert on the constitution and voting processes, both within Iraq's government and among its national electorate. Right now I'm also looking at the civil war question and the relations between the United States and the new Iraqi government."

"Sounds like you have a lot on your plate. What's your background that brought you to DIA?"

"I went to Middlebury College and studied political science, with a particular focus on the Middle East, which led me to study in Istanbul and take courses that allowed me to pursue that interest. After I was with the agency for a while, I volunteered to deploy to Iraq, where I spent six months doing a combination of tactical and strategic intel, and then I came here."

"That's very impressive. I'm glad you're with us."

"Yes sir, thank you, sir."

I don't remember the exact question, but he then asked me about my impressions of the office, and what I thought could be improved.

"I think, broadly, that there are two main facets of this office, and of any intel office, really: analytical and structural. In this office, I think there are challenges in both areas." Ugh. *Challenges.* I was off to a big euphemistic start.

"Structurally," I went on, "people here have very little faith in the administrative processes. Everything from security access and badges to space issues can take months to resolve, and that's if it gets taken care of at all. It's hard to believe that our work is a priority when basic issues like badges and access to vital programs and even cabinet space are ignored. And when this stuff doesn't get done, it's impossible for us to know whose fault it is, because everybody blames whoever is above them on the chain of command. Structurally, there's no accountability, and there's a lot that people should be accountable for."

"I've heard about some of these problems, especially space, and I want you to know that we're all working on it," he assured me.

"Yes sir, we've been hearing that for a long time, but there's been no action on it for literally years. I can say that the lack of space and resources is probably the most frustrating thing on a daily basis for analysts. And I understand why it's not a big issue for leadership: They don't have a problem in that arena. When they ask for something it gets done; it's the other 90 percent of us who it affects. We have enough analytical problems without resource deprivation affecting our ability to do a good job."

"Oh? Analytical problems?"

"Yes sir, besides the structural problems there are analytical difficulties. For example, I have about a dozen people on my chain of command up through the top of the office, all of whom have the power to make any edits they want, and few of them communicate with each other, so many times I have to try to figure out how to incorporate suggestions from multiple people who are at odds with each other. Further, the chain of command itself is so screwed up that often we don't know who's the final word on any given product."

"I don't understand." He frowned. "How can that be?"

"Let me give you an example. I write a paper on, say, intra-Shia fighting. When I'm satisfied with it, it goes to my team chief, who makes edits and then gives it back to me for revision. Once that's done, it goes to the rest of my team, and I work with them on another round of editing. Then it goes out to all the Strat analysts, and they all get a chop on it. After that, it goes to my SIA, SIO, and division chief, and I work with them to fine-tune it. At any point in this process, I might bounce it back and forth two or three times to make sure they're all satisfied with it. By now about twenty people have had the opportunity to read, make comments, and suggest edits, and virtually all of them outrank me."

"I see."

"And that's only the beginning, sir. At that stage the product hasn't even gotten out of Strat. So the comments there are mostly helpful, because they're analytical in nature. In fact, I should say that I have nothing to say but good things, unqualified good things, about my immediate teammates and leadership. The problems in the office are, I believe, in spite of them and not because of them. Juan, Evan, and Major Nimick, who used to lead Strat before he was banished, are all fantastic supervisors and I think they do a great job in the face of a lot of institutional pressure. But once it gets past them, the real fun begins, because there are five people at the office level who can still keep it from being published. Now, we all know how to deal with them individually. Their ideologies are so fixed that we can tailor products to meet their respective approval. But we never know who will edit it for release, so it's impossible to write for our audience."

"But your audience is the policymaker, not the office."

"Sure, but to get to the policymaker, it's got to get through the office, which is no small feat. We usually know generally what the office leadership will say, and we have to take that into consideration."

I explained the individual biases and ideologies of each of the office leaders, which I have already described, to emphasize how entrenched their views were.

"The only thing in common with all of them," I closed, "is that they all want us to be more optimistic. Apparently accuracy is less important than cheerfulness. It's the Tinkerbell theory, I guess: If we all just clap harder, everything will be okay." I wasn't sure how familiar he was with the plot of Peter Pan, but I figured I'd give the metaphor a shot.

"Why do you think that is?" he asked, his eyes narrowing.

"Well, sir, I don't know. You'd have to ask them. I can't speak to their motivations specifically. But as a logical analyst, I can think of two potential reasons. The first is a problem with passing bad news up the chain. Everybody knows that we work in an environment in which giving superiors bad news is dangerous and can have a detrimental effect on your career. It's entirely possible that people are concerned about their careers, and are therefore changing analysis to deal with that, which I can understand, though I don't think it makes it right. The other possibility is that those leaders honestly believe, despite all evidence to the contrary, that the consensus analytical opinions of our subject matter experts make things seem worse than they really are in a variety of areas. In reality, our eventual assessments tend to be either accurate or too cheery—virtually nothing ends up better than we predict—but I suppose it is possible that despite our excellent recent track record, leadership repeatedly believes we're misinterpreting that data even after we're proven right time and time again. If it's honest disagreement, I understand that, too, but that might be even worse than the first option."

"That's a serious statement." Clark shifted uncomfortably in his chair. "Are you accusing OIOs here of changing assessments based on political or career influences?"

"Like I said, sir, I can't read minds. I don't know what their reasons are for changing analysis in the same mistaken direction all the time, but those are the two most obvious potential reasons I can think of. If you want to know which it is, or what combination, you'd have to ask them, sir." I was matter-of-fact. I wasn't especially emotional about it, and I didn't want to undermine my own legitimacy by getting excited.

"That's very unusual . . . I find it hard to believe that those are influences."

"Sir, the atmosphere of pressure and influence is so pervasive, I don't think people recognize how insidious it is. Let me give you an example: I know for a fact that Mr. Kerik, the deputy office chief, instructed at least two analysts to tell you that there were no problems within the office except for a lack of billets. He met with these analysts and first asked them what they planned to tell you, and then he looked them in the eye and told them what to say. And maybe the worst thing was that nobody was especially surprised. Disgusted, yes, but not surprised."

"Oh my." Now I really had his attention. His eyes were dinner plates, eyebrows raised toward the ceiling. "That is extremely inappropriate."

"Yes sir, to say the least. And as I said, it's very indicative."

We talked for a while longer, but he seemed distracted. He asked what I would do if I were made head of the office for a day, a typical but reasonable management question, and I described what I thought would be a beneficial reorganization of the office. We also talked more about the leadership approach, especially the apparent inability (or unwillingness) of office-level analysts and managers to communicate about many of the internal issues. I also stressed that I was not a disgruntled employee, but rather one who wanted to see the problems addressed and rectified for the good of the Iraq intelligence effort. I also indicated that I enjoyed the work that I did, and was good at it, and I encouraged him to look at my evaluations if he had any concerns that I was criticizing leadership because of poor reviews. He never asked whether I planned to stay with the office.

Our meeting lasted nearly an hour, and when I came out other young analysts casually sauntered over to see how it had gone. When I recounted the conversation, they were shocked.

"Aren't you worried he'll mess with your promotions?"

"Dude, you're screwed."

"What if he tells Ben or Roger what you said?"

"I hope he does," I told them. "I hope he creates a shitstorm so big that nobody can ignore this debacle anymore, and some things start to get better as a result."

CHAPTER 18

Over the next week or two I began to tell a few trusted colleagues that I would be leaving. Because I had joked about it for so long, at first people didn't believe me, but I told them that I was serious, finally. I first notified Jose and my governance teammates, Andrew, Kate, and my boss, Juan, and I felt especially bad for Juan because he would have to pick up most of my responsibilities. I also wanted to assure him that my reason for leaving had nothing to do with my immediate leadership, and I thanked him for his help and guidance. He was a good guy in a tough situation, and it was not his fault that he got caught in the middle of so many squabbles. I then told Evan, the Strat intel supervisor, that I'd be giving my notice soon, and I let him know, too, how much I appreciated his personal and professional acumen. Of everyone in the office, he was probably in the most difficult position—too senior to be part of the analytical camaraderie, but not high ranking enough to win many battles against the office-level personnel. I told both Evan and Juan that I planned to finish up my outstanding projects before leaving, and I also asked them to keep my departure plans to themselves until I told Major Sebelius. I was not looking forward to that conversation, but I did wonder what he would say.

I was surprised when everybody's reaction was virtually identical: "Good for you!" they all said. "You're finally getting out, eh? That's great. Seriously, congratulations." It was as if they were all quitting vicariously, like my impending departure was an invitation to admit all the enmity people had built up. I was surprised at how unhappy they were; I'd known my coworkers were dissatisfied, but even at that point I had no idea how far it really went.

Soon after I informed my friends and close colleagues, I told Major Sebelius I needed to talk to him when he had a chance.

"I have a moment now," he said, "why don't you sit down?" He gestured to an open chair, which I dragged over to his desk. There were people all around; privacy was nonexistent due to the close quarters in which we worked.

"I just wanted to let you know, sir, that I've decided to leave the office. I've decided to pursue other opportunities, so this is my two-week notice."

"What? You're leaving? Why?" He was incredulous. His surprise demonstrated just how out of touch he was with his workers, but I felt no need to rub it in.

"I think it's time for me to move on."

"So what office are you going to?" He still wasn't quite processing it; he thought I had gotten a transfer to another division.

"No sir, I'm leaving DIA altogether."

"So you're going to the private sector?"

"I'm leaving the government, yes. So I guess what I need from you is just the information for how to do out-processing, what the steps are for me to separate from the agency."

In fact, I had already looked into the process for leaving so I wouldn't be blindsided by anything. I wanted to find out what to do about continuing health insurance, what happened to my accumulated vacation time, and generally how the process went. I talked to a few people who had left other offices, and I called our human resource department to get an idea of the procedures. I would still need my office, however, for many of the specifics, and I wanted to make sure I didn't leave anything out.

I also was talking to friends and colleagues in the foreign policy world to explore what I would do next. It was extremely difficult to process the idea that I would be unemployed, even for a short while, but two factors made me decide to leave without anything specific lined up for my next job: First, I had more than a month of vacation time saved up, and DIA would pay me for it in one lump sum after I left. With nearly six weeks of salary, I'd have time to decide where I'd land. Beyond that, I had some savings from my time in Iraq (when I wasn't paying rent), so although finances would soon become an issue, they were not an immediate concern. Second, and more important, I really wanted to leave. Whether I had something specific lined up simply didn't seem to matter. I was so dissatisfied with the office and the process that I was willing to take a risk, even one as significant as open-ended unemployment.

"Well," Major Sebelius stammered, "I don't really know what happens. Why don't you talk to Jamie"—a coworker who was leaving to go to another office—"about what to do?"

"Sir, he's staying within the government, which I'm sure is a much easier process than leaving completely. If you're not aware of the procedures, could you please find out for me and let me know?"

"Uhh, okay, I'll see what I can find out." Great. Even leaving was going to be difficult. I'd known I would have to figure it out myself, but at least the ball was officially rolling.

"I guess I need to know two things, then," he said, almost as an afterthought. "When you're leaving and where you're going."

I sighed. "I'm giving my two-week notice, so I'm leaving two weeks from today. And sir, no, you don't need to know where I'm going."

"Oh . . . right, okay. Well, I'll let you know what I find out."

Initially, to my surprise, it felt pretty terrible. I'd worked much of my life to get a job like the one I had just quit. I'd lived a life that would allow me to obtain a security clearance, I'd studied the Middle East for years, and I desperately wanted to work for my country. But not like this. Not providing cover for a morally and strategically bankrupt set of leaders, and not as part of a system that was inverting its vital purpose by fitting analysis to policy instead of the other way around. After a while, though, I felt relieved, like a weight had been lifted. I could—and would—pursue that long-term goal, just through a different route than I had initially planned. Still, it was definitely bittersweet.

Major Sebelius went off to do whatever he needed to do, to tell whomever he needed to tell, and just a few minutes later Strat had our afternoon meeting. At the end we would always ask if anyone had something to add, and I spoke up.

"As some of you already know, I've recently decided to leave DIA to pursue other opportunities. I'd rather you all hear it from me rather than through the rumor mill. I gave my two-weeks just this afternoon, and I'm confident that I'll be able to finish up my major projects and pass along anything else. It's been a privilege to work here, and my departure is no reflection on my team or my immediate leadership. I wish everybody the best."

Most people knew, so it wasn't a bombshell, but it definitely gave the whole thing an air of finality. Especially because I could tell the office leadership already knew: Just before the meeting, Jose told me, Kerik had been shouting at Major Sebelius in his office. Jose relayed the brief discussion.

"What! Why is he leaving? What did you do?"

"I don't know, sir, I—"

"You go find out why he's leaving! And find out what you can do to get him to stay!"

After the meeting I was besieged by the younger analysts, all of whom wanted to know what I was doing next. Virtually all of them said that they, too, were looking to leave, and my decision triggered a massive outpouring of frustration. For the first time, someone had openly expressed the wide-ranging concerns of the vast majority of the office, and people seemed relieved to have an open discussion about it. Adam, a team chief in the group that replaced our group in Iraq who was now back at the Pentagon, confessed that he was looking for another job, an admission that shocked me. He was well along in his career, pretty close to a high-profile leadership position. I expressed my surprise, and he looked at me sadly. "You can't help an organization," he said, "that doesn't want to help itself."

My coworkers, especially those of my generation, seemed to realize that perhaps even the unknown was a viable alternative to their unhappiness. This torrent of honesty did not go unnoticed by our leadership, and I was expecting some fallout.

During our meeting Roger had walked over, stood just outside our group, and glared at me for a minute or two before shaking his head and walking away. When the meeting ended, Major Sebelius walked over and told me we needed to talk. I went with him back to his desk.

"So there's just some more information I need to get from you, after talking to office leadership."

"Yes sir, no problem."

"So . . . why is it exactly that you're leaving?"

"It's a combination of reasons, really." I didn't want to get into an argument with him, especially because even if he did understand, which I knew he wouldn't, he didn't actually care; he was just asking because his bosses had told him to.

"Well," he tried again, "there are factors that are involved in all job changes, right? Like money, title, the work you're doing. Would you say those are part of it?"

"As you said, those are elements in all job changes. Would I like to make more money? Sure. Do I wish there were more—or any, really—promotion opportunities in the office? Absolutely. Do I think we sometimes get bogged down doing irrelevant work? I imagine everybody thinks that." Was I doing the Rumsfeld thing where he asked himself questions so he could give answers that took the "conversation" in whatever direction he wanted? Without a doubt.

Major Sebelius shifted uncomfortably in his chair, apparently steeling himself for an unpleasant question.

"Okay, um, well, what could we do to keep you?" he asked.

"What do you mean?" I wanted him to be specific.

"Well, what could we do to make you change your mind? If we could promise more money, or a different position, or let you decide which projects you wanted to do, would that make you change your mind?"

"Oh." I hadn't really considered the possibility that the office would entice me to stay. "Well, what can the office offer?" I knew that I did a good job, and I also knew they were worried about losing people, but I was still surprised that they were trying to bargain with me. "You know, sir," I added, "I don't really know what the options could be. I mean, we've always been told that the office doesn't control promotions, and the office doesn't control the workload, so what are the possibilities?" It was true—office leaders always claimed they had little ability to influence these issues.

"I don't really know." Of course he didn't, because he was a proxy.

"Well, I'll tell you what," I said. "I believe in keeping options open, and I never say never. Why don't you let me know what the possibilities are, and we'll go from there."

I was curious to see what they might come up with to get me to stay, and I figured there were two significant benefits to knowing. First, if anybody ever tried to get back at me for leaving by saying I was a bad worker, or that there was something wrong with my performance, it would be helpful to note that the office had tried to keep me when I resigned. More important, I wanted to tell all my colleagues exactly what I'd been offered to stay, because anything the office was prepared to give me, they could also give my coworkers. Still, I didn't think the office would come through, because there was simply neither the will nor the ability to make a real effort to keep employees happy.

Later that afternoon Kerik yanked me into his office.

"So I hear that you're leaving." He got right to the point.

"Yes sir."

"You're leaving DIA entirely."

I didn't reply. I had no love for Kerik, so I saw no reason to give him more information than necessary, and I was also afraid that he would blackball me in the think-tank community, where I knew he had extensive connections.

"You're going to the private sector," he prodded.

"Yes sir, I believe so."

"You know, people leave jobs for all kinds of reasons. Sometimes money, or title, or the work that they do." Apparently everybody was reading from the same script. "Or some combination of these."

I just sat there, and we stared at each other. What he said was true, but I wanted him to actually ask a question. I have something of a talent for enduring uncomfortable silences, and after several seconds, he broke it.

"So which is it?" he suddenly thundered, lunging forward in his chair. "Which one?"

"Sir, it's really a combination of those factors," I frowned, "but mostly I really just don't think this is a good work environment. We don't have enough resources, there's no SOP, everybody is unsure about what responsibilities are, and there doesn't seem to be much coordination or communication. It's difficult to continue in a structure like that."

"You know we have thirteens opening up"—he was referring to a government salary level for which many junior analysts applied—"and we would consider you a top candidate for one of those slots. You'd be interested in one of those." It was looking like all his questions were going to be presented as declarative statements.

"Sir, the office has heard about those positions opening up 'soon' since even before I got here. And even when they do open, the interview board has much more influence over hiring than the office does"—that was another problem—"and there are plenty of competitive applicants in the office." Plus the fact that bribery was not going to keep me around.

"What if we gave you a freer hand to choose the projects you wanted to work on?"

This wasn't a negotiation, it was a laundry list of imaginary options.

"Sir, I already mostly pick the projects I work on, but what I work on has nothing to do with what gets published. And I have no problem working on the taskers that come down—I volunteer to do many of them. It's what happens after the products are drafted that's the problem."

He did not take the bait.

"What are you going to do next?"

"I'm looking at my options. I'm not in any rush, but I've been talking to various foreign policy groups and think tanks."

"Oh, I know all those bubbas at AEI and Heritage and all of those places."

I didn't know whether this was an oblique offer to help or a threat to my future job prospects, but either way I was not about to correct his misconceptions about my political leanings, though I did think it was funny that he'd automatically assume I was looking at far-right institutions. It also said much about his ideological orientation.

"Yes sir," I said noncommittally.

"Well, I guess that's it."

"Yes sir."

In the following days the office leaders approached me with a weird combination of hope that I would change my mind and disdain that I would even consider leaving. In their minds, all the grievances of analysts were a result of our naïveté, and both Roger and Kerik would later tell my coworkers that I left because I "couldn't cut it" in the office.

I worked to complete various projects and papers over the next several days while also trying to figure out what I needed to do to leave. As usual, Major Sebelius was no help, and his "efforts" to find out the appropriate steps for departure were fruitless. I made phone calls, got signatures, and handled the mundane details required for separation from the massive government and intel bureaucracy. I had a little going-away party in the office, during which I thanked my coworkers and encouraged them to keep up the good fight—and, in fine office tradition, I told them they should blame me for any problems following my departure.

To my mild surprise, I stayed involved with the daily production schedule even in those last two weeks. I'd figured the office would cut off my computer access, take my files, and have me twiddle my thumbs for the remainder of my time, if only for security reasons. Most private companies restrict employee access upon resignation, but apparently not an agency whose workers have access to vital national security information. Go figure. I was happy to work up until the very end, however, and with just a few days before I departed, Roger asked to speak to me. I knew he would want to know the same things everyone else did—why I was leaving and where I was going—and I was willing to be honest if he was interested in hearing the answers.

As it happened, a colleague was also preparing to leave the office around the same time, though he was staying within the intelligence community. We were walking through the hall, joking about our respective impending escapes, when we rounded a corner and literally bumped into Roger. He looked at us, shook his head, and told us to come back to his office. I was actually happy that my coworker, James, was with me, because I knew he would confirm what I said.

"So what's the deal, guys?" he asked bluntly. It was an inauspicious opening.

James and I looked at each other, then at Roger.

"James," he went on, "you I can at least understand. You're staying within the intelligence community. But Alex, you're leaving totally? Did you get the opportunity of a lifetime, or something? Something you've always wanted to do?"

"No sir, I, uh, actually don't even have a job lined up. I just really wanted to leave, sir."

"Well, why? Seriously, tell me why."

"May I close the door?" Roger was the one person in the Iraq section who had an office with a door, and I didn't want people eavesdropping if he really wanted to know why I was departing.

"Of course," he allowed. "Go ahead." I shut the door and sat down. I took a deep breath, glanced at James, and started.

"Sir, I think there are serious analytical and structural issues within this office that prevent analysts from having the effect that we're intended to, and I don't feel like I can be a part of that process anymore. The morale here is universally terrible. Everything from our lack of resources to analytical interference is causing a gradual meltdown of the operation."

Roger sat back in his chair and interlaced his fingers behind his head, looking up toward the ceiling.

"Like what? What issues?"

I went through an account of the problems almost exactly the same way I had with Roger's boss, the new office chief, not long before. I talked about the lack of an analytical standard operating procedure, explained what happened to a product from drafting to publication, and tried to get across how unhappy the office was with the resource and supervisory situations. James's eyes just got wider and wider. Roger argued about a few of the points, but primarily he asked questions and listened. He was mostly passive, with the notable exception of when I talked about analytical adjustment.

"Wait, what do you mean analysis is adjusted by leadership?"

"Sir, modification of analysis, against the wishes of the analysts themselves, is so pervasive it has become a running joke in the office. I mean, we literally had a Wall of Optimism, which was just one big sarcastic joke on the fact that office-level leadership is constantly telling us that we're not being cheerful enough in our analysis."

"Did you ever think that maybe it's honest analytical disagreement? For example, I'm an optimist by nature, and I know that, and part of the way I look at things is because of that."

"Yes sir, it's certainly possible that the conflict is over honest disagreements, but when the analysts keep getting overruled about the same exact things but then *keep getting proven right later on,* it's very difficult for us to process having our analysis changed repeatedly in the same way it was incorrectly altered in the past. Very, very difficult for us to understand that. It's hard for us to believe that constant accusations that analysts are being too pes-simistic can always be honest disagreement. After all, if we were practicing bad analytical tradecraft, wouldn't we be off base in dif-ferent ways, not just the same thing all the time?"

James nodded his agreement, as he had repeatedly during the discussion. I was glad he was there to validate all this; it's much harder to dismiss two people than just one.

"Then why do you think these disagreements continue to occur?"

"I'm not a mind reader, sir, but I can think of two main possi-bilities for why senior leadership might have this tendency. Either they honestly believe that things are better than they really are, de-spite all assessment and precedent to the contrary, in which case I'm very worried about the analytical abilities of our OIOs. The other possibility that jumps out at me is that leadership may be re-luctant to give bad news up the chain of command due to ideolog-ical or career-related considerations."

I had fired the big guns, and I held my breath. I didn't have to hold it long.

"You just committed a cardinal sin!" Roger raged, jabbing a finger toward me.

I didn't blame him for his strong reaction; I had stated what many of us thought was true, but nobody had been able to say it to leadership, and I knew he'd be pissed. But I was a little confused. I hadn't committed a cardinal sin; I had accused others of one.

"Sir?"

"You suggested that analysis is influenced by personal or ideo-logical reasons. That *never* happens."

"Sir, please. Honestly. The WMD debacle? The debates over whether we're allowed to use the words *civil war*? You don't think it ever happens, at all?" The delusion was exasperating.

"Well, it doesn't happen in this office. Listen, you can't just ac-cuse people of influencing analysts like that."

"Really? Let me tell you a story about influencing analysts. You know how your new supervisor has been coming to meet with us to introduce himself as the new big boss and talk to people about the office? Well, before his first meetings, Colonel Kerik went to two analysts and told them what to say to Clark. He instructed them that the only problem in the office was a lack of billets, and he reminded them that you are a great leader. He said that three times, actually. How's that for no influencing of analysts?"

Roger sat back, deflated, and looked over at James, who nodded. I could see the wheels turning.

"Well, that's inappropriate," he muttered.

"Yup."

"Why didn't I know about any of this? Why didn't you tell me about these problems before deciding to leave?"

"Sir, I find it impossible to understand how these issues could possibly be a surprise to you. Analysts have communicated all of this up the chain of command, and like I said, we literally posted our concerns on the wall! Everybody knows about this stuff. Most of it has been discussed openly, and it's all well known to the SIOs. I guarantee you that if you ask people for their honest opinion, they'll tell you exactly what I have."

"Why didn't they just come to me? I have an open-door policy, you know."

Why do executives always talk about their open-door policies? Nobody is going to torpedo their career by walking into the boss's office to complain or elucidate problems they've already expressed to their immediate leadership. It would be career suicide, and in any case, if you tell your chain of command, it's their responsibility to communicate it further. I also knew from emails, such as the one previously quoted sent by Major Nimick, that the problems were no secret.

"Sir, nobody is going to jump to the top of the chain of command unless you seek them out to talk. We're all aware that the problems are widely known, and the difficulty isn't that the issues are unknown, it's that nobody is doing anything about them. If anything, they're being perpetuated and solidified. That's the worst thing of all."

We talked a little more, and James weighed in on related concerns, but I had said my piece. Roger kept telling me that I didn't have enough perspective on the situation, and I told him that if there were good explanations for the issues then nobody knew about them. My concerns were widely shared, I repeated, and if something wasn't done, my resignation would be just the beginning. As it turned out, my departure was indeed followed by massive defections and turnover in the office.

Afterward, I continued to have mixed feelings. Abandoning a ship speeding toward an iceberg, and citing the oncoming iceberg as the reason for departure, is good for the person who leaves and can be good for the ship. But abandoning it still doesn't feel great. Still, I thought I was making the right decision, and during my last few days many colleagues came forward to thank me for standing up for the analysts and outlining the concerns of the office in such a straightforward way. The story of my frank conversation with Roger had made it around the office, not from me but through James and even Roger himself, and it had become a minor rallying cry. I would not be around to see any eventual effects, but I left hoping to continue working for the safety and security of the United States in other ways.

On my last day, after finishing up all the administrative crap that Major Sebelius sprang on me at the last minute, I sent out one final email to my Strat teammates and office leadership.

Colleagues,

Today I depart DIA. I want to unconditionally thank so many of you who have taught and guided me during my time with the agency, and I'm tremendously grateful for the experiences and knowledge I've gained here. There are a tremendous number of bright, motivated people working on this problem set, and it was especially an honor to work with those of you in uniform. I particularly want to express my appreciation to all of you with whom I worked in Iraq; it was a time I'll never forget, and it will continue to motivate my efforts in future endeavors. I wish y'all the best of luck in facing a difficult issue, and as a (very soon-to-be) private citizen, I commend you for your efforts.

Most of you know my reasons for departing, and I see no need to bore the rest with my personal perspectives. But being in a position where I no longer have to worry about the consequences of honesty, let me say this: It worries me greatly that the commendable work done by so many people seems to be in spite of structure and leadership rather than because of facilitation by those elements . . .

Regarding analysis, I defer to Rick MacKenzie, who recently departed after 38 years here: "Something remains fundamentally wrong with analysis . . . One must sense a crisis in analysis, in the management of analysis, in the training of analysts and in the intellectual curiosity of analysts about their real profession—not area expert, but aide to national security problem solving . . . be true to the intelligence evidence. The indicators never are wrong. As an attorney I assure you that the lawyers do not win cases, the evidence wins it."

I implore subject matter experts to fight back against accusations of being "off message," "cynical," and the like, and I hope leadership at all levels will defend reasoned, judicious analysis against the harmful creep of ideology and careerism. In our problem set, it is often necessary to deliver news that will displease someone up the chain of command, but often the only way to prevent something bad from happening is to warn about it; even if something cannot be changed, at least it can be planned for. But that requires a too-rare combination of analytical rigor and leadership support.

Let me be clear: I do not leave angry. I just want to make sure nobody can say down the road that these things are surprising. I'm hardly alone in perceiving these issues, and it is my hope that raising them one final, public time will help call attention to problems that are entirely fixable.

I wish you all the best of luck in the future, and thanks again for being great coworkers and friends.

Very Respectfully,
Alex.

I logged off the computer, gathered my things, said last good-byes, and headed to the Metro. The next day I went to another site to turn in my badges and sign some last paperwork. I was officially detached from DIA.

CHAPTER 19

Most Americans remain unaware of the depth and breadth of the ongoing problems in the intelligence community, and even of just how bad things are in Iraq. To some extent, the lack of information about the changes in U.S. intelligence and military strategy is directly related to the dearth of news reporting on these issues. It is difficult to find credible, timely, and relevant news on Iraq, and even on intelligence and military policy in general. I was one of very few analysts who augmented classified reporting with unclassified information, and I was constantly scouring the media for insightful information. Television news was unhelpful, as always, a flow of talking heads with little knowledge and even less interest in getting into details or subtleties. Print media was inconsistent at best.

For whatever reason, the television idea of "balance" was, for a long time, to report casualties on our side (Bad News) and reconstruction or casualties on their side (Good News). There was even a grim cyclical nature to the reports; invariably we could count on "School Built in Iraq" to become, a few weeks later, a casualty report: "3 Coalition Soldiers, 18 Iraqis Dead in New School Blast." Broadcast media also reported major events, such as elections, government formation, and particularly relevant statements, but rarely explained the "how" and "why" along with the "what." Some long-form TV news managed to address some of the finer points, but mostly television presented a flood of events without context. And in any case, most people can read faster than others can talk, so people can consume far more news in print form than through broadcast, making TV doubly useless.

In turning to print media, I would at least peruse mainstream news outlets: *The New York Times, Washington Post, Los Angeles Times,* and magazines such as *Time* and *Newsweek.* There was some value there, but they, too, often reported events without contextual explanation. So if I read a piece about the latest surge in Shia–Sunni violence in the *Times,* the same story with minor variations was often repeated in all the major outlets. Still, I skimmed several corporate media websites every day: CNN, MSNBC, NY Times, the Post, LA Times, and Fox News, among others, to get a sense of the news cycle. Some commentators, primarily political conservatives, have criticized corporate media for neglecting to cover the good news in Iraq, but I found that the larger problem was not that the media didn't cover the good news, but that it did not cover much of *anything* of real depth in Iraq. While the debate went on over whether the media spent too much time reporting on casualties, a civil war raged. While the media dutifully reported the drafting of the Iraqi constitution, it failed to explain the many problems the document would likely cause. And so on.

The answer to the search for news both current and analytical, I found, often lay in nontraditional online media. Among corporate media, often the most interesting and helpful articles were op-eds, which actually took the time to proffer assessment of the news rather than just transcription of events. Some were better than others—I avoided Tom Friedman like the plague, for example, but regularly read Fareed Zakaria—but they were the best place to get unique and insightful perspectives on Iraq, the Middle East, and the so-called War on Terror. The logical extension of op-eds in traditional media was to online magazines and blogs. There were former intelligence professionals, professors, think-tank fellows, and people actually in the countries I worked on who wrote regularly online, and I sought out the best ones to inform my thinking, for both general knowledge and professional analysis.

The world of online news and analysis is as close as it gets to a true meritocracy. There is an advantage to being first, but if the writing is insightful, prescient, and/or entertaining, it finds an audience. Sometimes that audience is niche, to be sure, but I was stunned at the amount of interesting and helpful online writing on topics I needed to know about. I was already reading blogs on domestic politics, just for fun, and while in Iraq I made a serious effort to add foreign policy and Iraq-specific blogs to my reading list. Through links, searches, and happenstance, I stumbled across valuable sources. Sites written by Iraqis, such as IraqTheModel and HealingIraq, were regular reads, and they helped give a sense of what was happening on the ground, including what rumors and perceptions were common on the Iraqi street. Multipurpose sites sometimes had good analysis and frequently had relevant links. Online magazines, especially *Salon,* had some excellent original reporting, more in-depth and relevant than traditional media, and the best thing about all of these sites was that they linked to other articles and analysis; I often found important, detailed information simply by surfing from link to link.

Consistently the best source of news on Iraq and the Middle East was Juan Cole, a University of Michigan professor and editor of the blog Informed Comment, a treasure trove of information and insight. I read his site every day, and although I sometimes disagreed with his political perspectives, his analysis of the events of the region was precise time and again. Many of my papers owed much to his analysis, and although Professor Cole takes plenty of grief from opponents due to his frequent criticism of the Bush administration, intelligence agencies have quietly asked him to share his expertise with government officials of a variety of ranks and positions, and he has been kind enough to oblige. Thanks to the accuracy of Professor Cole and the other media sources I came to trust, my wide-ranging reading made me look good and, more important, led to accurate assessments that otherwise would not have been made—at least not as very serious, thoughtful arguments that had never been made in such detail or with such care.

Unfortunately, most people, even those who are ostensibly interested in the conflict, often fail to utilize these resources. Having been on the ground in Baghdad and in the nexus of strategic intelligence at the Pentagon, I think conservative-leaning news outlets, from Fox News to a variety of websites and commentators, tend to downplay negative aspects of the war, and individuals who rely exclusively on these news sources honestly believe that things are going better than they are. This creates an unfortunate situation in which a partisan divide is not just over issues, but over information, and both sides think the other is being disingenuous. It is interesting that conservative popular media tend to be news-oriented (Fox, Drudge, talk radio) while progressives tend to gravitate toward analysis (blogs, op-eds), and I think this divide has greatly—and regrettably—contributed to the political polarization over the Iraq war. Polling indicates that opinions about the Iraq war break far more along political lines than even Vietnam, and this may be largely because people are getting their news from different sources.

After I returned from Iraq, people always asked me what it was like. My friends and family wanted the story, of course, but even people I didn't know, who heard my friends and I talking about it in a restaurant or at a bar, would come over and ask me questions.

"What's it really like over there?"

"Are we winning or losing?"

"What's the truth?"

I would usually say something noncommittal, but I would also note that the media didn't report nearly all the problems and carnage that existed. Most people were interested to hear that perspective, and most were very eager to express their opinions as well. But some simply refused to believe me when I said things were bad. Even a response as vague as "It's as bad as it looks" caused some to angrily inform me that the media were conspiring to keep the truth—which was that Iraq was really doing quite well, I guess—from the American people. I would smile politely and extricate myself, but I was surprised at how many people passionately believed that the good news was being hidden.

The lack of insightful reporting on Iraq in the media, which continues unabated (especially on TV but also in most local newspapers), is bizarrely disconnected from the passion and priority granted to the war by most of the public. In my experience, the more information people have about Iraq, the more realistic (or, as my former bosses would say, "pessimistic") they are. In my office, where we constantly read reports straight from the ground, the general consensus—despite being overwhelmingly populated by conservatives—was that the Iraq project was a debacle, mainly due to incompetent leadership in the Pentagon and the White House. We joked that President Bush had finally set up the conservative religious government he dreamed of . . . only it was an Islamist one in Iraq rather than a Christian one at home. Good information on Iraq exists, but it has to be sought out, and as much of the media abdicate their responsibility to inform the public about these vital issues, it is imperative that people educate themselves—especially if they want to back up their opinions with reality-based information. Knowledge of the situation, from the average citizen all the way up to high-ranking government and elected officials, is key to fixing both the war in Iraq and how it is understood at home.

CHAPTER 20

The nature of intelligence work makes its processes and conclusions extraordinarily vulnerable to abuse, neglect, and mismanagement. The requirements of secrecy prevent transparency and drastically limit oversight, and this leaves room for dangerous actors and actions to damage the system. The lessons of 9/11, outlined by the 9/11 Commission and countless other experts, amounted to a few key, simple elements: The intelligence community needed, among other things, greater information sharing through both people and technology, less bureaucracy in lateral and vertical processes, a greater emphasis on human intelligence rather than technological efforts, and a culture that emphasized creative and aggressive analysis rather than groupthink. These are commonsense requirements, but from what I can see these aspects of intelligence are not getting any better; if anything, many are getting worse. My more-experienced colleagues shared this view, and follow-up reports from Congress and the 9/11 Commission have affirmed and elucidated the continuing problems.

The effort to determine whether Iraq had weapons of mass destruction is, of course, a stark example of how the process of intelligence can go terribly wrong. In fact, the entire lead-up to the Iraq war was a lesson in catastrophe, and those failures were largely a function of the kind of problems I saw and experienced as the war raged on. The role of the intelligence community is to observe what is true—what is reality-based—and explain the context of that truth, the important current elements of it, and what it most probably means for the future. Policy can then be made or adjusted based on that information. I cannot overstate the danger to national security and sane foreign policy when the process is inverted. When policy is made based on either ideological or political considerations, and then intelligence is expected to support that policy, the fundamental mission is completely undermined.

My colleagues who'd experienced the lead-up to the war bitterly recounted the ignored warnings and political pressures to avoid being "off message." Pentagon and Bush administration leaders were so intent on getting the information they wanted that they set up the now-infamous Office of Special Plans, a small intelligence outfit within DoD staffed with ideologues and administration loyalists.* The stories of intelligence cherry-picking and political pressures are well known today among government and Washington insiders, but the public remains largely unaware of these influences because intelligence agencies, and especially individual analysts, are unable to defend themselves against charges of blunders or incompetence.

The myriad problems with the Iraq war include intelligence failures, to be sure, but there are also massive failures of leadership at the highest levels. Those failures, rather than being addressed and corrected, are trickling down through the intelligence community and infecting the daily life and processes of an insular, conformist intelligence culture. One of the more counterintuitive aspects of intelligence is that people, especially leaders, tend to remember fights more than the results of those fights. That is, if an analyst goes against the grain, resisting the groupthink to stake out an independent position, the fact that the position was an outlier is remembered more than whether it ended up being right or wrong. Even when an analyst takes a minority position and ends up being right, the common perspective seems to be

---

* Hersh, Seymour. "Selective Intelligence." *The New Yorker.* 12 May 2003; "Report of an Inquiry into the Alternative Analysis of the Issue of an Iraq–al Qaeda Relationship," Senator Carl Levin, Senate Armed Services Committee, 21 October, 2004.

that because the analyst had an unusual view, he or she was looking at the information wrong *even when the analysis is proven
accurate.*

Groupthink is a term that is frequently tossed around, but it's
somewhat misleading. On the vast majority of issues, analysts
should be generally in agreement on their assessments. If there are
wildly divergent opinions on a topic, it probably means that there
is not enough information to make a knowledgeable and accurate
assessment. The problem isn't simply a matter of analysts agreeing
with one another, it's what happens when that majority turns out
to be *wrong*. In most cases, there is no effort to change the process
or perspectives that led to the inaccurate judgment, and as I found
out from personal experience, analysts who are proven correct are
given no more confidence or trust on future out-of-the-mainstream
assessments. Every single time I heard "That's too pessimistic," it
was a reminder that agreement with the majority (or even the minority, as long as it consisted of leadership) was more important
than past accuracy.

The intelligence community, particularly within the Department of Defense, is rapidly becoming a culture that values and rewards "good news" over candor. Telling your bosses what they
want to hear—which is usually whatever they think, though it can
also be what they hope—is the surest route to success. Even if you
are wrong, you're wrong along with your boss, and that boss is
likely to think something other than poor analysis caused the mistake. After all, who wants to believe that they've screwed up their
job, especially if an underling got it right? In terms of your career,
it is a dangerous thing to insist that you are right and your boss is
wrong. Even if you are ultimately correct, your boss is much more
likely to remember that you disagreed than that you were right.
And with little oversight either within or outside the intelligence
agencies, it is easy for these problems to continue.

As with any organization, the culture of the Department of
Defense is fundamentally established at the top. I used to underes-
timate the power of leadership, for good or for ill, but my experience in Iraq and at the Pentagon dispelled that misperception.

Leaders can make or break an operation, and one as massive and vital as our national defense requires an able boss. Secretary Rumsfeld, for example, repeatedly demonstrated incompetence, a dismissive and incurious nature, and a dangerous detachment from reality. He should have been fired long before his eventual departure, and it is beyond me how someone who presided over such an obviously disastrous war plan could be defended by any reasonable person, let alone retain his position for so long. The idea that you have to stick with a bad leader, sometimes defended by the statement "You don't change horses during a race," defies all reason. A presidency isn't one long horse race, it's a series of races, and if your horse sucks, you stop racing him. A more apt comparison is that of a sports team leader. Funny that many DC residents I know, for example, who steadfastly insisted that Rumsfeld had to stay, scream for the scalp of a Redskins coach if he presides over an unsuccessful season—or even just a handful of losses.

The former secretary's arrogance, disregard of facts, and obedience and subservience to Bush administration ideology were dangerous and harmful to American interests and security, and close advisers were no better. In particular, Stephen Cambone and his right-hand man, Deputy Undersecretary of Defense for Intelligence Lieutenant General William Boykin, were architects of mismanagement, dangerous ideology, and inattention to the problems in their respective areas of responsibility. The DoD intelligence apparatus faltered greatly under Cambone's supervision, and he is a notorious ideologue who pushed for irresponsible policies, including reactionary support for torture. General Boykin is best known for inflammatory comments he made in October 2003, when he said, while talking about hunting down Osman Atto in Mogadishu, "He went on CNN and he laughed at us, and he said, 'They'll never get me because Allah will protect me. Allah will protect me.' Well, you know what? I knew that my God was bigger than his. I knew that my God was a real God and his was an idol." *

---

* Cooper, Richard. "General casts war in religious terms." *Los Angeles Times*. 16 October 2003.

His wife of twenty-five years left him due to his religious fanaticism,* and he views the war on terror in apocalyptic terms. Not exactly a solid foundation for dispassionate analysis. These individuals are not in the public consciousness, but they have had tremendous influence just under the surface, and the United States cannot afford to have such people continue to screw things up.

In addition to significant adjustments in leadership, the intelligence community still needs the kind of changes recommended years ago by the 9/11 Commission. In particular, intelligence professionals (and their congressional overseers) must go back to basics. After big mistakes, in any kind of field, it is often helpful to review the building blocks necessary for success. This is not a revolutionary suggestion, and again sports come to mind. My basketball coach used to say the same thing, and if my team was having a tough time, he emphasized the fundamentals. Any loss was the result of getting outscored, of course, but if we had a losing streak, we didn't practice shooting; instead, we did hours of defense and rebounding drills.

In intelligence, winning is getting the right assessment and/or prediction. If an assessment is made that is ultimately inaccurate, the process taken to get there should be quickly and efficiently examined and corrected. I am not suggesting congressional hearings every time a minor error is made, but offices and divisions have to constantly adjust and steer their forward motion, and learning from mistakes, as simple as that sounds, is not currently a major focus at the analytical level. If we can learn from the little ones, hopefully we can avoid the big ones. Even more important is recognition and repetition of accurate analysis, *especially* when that analysis goes against the grain. If an analyst is accurate, that's great; if an analyst is uniquely accurate even when his or her colleagues are wrong, that is something special and worth examining and understanding.

Rick MacKenzie, the thirty-eight-year veteran of DIA, had a system of calculating the accuracy of assessments when it was possible

---

* Leiby, Richard. "Christian Soldier." *Washington Post*. 6 November 2003.

to objectively judge them, and he kept a constant running score of the performance of various offices. But I don't know how or when it was used, as we only heard it referenced a few times, mostly regarding other departments. Offices should track successes and failures, and they should do it down to the individual analysts. Anything that gets published should be vetted for accuracy at some later time, and if it was wrong, the reasons should be determined and taken into account for the future. Again, this would not require extensive processes or any kind of expansion of the already-burdensome bureaucracy—just fast internal checks to see how things are going. I respect MacKenzie's point that intelligence is a speedboat, needing correction on its way forward, but glancing back is different from dropping anchor to study the prior course.

More specifically, individual performance should be tracked and addressed. If there are analysts who consistently make the right calls, particularly if those assessments are unusual, those individuals should get more responsibility and credibility. Intelligence really should be a meritocracy, especially at the analytical level, where there are thousands of relatively undifferentiated workers. The only way to even attempt this is to track accuracy. It is virtually impossible to fire someone from government service, so it's not as if jobs would be on the line, but there would be a quantifiable basis for judging analysis. Further, it would also help reveal those who are coasting. There are unfortunate numbers of people in government, even in intelligence, who simply don't seem to do anything. Management does not want to deal with them, so they are ignored. Many eventually fail upward, often because a boss will provide a good recommendation just so the problem gets passed along. If analysis was tracked and evaluated on a regular basis, many of these issues could be properly identified and solved. Broad office-level analysis could be judged the same way as individual predictions, and evaluations of leaders and analysts should take into account the most vital part of the job: getting the assessments right.

Even if analytical problems can be fixed, however, there must be a receptive audience for the judgments. Exacting assessments are no help if they are rejected by supervisors who refuse to countenance viewpoints that oppose their political ideology or might irritate their bosses, and that culture must be addressed and fixed. This particular problem has to be addressed from the top down, and value must be shifted from confirmation of already present opinions to accuracy. While this may seem obvious, it is not happening.

Without changes, the mistakes and mismanagement within the intelligence community portend further failure and increased politicization. Before I left, the Iran issue was already the subject of much speculation and dark humor. A group of us shared emails with one another with the subject "Ba dum ba dum ba dum . . ." to indicate the drumbeat for war with Iran. Whenever we saw a report or assessment that tried to blame Iran for the massive U.S. mistakes in Iraq, we knew that the drumbeat was getting louder. Ba dum ba dum ba dum . . . The efforts to link Iran to many of the problems in Iraq were deeply disturbing, and they were part of the reason I decided to leave. Efforts to blame Syria were also increasing, and the general belligerence and dumbfounding attempts to turn one disastrous war into two or three baffled me. Once again, it was pressure from above to have intelligence conform to political ideology, rather than having intelligence inform policy.

The intelligence community is not beyond repair, but it is still broken. Greater bureaucracy and micromanagement are not answers; the issues are more cultural than tactical. And the culture is directly affected by leadership, including an unfortunate lack of high-level leaders in DoD and the intelligence community who are willing to push back against the menacing influences of careerism, apathy, and ideological conformity. I didn't work in government for thirty years, and I am not a journalist with high-placed sources, so I leave the detailed analysis of how and why it got this way to those with a top-down view. My ground-level experiences were enough to convince me that injurious influences, from both outside actors and internal pressures, are causing our intelligence agencies and military irreparable harm.

With the intelligence community at an imperative moment in

our nation's history, the next few years will be critical. Will this administration's gross politicization of the military and intelligence apparatus persist, or even become an established long-term practice? Will others in the 9/11 generation feel betrayed by the ruthless partisanship that took the place of promised concord in the wake of the greatest unifying event in the history of our country? My generational peers, far from being the slackers we are sometimes stereotyped as by purveyors of conventional wisdom, are engaging in service, volunteerism, and altruistic activities at record levels, but I do not see those efforts necessarily translating to participation in government and traditional civil service. The formative years of my peers were spent under unprecedented peace and prosperity in America. We were safe, we were secure, and we had limitless futures. That prospect was shattered over the course of one morning, forcing many of us to realign our priorities. I remember telling my friends after the attacks that 9/11 had changed everything, that it would affect our lives in ways we could not yet imagine, and they were skeptical. "How?" a friend asked. "What's really going to change?" I struggled to find the words then, but it gives me no pleasure that I can articulate the deeply problematic answer now.

At the top of the list are the thousands of dead and tens of thousands of wounded American soldiers. Among the rest of the ways our nation has changed is the continued failure of the intelligence community to properly address, analyze, and approach threats from the sinister forces that menace us abroad and at home. The IC is on its way to being permanently damaged. It has, to a significant extent, hunkered down to try to protect itself from the dual attacks of the executive and legislative branches of government, as both sides have used it in proxy battles against each other. Intelligence officials greatly distrust Congress because it leaks information nonstop (on a bipartisan basis) and tends to blame the intelligence community for failures of law or policy; likewise, they distrust the executive branch because the president and his cohorts are also quick to lay blame upon intelligence when bad policy turns into bad results. The relationship between Congress and the

IC must be repaired, and it can be, but only through cutting down on leaks and increasing communication between intelligence officials and congressional members and staffers. If Congress better understood the people and processes of intelligence, it could better evaluate successes and failures, and it might even make appropriate laws to govern the intelligence community. To do so, members and staffers must have contact not just with the highest-level leadership but also with analysts and managers from relevant offices and sections, and they must exercise their vital powers of oversight. Intelligence is necessarily shrouded in secrecy, which makes it all the more important that its designated overseers take oversight responsibility seriously.

More important, the executive branch must stop treating the intelligence community as a political extension of the West Wing. A strained relationship between Congress and the IC is unfortunate but somewhat understandable given the daily partisan conflict, but an intelligence community that has to fight political influence from the executive branch is a debacle. Partisan hacks are not effective leaders, as Porter Goss's disastrous (though mercifully short) stint as CIA director demonstrated, and the CIA practically revolted against his autocratic and ham-fisted efforts to make the agency a subsidiary of the administration. Stories of high-ranking administration officials such as Vice President Cheney, former UN ambassador Bolton, and others attempting to intimidate analysts and influence intelligence are as shocking as they are damaging to the culture and process of analysis, and those kinds of practices are antithetical to having a trustworthy and legitimate intelligence community. Among senior officials, there is a very real fear that personal revenge could be enacted in response to differences in judgment, as in the destructive outing of CIA operative Valerie Plame.

The dangerous effects of politicizing intelligence are already apparent. Career considerations weigh heavily upon any decision to give bad news to a boss, institutional pressures to avoid "off-message" analysis are significant and increasing, and the morale, especially among young people, simply cannot be underestimated.

After I departed, the governance section experienced nearly 100 percent turnover, and the entire Strat division had around 50 percent—all in less than a year. In a matter of months, virtually all the institutional knowledge disappeared, and this is not unusual, particularly in offices that deal with the most crucial subjects: Iraq, counterterrorism, the rest of the Middle East. My former office has been shuffled around, but there are still problems with resources, leadership, and direction, and the pattern is repeated throughout the IC.

Many of my colleagues have gone on to other high-minded jobs, including teaching, nonprofit work, think tanks, and policy development, and many of them work abroad. It's not that they couldn't cut it, or didn't have the stomach (or bank account) for long hours and little pay; it's that they—we—did not feel we were being utilized in a positive way. My generation has focus, expertise, and energy to spare, but we are being turned off by the millions due to the deficiencies of the Bush administration and its enablers. Even with the absolute disasters of Bush administration foreign policy, including Iraq, North Korea, Darfur, Iran, and South America, the most damaging long-term strategic catastrophe may very well be the alienation of much of the next generation of policymakers, analysts, and advisers. This alienation is not a partisan affair, either; many of my now-departed colleagues are conservative, and some of the people in my office who were most dissatisfied with the Bush administration were Republicans who felt especially angry at being betrayed and damaged by members of their own political party.

I worry even for the future of those who still believe that our international efforts are advancing American interests: At some point either they will come to the realization that they were wrong, and were in fact misled by the people and ideologies they trusted, or their delusions will prevent them from becoming legitimate contributors to policy and the discourse that surrounds it. The effort against terrorists and their ideology is one likely to continue for generations, and the most effective endeavors will be those that hold true to the idea that American partisanship stops at the water's edge. The war on terror is a battle between openness and isolation, progress and regression, and we cripple our cause when we engage in tactics and strategies that represent the worst of American power. We can once again be a shining example in the international community, but we must rebuild concurrently from top to bottom and bottom to top. And we'll need good people to help effect those necessary changes.

I continue to believe in public service, and I know that those in the military, the intelligence community, and the government as a whole continue to work for the security and progress of America. I also hope and believe that my departure from the Defense Intelligence Agency is a temporary absence from government service. Americans, especially the younger generations, can protect our physical security as well as the American tradition of benevolent government and internationalism, but only if we are as committed to our cause as our enemies are to theirs. I hope military and intelligence professionals of all ranks and backgrounds will strive to place their country's interests above politics, although I know all too well how difficult it can be to exist in a dysfunctional and manipulative environment. Finally, I hope the American people demand greater accountability, transparency, and effectiveness from their leaders, both elected and in civil service. Without brave individuals within and outside the system to call for improvement, a small minority of destructive actors will continue to cripple the future of U.S. national security. I recognize and cite these issues not in spite of my patriotism, but because of it. We are far down a dangerous path, and I very much hope it is not too late to change direction.

After I departed DIA, several of my coworkers pressed our leadership to make changes based on the general sentiments I had voiced. In response, leadership gave the impression that I had left simply because I "couldn't cut it" and that changes were unnecessary. The top-level supervisors said my impressions were outliers, implying that I'd left because I was bad at my job. In anticipation of others wondering if this kind of explanation for my account is accurate, I have attached my most recent performance evaluations prior to my departure. One covers my time in Iraq, the other my subsequent time in the Pentagon. I offer them so readers can judge for themselves.

Security Classification: UNCLASSIFIED

DIA PERFORMANCE APPRAISAL

A. IO-12

Privacy Act: This form is subject to the privacy act safeguards and any abuse may subject the violator to disciplinary action, a fine up to $5,000.00 or both (P.L. 93-579) A

1. NAME: (Last, First, Middle Initial)			2. SSN:	3. POSITION TITLE, PAY PLAN, SERIES, GRADE:
Rossmiller	Alexander	J		

4. DIRECTORATE/ STAFF SYMBOL AND OFFICE TITLE:

5. PERIOD COVERED:
11 Sep 2005   31 Jan 2006

6. JOB DESCRIPTION:

Serves as an intelligence analyst for the Governance Team, Strategic Issues Division (SID), Office of Iraq Analysis (OIA), Directorate for Analysis (DI), performing operational/strategic-level analysis on Iraq in support of the Joint Chiefs of Staff (JCS) J2. Provides critical strategic analysis to senior Department of Defense (DoD) policymakers. Develop all-source intelligence products for dissemination throughout the Intelligence Community (IC). Coordinates within the Defense Intelligence Agency (DIA), the Joint Staff, Multi-National Forces — Iraq (MNF-I), and Central Command (CENTCOM). Provide Political-Military related briefing to the IC, Congressional Committees, and Executive Branch. Demonstrate proficiency with intelligence software in support of intelligence analysis.

7. CORE PERFORMANCE ATTRIBUTES: (Place the appropriate mark on the box to the right of the core performance attribute that best describes the employee's achievement level - (+) for employee's strength; (x) for proficient; (-) for developmental need. Mark only one box per attribute. See instructions page for guidance on completing attribute score.)

7A. CUSTOMER SERVICE (ALL)	ATTRIBUTE SCORE 94	(+)	(x)	(-)
Seeks customer interaction/ interacts well with customers		◆		
Anticipates & fulfills customer expectations		◆		
Is courteous & respectful		◆		
Delivers quality products & services		◆		

7B. COMMUNICATION (ALL)	ATTRIBUTE SCORE 94	(+)	(x)	(-)
Writes effectively		◆		
Speaks effectively		◆		
Obtains feedback to ensure understanding		◆		
Listens effectively		◆		

7C. RESOURCE MANAGEMENT (ALL)	ATTRIBUTE SCORE 92	(+)	(x)	(-)
Optimizes use of assigned resources/ properly accounts for property		◆		
Uses/ manages duty time effectively		◆		
Generates/ accepts new work efficiency methods		◆		

7D. MISSION ACCOMPLISHMENT (ALL)	ATTRIBUTE SCORE 94	(+)	(x)	(-)
Displays appropriate knowledge/ expertise/ sound judgment		◆		
Accomplishes priorities with a sense of urgency		◆		
Practices appropriate security awareness		◆		

7E. TEAMWORK (ALL)	ATTRIBUTE SCORE 93	(+)	(x)	(-)
Subordinates personal role to achieve results (all)		◆		
Enhances/ recognizes the performance of others (all)		◆		
Forges/leads/sustains teams (for results) (GG 12-15)				
Understands agency and IC goals and sets goals that optimize employee performance (GG 12-15)				

7F. SUPERVISION (SUPERVISORS ONLY)	ATTRIBUTE SCORE	(+)	(x)	(-)
Supports & promotes DIA objectives; is loyal and ethical				
Ensures a climate of fairness, respect & inclusion				
Establishes performance expectations; counsels, evaluates, and mentors employees				
Resolves conflicts fairly/ promptly with an eye to achieving "win/win"				
Models organizational cohesion & morale				
Leads pro-actively; achieves EEO & EO objectives				
Motivates effectively, trains, develops & ensures safe environment for subordinates				
Ensures timely and proper recognition of subordinates' performance				
Makes hard choices in ranking subordinates and achieving CA-21 goals				

8. RATER'S LIST OF EMPLOYEE ACCOMPLISHMENTS: (Using a Dash Symbol (-), list the accomplishments considered most significant for this employee.)

- Completed six-month volunteer deployment to Iraq, redeploying with OIA, serving the Joint Staff and the DI as an Iraq Strategic Issues analyst. Supported senior-level customers, including the President, Secretary of Defense, and Chairman Joint Chiefs of Staff.
- Produced over 20 focused and timely items for JCS J2 consumption, including over 15 briefing slides and numerous Executive Highlights and Notes in Brief between November 2005 and January 2006. Personally briefed the JCS J2 on seven occasions in support of current intelligence for submission to the CJCS.
- Authored over 15 written products, including Information Memorandums, Defense Intelligence Assessments, Information Papers, Defense Analysis Reports, Response Memorandums, and internal memoranda, primarily on Iraqi election implications, government formation, and constitutional issues.
- Wrote assessment products based on direct taskings for specific customer requests including DIA Director LTG Maples, NESA Director BG Thornhill, DI Director Sheck, and Undersecretary of Defense for Intelligence Dr. Cambone.
- Created slides for and briefed foreign government delegates for various foreign exchange and briefing programs, including Israel, United Kingdom, Morocco, and India, regarding issues.
- Attended and participated in various conferences and meetings that addressed current information regarding Iraq governance, Middle East political developments, and insurgency issues.
- Developed strong working relationships with analysts in DIA and other elements of the IC and DoD, allowing for involvement in meetings with senior customers and deployed personnel.

Security Classification: UNCLASSIFIED

9. RATER'S COMMENTS (Using a Dash Symbol (-), list the significance of the employee's accomplishments annotated in block 8.)

- Mr. Rossmiller is a self-starter, confident of his abilities and work. He volunteers to tackle any assignment without doubt or hesitation. He works zealously to complete each task as perfectly as possible. His keen analytical mind and ability to adapt to changing situations make him highly effective in any situation.
- He is meticulously accurate with a great sense of responsibility for the quality of his work. He always volunteers for additional work to help others and increase his own potential, skill and worth.
- Mr. Rossmiller's ability to communicate a complex and dynamic problem into manageable and easily understood intelligence products provided senior military and civilian DoD officials, and foreign officials, a broadened perspective of the December 2005 election results in Iraq.
- Completely self-reliant, he strives for perfection and sees all projects through to their successful conclusion. He is one of the most prolific producers of intelligence products in the Division.
- Mr. Rossmiller is an extremely talented intelligence analyst who has unlimited potential. He performs well above his current pay-grade and completes all tasks in an exemplary and thorough manner. I highly recommend his continued accelerated promotion, and selection as a full time student to the Joint Military Intelligence College in order to further enhance his professional development.
- He is a rising star in the intelligence community.
- I strongly recommend Mr. Rossmiller for a Directorate/Special Officer Bonus

10. RATER'S RECOMMENDATIONS: (Enter an "X" in the box or boxes that best describe your recommendations.)

Sustain Current Assignment	Higher Leadership	More Senior Technical	Command Representative	Training & Education
[X]	Agency Wide [ ] Discipline Specific [ ]	[ ]	[ ]	Senior Service School/ JMIC [X] Technical [ ] Command and General Staff [ ] Leadership [X]

11. OVERALL PERFORMANCE RATING: (Enter an "X" in assigned numerical rating in the box below):

RATER'S SSN:

Counseling Required [ ]

Top Performer		Superior Performance											Meets Expectations												Unsatisfactory

30	29	28	27	26	25	24	23	22	21	20	19	18	17	16	15	14	13	12	11	10	9	8	7	6	5	4	3	2	1
					X																								
0	0	0	0	0	2	1	0	0	0	1	0	0	0	0	0	0	0	0	0	0	0	0	0	0	0	0	0	0	0

Rater Profile

Date / Time Stamp:

12. REVIEWER'S COMMENTS: (Emphasis on potential for increased responsibility.)   [ ] Reviewing Official has been assigned for less than 90 days.

- Mr. Rossmiller is an efficient and highly knowledgeable intelligence analyst whose performance, singularly and collectively, has been outstanding. He demonstrates unbound ability and capacity to successfully assume positions of greater authority.
- Alex has the strength of mind and character to accept and meet challenges well beyond the scope and range of his contemporaries.
- Continue to develop with leadership and analytical training and education.
- A top candidate for a Directorate-level bonus!

13. REVIEWER'S RANKING OF POTENTIAL: (Enter an "X" for assigned ranking in the box below)

Concur with rating [X]   Nonconcur with rating [ ] Comments attached

REVIEWER'S SSN:

	UNLIMITED						OUTSTANDING								GOOD						LIMITED				NONE

30	29	28	27	26	25	24	23	22	21	20	19	18	17	16	15	14	13	12	11	10	9	8	7	6	5	4	3	2	1
					X																								
0	0	0	0	0	2	4	5	0	0	1	0	0	1	0	0	0	0	0	0	0	0	0	0	0	0	0	0	0	0

Reviewer Profile

Date / Time Stamp:

14. RATER'S SIGNATURE:	15. SSN:	16. DATE: 22 Feb 2006 13:43
17. REVIEWER'S SIGNATURE:	18. SSN:	19. DATE: 23 Feb 2006 15:45
20. RATEE'S SIGNATURE: Rossmiller Alexander J		21. DATE: 24 Feb 2006 14:06

DIA FORM 124 (03-03)

DIA PERFORMANCE APPRAISAL SUPPORT FORM

| A. |
| IO-12 |

Privacy Act: This form is subject to the privacy act safeguards and any abuse may subject the violator to disciplinary action, a fine up to $5,000.00 or both (P.L. 93-579)

1. NAME: (Last, First, Middle Initial)			2. SSN:	3. POSITION TITLE, PAY PLAN, SERIES, GRADE:
Rossmiller	Alexander	J		

4. DIRECTORATE/ STAFF SYMBOL AND OFFICE TITLE:	5. PERIOD COVERED:	
	07 Feb 2005	10 Sep 2005

6. PERFORMANCE EXPECTATIONS: ☐ Assignment spans a period of 30-89 days and only a Supplemental form is required.

MISSION ACCOMPLISHMENT

• Contributes to the analytical activities of the HUMINT Support Team by producing scheduled and ad hoc products, identifies information gaps and proposes collection requirements to meet current and anticipated intelligence needs and evaluates the intelligence collected in response to requirements
• Ensures the quality, relevance and timeliness of finished intelligence products that are provided in support of DIA HUMINT collection within Iraq
• Advises Team Chief or SIO of key issues and project milestones as they occur; provides sound recommendations to address problem areas; demonstrates innovation/creativity.
• Critical work to meet mandatory suspenses is always completed on time. Completion of other work may be occasionally delayed, except where delay would impact mission accomplishment.

CUSTOMER SERVICE

• Communicates clearly, courteously and effectively with customers.
• Solicits customer requirements and feedback on an on-going basis, incorporates feedback into products and notifies Team Chief and the SIO.
• Reviews customer requirements, makes acceptance/declination recommendations to Team Chief or SIO, and notifies customer of decision in a timely manner, according to mission requirements. Notifies customers as soon as possible if circumstances prevent the meeting of suspense.
• Works with reports officers, case officers, and appropriate members of the Combined Intelligence Operations Center regarding IIR evaluations, SDRs, HCRs, and TSCRs.

COMMUNICATION

• Products conform to established formats and are grammatically correct; are clear, complete, concise, accurate, timely and tailored to meet the needs of the audience; and reflect analytical ability and substantive expertise commensurate with grade/tenure. Significant problems in products should be rare. Products should be returned not more than once for correction.
• Alerts Team Chief or SIO to significant events/ substantive developments/ and problems on the day of occurrence and takes responsible follow on actions. Provides notification through chain of command. Backbriefs chain as soon as possible when circumstances demand bypassing.
• Products are coordinated with other organizations as required.
• Understands and implements established digital production procedures to meet customer needs.

TEAMWORK

• Treats colleagues with candor, honesty and respect. Responds professionally to criticism and uses as vehicle for improvement. Personal interactions foster cooperation, productivity and mission accomplishment. Listens well.
• Provides direct assistance to Team employees to ensure all timelines are met.
• Displays positive attitude. Supports HST and MNF-I C2X mission, goals, and priorities.
• Assumes responsibility and accountability for all actions.

RESOURCE MANAGEMENT

• Uses and manages time effectively.
• Looks for more efficient ways to accomplish mission – examples include templates, digital production, networking, and analytic tools.

7. RATER'S SIGNATURE:	DATE:
	26 Jul 2005 16:55

8. RATEE'S SIGNATURE:	DATE:
Rossmiller Alexander J	27 Jul 2005 08:52

DIA FORM 124-1 (03-03)

9. MID-TERM REVIEW:

Alex, you have excelled during your six-month deployment to Iraq in support of Operation Iraqi Freedom. You quickly adjusted to the demands of living and working in a combat environment and immediately assumed the duties associated with providing professional analytical support to DH collectors and case officers, as well as developing actionable intelligence packages for combat units in theater. Your dedication to the mission was unwavering and key to the success of our HUMINT Support Team.

You exceeded my expectations for a DIA, GG-9, intelligence analyst. While serving as a principle analyst for a critical Iraqi government source, your work was essential to the development of over 140 actionable intelligence packages. Through your mission first attitude and selfless work ethic, you ensured that the Overt HUMINT Support Team remained customer and operationally focused.

You have an excellent grasp of the research tools (M3, C2X Portal, Pathfinder, Analyst Notebook, etc.) needed to provide quality, all-source analytical support to the DH detachment and our supported action units. You have been performing well above your current grade, in both the quality and quantity of your work. Additionally, you have adapted very well to changes in our mission focus and production requirements.

Alex, the intelligence products you produce are consistently professional, comprehensive, well researched, and pertinent. You have received compliments on your work from the HUMINT Support Team Leadership, other analysts within the Combined Intelligence Operations Center, as well as combat units and other governmental agencies.

10. RATER'S SIGNATURE:	11. DATE:
▬▬▬▬▬▬▬▬▬▬▬▬▬▬▬	29 Jul 2005 10:45

12. RATEE'S SIGNATURE:	13. DATE:
Rossmiller Alexander J	29 Jul 2005 19:50

☐ Employee elects not to submit accomplishments

14. EMPLOYEE'S ACCOMPLISHMENTS: (Employee: Using a Dash Symbol (-) list your most significant performance accomplishments.)

- Created over 50 actionable intelligence packages, including names and descriptions of individuals, imagery, group associations, and locations of target. This intelligence was shared with military action units throughout the theater, resulting in dozens of insurgents being pursued, detained, and incarcerated.

- Facilitated the movement and processing of over 50 detainees suspected of anti-Iraqi forces (AIF) activity. Assisted in organizing the in-processing structure, provided support to direct action units to draft sworn statements to enable detention at long-term facilities, and contributed analytic support to initial detainee screenings and interrogations.

- Facilitated feedback process for intelligence gathering before, during, and after direct action operations. Talked with direct action unit individuals, Iraqi special forces operators, collectors, sources, S2 (intelligence) staff, and Judge Advocate General (JAG) officers regarding the intelligence roles and responsibilities in the pre- and post-operation analysis of military action.

- Created, managed, and maintained several databases utilized to track and analyze HUMINT reporting and corresponding military missions. These tracking mechanisms included a geo-coordinate database which included biographical and geospatial information on more than 500 suspected insurgents.

- Authored detailed analysis of assassinations of local political, religious, and social leaders (described as "Tier III" individuals) in Iraq, explaining the detrimental effects of continued and increased assassination attempts and successes against Tier III targets. Provided potential solutions to decrease assassinations and mitigate the negative results when they do occur. Published 04/05.

- Authored Information Memorandum on the threat from fuel tanker trucks in theater. Provided the intelligence community with a feasibility study on the danger of detonation of tankers by IED, VBIED, or suicide bombing and presented options for prevention and detection of insurgent activity related to tanker attacks. Published 08/05.

- Developed all-source link analysis with collectors to facilitate the improvement of collection priorities, methods, and analysis. This analysis provided the identification of key intelligence gaps and HUMNIT collection opportunities to support Multi-National Force – Iraq (MNF-I) priority intelligence requirements and the corresponding analysis of the Iraqi insurgency.

- Authored evaluations of more than 50 Intelligence Information Reports (IIRs), providing essential feedback to DH HUMINT collection on the accuracy and value of each source's reporting, as well as including guidance for future collection efforts. This feedback led to more efficient and effective HUMINT collection and reporting.

DIA FORM 124-1 (03-03)

DIA PERFORMANCE APPRAISAL

	A. IO-12

Privacy Act: This form is subject to the privacy act safeguards and any abuse may subject the violator to disciplinary action, a fine up to $5,000.00 or both (P.L. 93-579): B

1. NAME: (Last, First, Middle Initial)	2. SSN:	3. POSITION TITLE, PAY PLAN, SERIES, GRADE:
Rossmiller Alexander J		

4. DIRECTORATE/ STAFF SYMBOL AND OFFICE TITLE:	5. PERIOD COVERED:	
	07 Feb 2005	10 Sep 2005

6. JOB DESCRIPTION:

Forward deployed to Baghdad, Iraq to serve as an all-source analyst for the Multi-National Force-Iraq, C2X, HUMINT Support Team operating in the Combined Intelligence Operations Center on Camp Slayer. Conduct in-depth research and analysis on the Iraq insurgency, to include insurgent tactics, techniques and procedures; monitor and assess the role of assassinations and kidnappings in support of the insurgency; and identify significant collection gaps, opportunities, trends, and threads. Support HUMINT operations through source validation and objective evaluation of HUMINT reporting. Provide continuous, direct analytical support to HUMINT collectors through the use of IIR evaluations, SDRs, and HCRs. Additionally, serve as a member of a three-man Direct Action Cell, which develops actionable intelligence packages for US and Coalition Special Forces to kinetically target insurgents and their enablers.

7. CORE PERFORMANCE ATTRIBUTES: (Place the appropriate mark on the box to the right of the core performance attribute that best describes the employee's achievement level - (+) for employee's strength; (x) for proficient; (-) for developmental need. Mark only one box per attribute. See instructions page for guidance on completing attribute score.)

7A. CUSTOMER SERVICE (ALL)	ATTRIBUTE SCORE 92			
		(+)	(x)	(-)
Seeks customer interaction/ interacts well with customers		◆		
Anticipates & fulfills customer expectations			x	
Is courteous & respectful		◆		
Delivers quality products & services		◆		

7B. COMMUNICATION (ALL)	ATTRIBUTE SCORE 90			
		(+)	(x)	(-)
Writes effectively		◆		
Speaks effectively		◆		
Obtains feedback to ensure understanding			x	
Listens effectively			x	

7C. RESOURCE MANAGEMENT (ALL)	ATTRIBUTE SCORE 87			
		(+)	(x)	(-)
Optimizes use of assigned resources/ properly accounts for property			x	
Uses/ manages duty time effectively		◆		
Generates/ accepts new work efficiency methods			x	

7D. MISSION ACCOMPLISHMENT (ALL)	ATTRIBUTE SCORE 87			
		(+)	(x)	(-)
Displays appropriate knowledge/ expertise/ sound judgment		◆		
Accomplishes priorities with a sense of urgency			x	
Practices appropriate security awareness			x	

7E. TEAMWORK (ALL)	ATTRIBUTE SCORE 95			
		(+)	(x)	(-)
Subordinates personal role to achieve results (all)		◆		
Enhances/ recognizes the performance of others (all)		◆		
Forges/leads/sustains teams (for results) (GG 12-15)				
Understands agency and IC goals and sets goals that optimize employee performance (GG 12-15)				

7F. SUPERVISION (SUPERVISORS ONLY)	ATTRIBUTE SCORE			
		(+)	(x)	(-)
Supports & promotes DIA objectives; is loyal and ethical				
Ensures a climate of fairness, respect & inclusion				
Establishes performance expectations; counsels, evaluates, and mentors employees				
Resolves conflicts fairly/ promptly with an eye to achieving "win/win"				
Models organizational cohesion & morale				
Leads pro-actively; achieves EEO & EO objectives				
Motivates effectively, trains, develops & ensures safe environment for subordinates				
Ensures timely and proper recognition of subordinates' performance				
Makes hard choices in ranking subordinates and achieving CA-21 goals				

8. RATER'S LIST OF EMPLOYEE ACCOMPLISHMENTS: (Using a Dash Symbol (-), list the accomplishments considered most significant for this employee.)

- Volunteered for a six-month deployment to Iraq in support of Multi-National Force-Iraq, as part of a HUMINT Support Team, which was responsible for the capture or death of more than 150 key insurgents in Iraq.
- Quickly adapted to the hardships and stresses of living and working in a combat zone. He was able to maintain his mission focus, intellectual capabilities, and positive attitude despite the adverse conditions.
- As a member of the Direct Action Cell, researched, developed, coordinated, and passed more than 50 actionable intelligence packages to Special Forces units, which directly resulted in the capture of 17 known insurgents and diminished insurgent capabilities across Iraq.
- Supported a large-scale direct action mission, which facilitated the movement and processing of dozens of detainees suspected of insurgent activities, to include researching and cross-referencing names, organizing the in-processing procedures, and providing analytical support for detainee screenings and interrogations.
- Authored responses to RFIs regarding trends and implications of the assassinations of local political and religious leaders in Iraq, the assassination of a high-ranking Iraqi official, and the assassination of a U.S. State Department official.
- Key contributor to a General Officer briefing on the assassination tactics, techniques, procedures, and command and control practices of an Iraqi militia group.
- Coordinated with direct action unit leaders, Iraqi Special Forces, DH and military HUMINT collectors, sources, C2/S2 staffs, and military lawyers regarding intelligence roles and responsibilities. Remained involved the intelligence cycle from initiation through the after action reviews.

9. RATER'S COMMENTS (Using a Dash Symbol (-), list the significance of the employee's accomplishments annotated in block 8.)

- Alex greatly exceeded my expectations for an intelligence analyst of his grade and experience, he is truly a professional and an asset to DIA and the Intelligence Community. He excelled throughout his deployment to Iraq in support of C2X, Combined Intelligence Operations Center (CIOC), Multi-National Force-Iraq. His dedication to the mission was unwavering and key to the success of our HUMINT Team.
- Quickly adapted to the demands of living and working in a combat environment and immediately assumed his duties as a member of the HUMINT Support Team and Direct Action Cell. Through his immediate mission focus and committed work ethic, Alex developed more than 50 actionable intelligence packages for theater Special Forces units, which directly resulted in the capture of 17 known insurgents.
- Authored responses to RFIs regarding trends and implications of the assassinations of local political and religious leaders in Iraq, the assassination of a high-ranking Iraqi official, and the assassination of a U.S. State Department official.
- Alex's analytical products on insurgent assassinations and kidnappings were of great value to the combat leaders and policy makers in Iraq. His products contributed to MNF-I's better understanding of the role assassinations and kidnappings play in the greater picture of the Iraq insurgency.
- Alex's analysis is consistently professional, comprehensive, well researched, and pertinent. His work repeatedly received the praise of the CIOC leadership, DH collectors, U.S. and Coalition Special Forces, Iraqi Special Forces, and other intelligence community analysts operating in Iraq.
- A financial bonus is recommended and well-deserved for Alex's accomplishments during this deployment.

10. RATER'S RECOMMENDATIONS: (Enter an "X" in the box or boxes that best describe your recommendations.)

Sustain Current Assignment	Higher Leadership		More Senior Technical	Command Representative	Training & Education	
X	Agency Wide ☐		☐	☐	Senior Service School/ JMIC ☐	Technical X
	Discipline Specific ☐				Command and General Staff ☐	Leadership ☐

11. OVERALL PERFORMANCE RATING: (Enter an "X" in assigned numerical rating in the box below):

RATER'S SSN: ▮▮▮▮▮▮▮

☐ Counseling Required

Top Performer	Superior Performance					Meets Expectations																				Unsatisfactory			
30	29	28	27	26	25	24	23	22	21	20	19	18	17	16	15	14	13	12	11	10	9	8	7	6	5	4	3	2	1
						X																							
0	0	0	0	0	0	1	0	1	0	0	0	0	0	0	0	0	0	0	0	0	0	0	0	0	0	0	0	0	0

Rater Profile   Date / Time Stamp:

12. REVIEWER'S COMMENTS: (Emphasis on potential for increased responsibility.)   ☐ Reviewing Official has been assigned for less than 90 days.

Mr. Rossmiller demonstrated tremendous potential to serve in positions of greater responsibility, and exceeded all expectations while in Iraq. Mr. Rossmiller possesses the requisite skills and knowledge to serve at the next higher grade. Assign to the Agency's toughest analytical projects where his research skills will prove invaluable. Send at the earliest opportunity to Service Command and General Staff College or civilian equivalent. Clearly deserving of an Office-level performance award or high cash bonus.

13. REVIEWER'S RANKING OF POTENTIAL: (Enter an "X" for assigned ranking in the box below.)

REVIEWER'S SSN: ▮▮▮▮▮▮▮

Concur with rating X   Nonconcur with rating ☐ Comments attached

UNLIMITED						OUTSTANDING										GOOD						LIMITED				NONE
30	29	28	27	26	25	24	23	22	21	20	19	18	17	16	15	14	13	12	11	10	9	8	7	6	5	4	3	2	1
							X																						
0	2	2	1	0	1	1	1	2	1	0	0	0	0	0	0	0	0	0	0	0	0	0	0	0	0	0	0	0	0

Reviewer Profile   Date / Time Stamp:

14. RATER'S SIGNATURE: ▮▮▮▮▮▮▮	15. SSN: ▮▮▮▮▮▮	16. DATE: 31 Mar 2006 16:05
17. REVIEWER'S SIGNATURE: ▮▮▮▮▮▮▮	18. SSN: ▮▮▮▮▮▮	19. DATE: 03 Apr 2006 07:01
20. RATEE'S SIGNATURE: Rossmiller Alexander J		21. DATE: 03 Apr 2006 11:21

DIA FORM 124 (03-03)

ACKNOWLEDGMENTS

Someone of my youth and inexperience in the writing profession does not publish a book without a lot—*a lot*—of help. This project is the result of the combined efforts of a stellar team, and I have tremendous appreciation and respect for those who shepherded me through the process. Countless individuals along the way took a chance on a young, unproven author, writing about controversial events and issues, and I hope I have come through for them as they did so many times for me. Many thanks to my agent, Eric Lupfer, who provided excellent guidance and reassurance throughout, and to Jonathon Jao and Ron Doering, who saw value where others did not and helped turn a story into a narrative. Thanks also to my attorney, Mark Zaid, who helped me navigate the legal land mines of the government approval process.

In addition to my appreciation for those who were part of the practicalities, I feel an overwhelming debt of gratitude to those who helped shape me as well as the development of this work. First and forever foremost, my parents, whose support and counsel has been important beyond valuation; my siblings Clara and Charlie, each a testament to the worth of family; my friends and confidants Jena and Justin, who support me but also, more important, tell me when I'm being an idiot; and Silvia, whose benevolence and insight are unmatched. My gratitude also to the tremendous friends who helped keep me sane while I was in Iraq, including Alex M, Audrey, Clyde, Danielle, Finny, Jason, Libby, Maggie, Russell and Betsy. And to Denis, who created a crucial initial opportunity.

Thanks to my friends and coworkers from life after DIA, many of whom provided help on this project. John, Joe, and all the readers at Americablog, who took a chance on an upstart writer on one of the highest-trafficked sites of its kind; to Eric Saar, whose *Inside the Wire* was an inspiration and whose advice was priceless; to Dave, Ezra, Karl, and others in the progressive community who provided kindness and help when it was of no benefit to them; to Rand, Ilan, and Moira at the National Security Network; to Rachel, who provided a crucial shortcut for this book, and the rest of my fine colleagues at the Truman National Security Project; to AJ and the staff at the Helix, who provided liquid celebration or consolation depending on the day.

A most heartfelt acknowledgment to my colleagues and co-workers at DIA and in the military. I have never encountered a finer group of people, and failures of leadership should not be confused with deficiencies among the ranks. The daily sacrifices of those who make it their lives to serve this country and its citizens make our nation the greatest in the world, and it was a privilege and a pleasure to be a part of that community. I hope we soon have leaders who accord these men and women the respect and treatment they deserve.

I would also like to mention a few people who have never heard of me and probably never will, but whose work provided moments of happiness and levity when I most needed them, particularly in Baghdad, where they helped me keep sane. So, with apologies for being self-indulgent, I'd like to thank Kelly Clarkson, Bill Simmons, the Dixie Chicks, Metallica, J. K. Rowling, Evanescence, and Scissor Sisters. One tends to gain a special appreciation for entertaining diversions when explosions rule the night.

Finally, I owe a great deal to all those who have doubted me, who didn't think I could accomplish my goals. There is no greater motivation than failure; every disappointment, every rejection, every doubt remind me how important it is to never stop working.

A. J. Rossmiller, a fellow at the National Security Network, served with the Defense Intelligence Agency for nearly two years. For his work in Iraq, he was awarded the Joint Civilian Service Achievement Award and the DIA Expeditionary Medal for valorous and meritorious service. He is a contributing editor at Americablog.com, and his writing has been featured or cited in a wide variety of news and commentary outlets. Rossmiller is currently an adviser and consultant for various foreign policy and security organizations, and is a member of the Truman National Security Project. He is a regular commentator on the Alhurra television network, a U.S.-government–run channel that broadcasts in Arabic to the Middle East. A. J. can be reached at ajrossmiller@stillbroken.com.

ABOUT THE TYPE

This book was set in Sabon, a typeface designed by the well-known German typographer Jan Tschichold (1902–74). Sabon's design is based upon the original letterforms of Claude Garamond, and was created specifically to be used for three sources: foundry type for hand composition, Linotype, and Monotype. Tschichold named his typeface for the famous Frankfurt typefounder Jacques Sabon, who died in 1580.